Shanta Gokhale—writer, translator and critic—writes in Marathi and English and also translates between the two languages. Gokhale has written two novels in Marathi, *Rita Welinkar* and *Tya Varshi*. Her most recent non-fiction book is her memoir, *One Foot on the Ground*. She has translated *Smritichitre: The Memoirs of a Spirited Wife* by Lakshmibai Tilak and the novel *Kautik on Embers* (*Dhag*) by Uddhav J. Shelke. Apart from these she has also translated plays by Vijay Tendulkar, Mahesh Elkunchwar, Satish Alekar, G.P. Deshpande, Premanand Gajvi and Makarand Sathe. Shanta has received the Sangeet Natak Akademi Award for her contribution to the performing arts; the Maharashtra State Award for the best novel of the year (for *Rita Welinkar* and *Tya Varshi*); the Sahitya Akademi Award for translation; and lifetime achievement awards from Thespo, Tata Literature Live! and the Ooty Literary Festival.

Jerry Pinto is the author of the novels *The Education of Yuri*, *Murder in Mahim* and *Em and the Big Hoom*, and the non-fiction book *Helen*. He has also published landmark translations from Marathi and Hindi, among them: Baburao Bagul's story collection *Jevha Mi Jaat Chorli Hoti* (*When I Hid My Caste*); Sachin Kundalkar's novel *Cobalt Blue*; and the memoirs of Daya Pawar (*Baluta*), Malika Amar Shaikh (*I Want to Destroy Myself*), Vandana Mishra (*I, the Salt Doll*), and Swadesh Deepak (*I Have Not Seen Mandu*). Among the awards Jerry has received are the Windham-Campbell Prize, the Sahitya Akademi Award and the National Award for the Best Book on Cinema.

The Engaged Observer

The Selected Writings of

SHANTA GOKHALE

Edited and with an Introduction by

Jerry Pinto

SPEAKING
TIGER

SPEAKING TIGER BOOKS LLP
125A, Ground Floor, Shahpur Jat, near Asiad Village,
New Delhi 110049

Published by Speaking Tiger in paperback 2018

ISBN: 978-93-88070-49-2
eISBN: 978-93-88070-50-8

10 9 8 7 6 5 4 3 2 1

Typeset in Minion Pro by Jojy Philip, New Delhi
Printed at Sanat Printers, Kundli

Contents

On This Grand Nation

On Writers and Writing

On Marathi Culture

On Music

Fiction

Shakespeare Take Two

Introduction
Shanta Gokhale as Mercury

Quite early in your career as a writer, you're supposed to be able to catch a person in a telling phrase, a noun phrase in apposition, as we would say in the business had we any concern at all for grammar. 'When I was talking to Shanta Gokhale, the award-winning novelist…' I might say for instance, and get on with it. The problem with Gokhale is that as soon as you write 'award-winning novelist', you want to add 'and translator'. Then you are reminded that she is 'playwright' but that doesn't quite fit either because she is also a theatre critic of high standing. Only 'critic' doesn't sum up her achievements there, so perhaps the word 'theatre historian' might work, considering her books on Marathi theatre, the edited works on Veenapani Chawla, Satyadev Dubey and the theatrical spaces that nurtured Mumbai's experimental theatre. And then you are reminded that one of her many avatars was as the Arts Editor of a national newspaper where she nurtured talents as diverse as Ranjit Hoskote, Arundhathi Subramaniam, Himanshu Burte and even one Jerry Pinto. This, you think, is beginning to sound quite absurd but then there is also the Shanta Gokhale who writes scripts for documentary films and for feature films, who has been producer on a number of award-winning films. She has taught English to commerce students and nurses; been a Public Relations Executive for a pharmaceutical company, she has edited encyclopaedias; been a member of the board and advisor to a slew of institutions, from the National Centre of the Performing Arts (NCPA), Mumbai, to the National Gallery of Modern Art (NGMA), Mumbai. But most of all, she is Mumbai's best loved and most easily accessible sounding board. She always seems to have the time and energy to listen to almost anyone with a play or a poem or a translation or even a novel to test-read, an idea to talk about, a project to bounce around.

Shanta Gokhale resists definition. And this may be one reason why even after I had marshalled all that was available of her writing and looked at it, I almost despaired of ever being able to put together a reader that would sum up her work in the world of words. Because Shanta Gokhale is mercury.

~

And so it should not be surprising that conversations with her never follow the routine paths you can take with other people who will simply follow you into the thickets of your emotional state. If you're angry, they'll be angry with you. If you're happy, they'll be happy with you. This is not because they empathize or understand or even agree, but because it is polite and emotionally manageable to do this. With Gokhale, you will get an honest and clear-eyed hearing. She will listen to you, ask questions and then tell you what she thinks. This is a rare thing: the ability to offer one's interlocutor the gift of engaged attention. It is probably what makes her such a fine journalist. She does not lose her balance easily but you get the feeling that it is not an act; it is the effort of a civilized mind seeking to find a civilized way to disagree.

After reading one of her columns, my friend Sameera Khan, a journalist, rang up and asked me: 'How does she do it? How does she manage to make criticism sound so objective and rational? I want to go out and buy X's book now and read it.' Another friend, whose book had been turned into a play, told me that Gokhale had written him an email that told him exactly what was wrong with the play, but so nicely, he said, that he didn't mind at all. I asked him to share the email because I sometimes can offend people when I am trying to pay them compliments. I wanted to see if I could learn something; unfortunately he never did.

Shanta Gokhale has a rare knack: the ability to distil an

argument and to then infuse it with just the right amount of emotion. This is something precious in our world where ranting and name-calling seem to have become the chosen method by which opinions are exchanged. This makes her an excellent social commentator and much of the work by which she is known is in this area. I hope therefore to present a taster of the moveable feast that is Shanta Gokhale.

~

Shanta Gokhale was born in 1939 into a middle-class family of parents who could not be classified as ordinary. Her father, G.G. Gokhale was an Assistant Editor with the Bennett Coleman Group but somehow found the money to send both his daughters to England to study. However, she was already writing before this and writing compulsively.

'I began writing when I was twelve. I felt a compulsion then to feel out what I was all about. A thought expressed on paper was concrete proof of what you were. When I put thoughts on paper, as many young people do, I recognized that I got a particular pleasure out of choosing certain words above others and putting them together in a certain way that wasn't just about making sense. This kind of writing was therefore a solitary exercise,' she says.

But then she went away to England and that meant an 'early separation from family. Writing letters home was a duty. But the joy of saying things in words went beyond duty. I told myself then that I could write. "Being able to do" was a motivating feeling and I began to write for pleasure. Every idea became a piece of writing. Sometimes I sent it to a newspaper or magazine. Sometimes it stayed in my notebook.'

Gokhale was still at Bristol University when her writing career began. 'My first ever contribution came out of a letter that I wrote to my father. He showed it to M.V. Mathew of the *Times of India* who said he would like to publish it. When that appeared, I was still in college and I thought: "Oh, that's how people get printed in newspapers." Mathew told my father that I should write about things that might be relevant and he would print them if he thought his readers would be interested. So I wrote about Rag Day, an annual fund-raiser in which the students of the university got dressed up as witches and wizards and suchlike and got on to a float and raised money from the town, the only occasion on which Town and Gown hobnobbed with each other, the students of the university being otherwise quite insular. Then I wrote about the fifteen-day trip I took with other students to Italy and my trip to Scandinavia. So that's how I began. I suspect it was partly because at the time there was an adoring interest still about things that went on in vilayat—otherwise what interest would a mainstream Indian newspaper have in Rag Day at Bristol University? I suppose it was also because it was a small world in which everyone knew everyone else. The media explosion was some years away,' she says.

Gokhale graduated from Bristol University in English Literature and came home to find that there were two options open to a woman with such a degree: she could write advertising copy or teach in a college. A family friend, the late legendary professor M.V. Rajadhyaksha, told her of a maternity-leave vacancy as a lecturer in Elphinstone College and that was where, she says, she discovered her vocation as a teacher.

Marriage intervened and she left Bombay to travel as Navy wife to Vijay Shahane, a man she chose because he was pleasantly addicted to reading. 'That this reading didn't translate into thinking was not Viju's fault. It was mine for assuming it did. He read like a reflex,' she remembers. Yet when she talks about those days, she makes it sound like it was some kind of crazed city-hopping picnic, where you filled up your boxes and moved into houses and other Navy wives came to your aid with things they didn't need.

Perhaps it isn't about just making lemonade, perhaps you also have to be able to focus on the lemonade moments.

~

It was the poet Nissim Ezekiel who reminded Shanta Gokhale that she was bilingual. Gokhale was in Vishakhapatnam in The New Entry Camp, an unlikely Navy wife with two young children, Renuka and Girish. This was where she began to translate, a peremptory challenge issued by Satyadev Dubey which she recounts in her essay on this polymorphous and confusing figure who galvanized Indian theatre for decades:

> 'In 1971, I was in Vizag. Girish was two years old. I wrote something, it was not a poem, but something close. I sent it off to Nissim Ezekiel. Poor Nissim, he was flooded with everyone's efforts and he was so kind. He wrote back and said, "You have a good prose style, you should write prose. And why don't you write in Marathi?" This letter was a catalyst. There were two or three stories going around in my head and I thought: Maybe I could write these in Marathi. And so I wrote three stories and sent them to Purshottam Atmaram Chitre, editor of *Abhiruchi*, father of Dilip Chitre. Now, he was Chitre Kaka to me, my father's friend, a regular at Lalit Estate and so he published two and sent one off to *Satyakatha*. After those three stories, I knew that I had Marathi in me as a creative language.'

Although there is nothing in her manner that suggests the tectonic shifts her life must have been taking—moving homes, moving identities, moving languages—it becomes clear in retrospect that she was ready to move on.

'My father died in March 1967 and my entire life began to change. Aai had to eventually sell the house that he had built as a retirement home in Talegaon; she came and stayed with me in Vishakhapatam where Viju was posted. Girish was about seven months old. She saw what my life was like with Viju and she said, "Was it for this that your father sent you abroad? What kind of life are you living?" When she returned to Bombay, she wrote me a letter enclosing an advertisement that H.R. College* had put in

* Hassaram Rijhumal College of Commerce and Economics, known in Mumbai by its initials.

a newspaper, an ad for a vacancy as a lecturer. "Apply for this," she wrote, "come back home."'

In 1974, she came back to Bombay and took up a job as a teacher of English at H.R. College. During this period, she only had the time to write commissioned pieces.

'After coming back, there was absolutely no time to do anything that was not about earning money. I was teaching at H.R. and I was giving tuitions. Five students: a Girgaon Brahmin girl; a Gujarati Modi girl; a Gujarati Jhaveri girl; Zehraben, a Dawoodi woman from the royal clan; and a Japanese woman. I helped the first three with their college work; the latter two were for English conversation. The Japanese woman was the most difficult of the lot. We came from different worlds so we had very little to talk about until we hit upon the Kobe steak. She would wax eloquent about it, how the cows were treated, which cuts were the best and her English improved quite dramatically. And I was teaching English to nurses at the J.J. Hospital.'*

These varied interests and avocations brought more writing her way.

'Some of it was because I was part of the women's movement and so the two women's magazines—*Femina* and *Eve's Weekly*—called on me to contribute. And then there was also my theatre connection. Dubey told Dharamvir Bharati, who was the editor of *Dharamyug*, that I would be the right person to interview Jennifer and Shashi Kapoor about Prithvi. (They translated it into Hindi.) And I was quite happy to earn those little extras. Middles brought you five hundred rupees; and since I was earning only four thousand rupees at H.R. College, every little helped and there was no time to write on spec.'

In 1977, she joined the women's magazine *Femina* as a Sub-editor. This was also where she met Olga Valladares, who gave Shanta her first column.

---

* Jamshedjee Jeejeebhoy Hospital in Byculla, South Mumbai, a legendary teaching hospital.

'Olga Valladares was leaving *Femina* because she hated everyone there and they hated her right back, but she loved me and I loved her. She was going to the *Evening News of India*, the tabloid from the Times of India Group, and she was to be the Features Editor. She asked me if I would write a column for women. The slug was: "Milady's Boudoir". I said, "Olga, I'd love to do it but not under that name." She said, "Change it to whatever you want," and "Woman to Woman" was born. I wrote that column until I left to join Glaxo.'

Shanta was a Public Relations Executive at Glaxo. This may sound like a punishment posting but not to hear her talk of it. She remembers that she made lots of friends, many of whom are still in touch; she started a theatre group for the workers, editing plays down to thirty minutes so that they could be enacted in the staggered lunch timings. Around this time, the compulsion to write came back. She talks about her first play *Avinash*[*] as something that haunted her until she had to write it.

'I wrote *Avinash* in 1982 in a single day when no chore or duty stood between me and the writing. Once written, it stayed in my drawer. Satyadev Dubey got wind of it in 1988 and demanded to read it. Within six months it was on the stage.' *Avinash* deals with a family struggling to come to terms with the alcoholic and manic-depressive Avinash, who lives with them but is kept in his room at all times. The play becomes a pressure cooker of unspoken horrors, with Avinash as the central character who the audience never sees.

Her first novel, *Rita Welinkar*,[†] was born during that time too. 'The novel developed out of experiences I had had at Glaxo, conversations I had with other women there. Many of my friends were having relationships with married men. The women, I noticed,

---

* *Avinash*, together with *Party* by Mahesh Elkunchwar and *City Lights* by Manjula Padmanabhan was published as *City Plays* (Seagull Books; 2004). This is the English version as translated by Shanta herself; the original was written in Marathi.

† *Rita Welinkar*, 1990, was translated into English by Shanta and published under the same name by Orient Longman in 1995. It won the V.S. Khandekar Award for a novel in Marathi. Renuka Shahane directed the eponymous film version in 2009.

were always sure of their commitment. The men never were. I began to deal with the issue inside my head, I suppose.'

~

Rita Welinkar began in English. 'I wrote four chapters and nothing was happening. I set it aside and said to myself, "Perhaps you're just not cut out to be a novelist." But the characters had already been born and so had their stories. I began to tell myself this story and I realized I was telling it to myself in Marathi. That's when I asked myself, "Is this the language in which I'm supposed to write this story?" And when I started again and wrote the first line in Marathi, I realized I had the language right, never mind the story,' Gokhale says.

'I began writing it in March 1984. If I had had a month to myself, I would have been able to finish the novel in that time. But I didn't have a month to myself. I was a mother and I was working at a corporate job and I was editing plays for the workers to perform. I remember when I wrote the last part. It was in 1986, when my mother was in hospital, dying of cancer of the colon. She was sedated most of the time and I sat by her side and wrote as she slept. I sent the novel out in 1986 and Granthali sat on it for two years. Then Shri Pu [Shrikrishna Purushottam] Bhagwat of Mouj said to me, "I hear you have a novel." I said, "Granthali have been sitting on it for two years." He said, "Can you pull it out from under them? I'd like to have a look." Mouj first published *Rita* in their Diwali special issue and then it came in 1990 as a novel.'*

It is an angular novel. Rita is born in a patriarchal family that is shabby genteel and pretentious; she is suffocating inside it and decides to get a job in order to help her family. At her office, she meets Salvi, an older man, and begins an affair with him and continues even after she discovers that he is married.

---

* The Diwali ank has a special place in the history of Marathi publishing. Often entire novels were published in these magazines. *Rita Welinkar* was published in Mouj's 1989 Diwali ank.

'Male readers loved it. The women didn't talk to me about it. I suppose it was because the book was written from the point of view of the Other Woman. And however rebellious the women were, there was always this question about freedom of choice. If a woman is free then why does she need to adhere to the formality of a paper by which the patriarchy declares that in its eyes X is married to Y? But when a woman found that her husband was having an extramarital affair, it hurt. At bottom, it hurt. I was later to become the Other Woman for Neela Bhagwat when Arun Khopkar and I began to see each other. He was married to her. And later when Arun was married to me and began to philander, there were women who became the Other Woman to me. It's a different thing that Neela and I are now friends. I should have been the thorn in her side but we managed to get over that. But I can see now why women really didn't want to talk to me about it. I did get a very good review in the *Times of India*, from Freya Taraporewala, the last review on the books page edited by Adil Jussawalla when he was there. I may not have been the first at anything, but I was very good at being the last.

'Much better feedback has come since then. It is now seen as a feminist book and specially since there is a translation, it goes into translation studies as well. That may be why it's still on the shelves: in Marathi and in English.'

~

In between, Gokhale would find time to do *Playwright at the Centre: Marathi Drama from 1843 to the Present* (Seagull Books; 2000). This is the kind of work one undertakes, I would have thought, only after one has been commissioned to do it. 'Nobody asked me to do *Playwright at the Centre*; I knew I had to do it if only to address the non-Marathi Indian reader who always had the same questions about Marathi theatre: how come you have so many writers? Why is your visual sense in theatre so poor? I had hunches about the answers to both questions but I needed to explore them. I felt I owed it to my theatrically rich State to put out there what I knew and what I discovered in the course of my research. It was a way of talking at length to my theatre colleagues in Bengal and Karnataka and Delhi and Chennai.'

It is a magisterial work that still remains indispensable to anyone who wants to understand the theatres of modern India. The book she edited, *The Scenes We Made: An Oral History of Experimental Theatre in Mumbai* (Speaking Tiger; 2015), makes an excellent companion volume.

~

Many years would elapse before the second novel, the much more ambitious *Tya Varshi* (The title literally means 'that year', but was translated as *Crowfall* in English). Its protagonist Anima has lost her husband to the riots and maintains a precarious relationship with her mother who lives in their village home. Art, music and friendship sustain her. This is a novel about cosmopolitanism but it never becomes an account of superficial sophistication. This is the space where an artist wakes up to confront his terror, the loss of muscle control; and the wrong raga at the wrong time of day can bring down the vitriolic wrath of a guru.

'I remember you telling me,' I remind her, 'about how the idea for a novel started with the image of an old woman on her deathbed and some other women around her...'

'With a novel, an image can be a starting point. You use the image and then as the story opens out and the characters begin to come alive, you may actually come to the point where you say to yourself, "What happened to that poor old woman on her deathbed?" For, there may come a stage when you have to let your starting point go. For instance, *Crowfall* began with my depression over the suicide of the artist Girish Dahiwale.* Through the fog of that sadness, I began

* Girish Dahiwale (1974–98) was held to be one of the promising artists of his generation. Some of his work can still be viewed on the internet, including his film *Vakratunda Swaha*.

thinking about the sudden rift that had opened between academic realism and modern painting; and then between modern painting and installation art and new media. There was a whole generation of artists who had been put through the formal grind at the Sir Jamshedji Jeejeebhoy School of Art and then came out into the world to find that something entirely different was happening. That was where *Crowfall* began. Then other artists came in with other problems and I began to realize that there wasn't enough there. I was also haunted by something the artist Deepak Shinde said to me. He had fought a terrible battle with his family, essentially a farming family, to come to the city and join the J.J. School of Art. When he was there, he gave himself entirely to painting. Then he came out and found that art had gone cerebral; there was no room for the kind of figurative work that was his strength. I remember his face, such a lost and desperate look.'

~

A large amount of Gokhale's written work has vanished into cinema. That's what happens to words in cinema: they vanish.

'The beginning of my association with films goes back to the days of Anandam, a film-viewing club which had regular screenings at the Ramnord Laboratories in Worli. The moving force behind this was a man called Gopal Dutia who used to be with Glaxo. Later, he got caught up in the 1970s "Back to the Villages" programme and he dropped out of sight. He was very keen on film and I saw some memorable ones at this film club.'

Her second marriage was to the film-maker Arun Khopkar, with whom she was collaborating even before they were married. 'He was making a film called *Nirnay*, for the Family Planning Association. I did the costumes for that. I suppose there were discussions and I was involved in those but the costumes for a documentary don't need much expertise; you only need common sense. But even before I met Arun, I had done a script for Govind Nihalani about the building of the atomic reactors at Trombay.'

One of the most interesting films of the Khopkar oeuvre is *Figures of Thought* (1990) which has Bhupen Khakhar, Nalini Malani and Vivan Sundaram in a creative jugalbandi with the director. Shanta remembers a moment when Khakhar visited and sang an old Gujarati song.

'I told Arun you must have him sing this song in the film and so he does. *Colours of Absence* [1993], a documentary based on the work and life of the artist Jehangir Sabavala, was my first script, perhaps. By then, I had done that script for Govind so I felt a little more confident about my abilities. I was a writer and here was a form I could work with. It was a form that interested me as well and Arun was never a very enthusiastic scriptwriter. It sort of became a joint venture at the time. We would discuss ideas and then choose one and I would write a proposal for the Ministry of External Affairs which was then sponsoring films on the arts. And when the funding did come through, I would automatically become the scriptwriter.

'There was also a story package that we worked on together for the Family Planning Association. This was at the time when the grand old lady of family planning in India, Avabai Wadia* was still around. So was Dr Mahinder Watsa, an old Glaxo hand.† The concept was that of a young couple who were planning to get married. They go to meet a doctor and ask him a question and from the answer, the film would take off. Anurag Kashyap played the young man. He was an up-country innocent at the time and he said he had learned quite a lot from the film.

'Then there was a film that I suggested. I heard that the puppeteer

---

* Avabai Wadia (1913–2005) was the founder of International Planned Parenthood Federation and the Family Planning Association of India. Her memoir is called *The Light Is Ours: Memoirs and Movements* (2001).

† Dr Mahinder Watsa is in his nineties and is one of the best known of India's sexologists for his columns in which he answers readers' questions with his trademark wit. He is the subject of the documentary film *Ask the Sexpert* (2017, Vaishali Sinha)

Ramdas Padhye had the original puppets that Vishnudas Bhave had handed over to Bhalchandra Pendharkar and he had them in a loft somewhere. He was himself a hand puppeteer so he did not know how to manipulate Bhave's puppets but he taught himself and chose some of them and did a show of one of the plays from his oeuvre, *Sita Swayamwara*. So I scripted a film for the Public Service Broadcasting Trust. No scriptwriter is ever happy with the way a film works out, with the final product, but in retrospect, I think it tells the story and it has a good story to tell. Meanwhile, I did two scripts for Nandan Kudhyadi; one on the painter Raja Ravi Varma and the other on the poet Vinda Karandikar.'

When her marriage to Khopkar ended, the association continued. 'When his infidelity had grown to the point that I could no longer take it, I wanted him to leave my home but he had nowhere to go. My friends urged me to throw his luggage out on the street but that didn't seem like something I could do. But since we had decided that we were no longer together but we were still living in the same house, I thought it best if we had some creative thing going or it might have been intolerable. So I suggested that he take the plunge and make a feature film. As usual I had many ideas but none of them interested him. So finally I said, "Why don't you tell me what you want to do and I'll take it from there?" He was reading a lot of Gogol in those days and said he would like to do a Gogolian story. When he settled on the quarrel between the two Ivans, I was very happy because it was a story I loved. He was not keen on scripting so he left me alone to do it. He wasn't keen on doing the shot breakdown either. I had to push him to do it, but finally I did that independently too.'

The result was a cheerful romp of a film released in 1996, *Katha Doan Ganpatraonchi* (The Story of Two Ganpatraos), illuminated by two comic talents Dilip Prabhavalkar and Mohan Agashe.

Practically the last film Khopkar and Gokhale did together was *Narayan Gangaram Surve* on the lok shahir, the people's poet, released in 2002.

'The Surve film began with me,' Gokhale recounts. 'I remember

Surve and I were both at some conference or meeting or event—I've forgotten what—at the Yashwantrao Chavan Centre and we were walking down the road, past the ministers' cottages at Nariman Point. Up ahead, there were four or five men, obviously of the working class. They saw Surve and their faces lit up with huge smiles. They came up and talked to him, greeting him without obsequiousness. And he too responded, patting one on the back, chatting naturally and spontaneously. Into my mind came the phrase: the people's poet. I came home and told Arun, this is a film I want you to do. Of course, I knew Surve's poetry. I knew he was an interesting man with an interesting story to tell. I also knew that there had been three other films made on him, including one by Dilip Chitre but I thought there was room for another. Arun didn't need much persuading; he was more than willing because Surve had been part of the Little Magazine movement but I had to fight hard to make the kind of film I wanted to. Arun kept saying the script was too complex because it would have Surve and it would have an actor playing Surve—this was because the poet himself was not up to rushing about the city and shooting at different locations. I finally said, "If you want to make a Sahitya Akademi or Films Division kind of documentary on him, then I'll do that one too," and I gave him both. Luckily for me and for the film, I think, Arun had a beautiful young female assistant who read both and said, "Of course we have to do this one with the actor and the real poet," and once a beautiful young female assistant had spoken, Arun was all over the script.

'This was the film that came closest to my conception and visualization of it. With one caveat. I believed that Surve had influenced Marathi poetry and Dalit poets and I wanted to have a few of these young men come together, as they do, and sit and talk about Surve. But for some reason, the production team could not pull this off and finally what we have is two poets stiffly reading out their poems to Surve which was not my idea at all. But there were many other things that were added, images that were created, that were magic; this was where I felt the scripted word had come closest to the visual language. I believe Arun gave himself completely to the film. I insisted that Narayan Surve's wife should also be in the film. Arun said that it would be problematic, she couldn't speak. I said, "Nothing of the kind. There is a poem addressed to her. And when Surve went underground, when he was in jail or in court or in the police station, she held things together. And he was hugely appreciative of her. She was a comrade in every sense of the term and she had to be in the film. Besides, she has a wonderful story about how they got married and she has told us the story so we know she can tell it." When Krishnabai was approached, she said, "I'll do it but Shanta-tai, you have to stand behind the camera and I will talk to you." I did and she did.'

I wanted to put in some of the film work into this book but there was just no space. Besides, the films are out there and her contribution to them should be evident to anyone who has seen them.

At the time of writing this, Ms Gokhale was struggling with a script for Govind Nihalani.*

~

It seems as if there hasn't been a time when this city has not had a column by Shanta Gokhale. I remember reading her in the *Sunday Mid-day*, in *the Times of India*, and lately in the *Mumbai Mirror*. And she also wrote in Marathi.

'Aroon Tikekar was editor of the *Loksatta*, the Marathi newspaper of the Indian Express Group and he was very persuasive. The group had a policy of one-year slots; at the end of the year, they would approach you again. At the end of the first year, he did ask me to continue but I refused. Then a year later, he asked me to do something on manners and that seemed like fun. I enjoyed writing about sitting in an airport and being rocked up and down because the man at the far end was shaking his legs vigorously,

* The film is *Ti ani Itar* (She and the others), 2017.

unconsciously. After I wrote that column asking why people shake their legs like that, I went to the goldsmith Bhadekar, down the road and when I walked in his wife burst out laughing and pointing to her husband, she said, "He shakes his legs," the poor man shrank into himself.'

And of course, there is the accusation that columnists want to mould public opinion. Shanta is honest in her answer: 'I'd love to. It's my space. The thing is, I believe in discussion. So when I write, I try to put down as many facts as I think are pertinent. Then I state what my opinion is on those facts. I am perfectly happy for my reader to have another opinion and I can only hope that this different opinion is based on facts too. From the feedback I get, I know that a lot of my readers seem to agree with me. But when you are reviewing something, you know you're on difficult ground because you are stating your opinion and artists of every kind can be very touchy. I recently wrote a critical review of a dance performance by Anita Rathnam and I was very surprised to get a long letter from her. She said that she had taken note of what I said; that she was going to try and tackle the shortcomings I had pointed out. I wrote back that I was happy to hear that because most artists don't want dialogue. But she said there are some people that we respect for their opinions and you are one of them. Well then, if one has acquired such a reputation that is a good thing.

'I wrote a column on Leela Samson once and several people rang me up to say that I had not mentioned that she couldn't quite hold the Nataraja pose. Yes, I did notice the wobble. But I did say that one looks for different things from a sixty-year-old dancer and from a young one. Because at the end of the day, it is about the body.

'Whenever I write a critical review of a film, one of the people involved will call me up and say, "Can you even begin to guess how much work went into the making of the film?" To which my answer is, "Every film-maker puts a huge amount of work into the film s/he is making. But that is not the point. The film is." And the next line is: "But So-and-So loved it." To which I can only say: "It is good for an artist to receive mixed feedback. Now you have to put my opinion next to So-and-So's and see what you get".'

~

In her study at Lalit Estates, Dadar, Shanta Gokhale and I are discussing the essays she and I are supposed to write for an international magazine.

'I've chosen a big topic,' she says. 'Because I'm no good at filling up.'

I thought it might make a good place to start. What does this mean: filling up?

'You get an idea. You think, "Oh, this might make a great story or a column." But when you get down to it, you find that it needs to be expanded. This is easily done if it is an argument, but that's not what I'm talking about here. This is something fluffier. You have to think up metaphors, you have to put in images, you have to add quotes and for that you have to have a good memory, which I do not have. That is called filling up. I have so many ideas that flit across my mind. I have learned over time to enjoy these and to let them go. In a book I have, called *The Creative Process: A Symposium* [Edited by Brewster Ghiselin, University of California Press; 1952], many people from mathematicians to artists to writers talk about their processes. One of these is Katharine Anne Porter, a short-story writer. She says that it was pointed out to her that she could not describe, her short stories lacked descriptions. So she set herself an exercise. She went out and sat down somewhere on a hill or something and looked around her with the intention of going home and describing things. When she got home, she tried and found that she could not do it; she could not describe what she had seen. And she decided that there were some things she could do and some things she couldn't. And that is why I say I can't fill up.'

This may be one of the secrets of her writing. If you are unable to fill up, you have to say what you want and end there.

One of the pleasures of working on this book has been, of course, talking to Shanta, going over, asking where the pieces were, going with her to the Mumbai Marathi Granth Sangrahalaya to locate her pieces for the weekly newsmagazine *Saptahik Sakal*, choosing them, and in some cases translating them.

So you will see the range of work here is quite astonishing. So are the tonalities. There is compassion and there is savage satire.

~

And of course, I discovered Shanta Gokhale's fiction.

One of the problems was simply making sure that I had read whatever work was available. The first piece that Gokhale wrote appeared in 1976. The last appeared a few months before the time we closed the book. That's forty years of a committed engagement with the word in two languages.

(Gokhale herself is not particularly interested in her own archive. Through the course of the making of this book, we would be talking about something else when she would mention some work she had done with this magazine or how that issue of a Diwali ank—a special issue—had carried a story and off we would go again, looking for material.)

Gokhale shines in her non-fiction but her fiction has an equally quiet power. She shapeshifts effortlessly, inhabiting the loafer, the ageing man about town who must compete with younger men, the little boy from a chawl who is compelled to become a goddess and enters into dialogue with the god. This section makes one wish that she had found more time to write short stories. There are others which could not be included here and still others which may be found.

And finally there is another register here, and this is where you see what a fine poet Gokhale might have been had she continued to try and write poetry. This is in the last section, the two beautiful takes on Shakespeare. *I Am Not What I Am* takes off from *Othello*, and begins to ask big questions, not just about jealousy, but about the nature of evil and how much we have to be complicit in order for it to work. I should love to see this made into a short film.

Rosemary for Remembrance, a work conceived for Arundhati Nag at the Rang Shankara, Bangalore, and which for one reason or another was never performed there. When I read it I thought it an interesting work that should find an audience and so it was staged for the Kala Ghoda Arts Festival, Mumbai, 2014, directed by Arghya Lahiri with Dolly Thakore and Devika Shahani-Punjabi in the lead roles. The Jehangir Sabavala Foundation gave us a grant that made it possible. What struck me there was her ability to invent convincing backstories for the two women in a play dominated by men and their bloody deeds. Hamlet may be the Bard's greatest achievement but that cannot be said for how he treats the women in the play. And it isn't as if he hasn't got some rather good women characters: Cordelia in *King Lear*, Portia in *The Merchant of Venice*, Beatrice in *Much Ado about Nothing*. But Gertrude seems to exist only to create the trouble; and Ophelia, although she has become something of a Romantic/Pre-Raphaelite staple, seems bloodless. Shanta brings both these women to life; she gives Gertrude a backstory and a rather grim take on what it means to be a queen without a king. She infuses Ophelia with love and blood and she points out something I had never seen: Hamlet's last words as heard by his mother.

'Odd,' I said when I had read the play. 'I never saw that.'

'You're not a woman,' she said. 'How would you?'

~

About my choices.

In some cases, I have violated an unspoken rule anthologists have: no repetition of subjects. But when you read the trio of pieces on Pandit Mukul Shivputra, you will see many of the things I consider so important about Shanta Gokhale's work: her method of elucidation by carefully worked out analogies (and from a breath-taking range of subjects, architecture, painting, dance and the novel), her commitment to the arts, her memory for these moments and her ability to make complex aesthetic moments comprehensible while never dumbing down the subject. With Sheila Dhar, I see this as some of the finest non-technical writing on music to have happened in this country.

I have enjoyed the way some of these pieces talk to each other. Consider her careful and civilized evisceration of Pramod Navalkar's belief that when women stop cooking, Indian civilization will end; then look at what Gertrude tells Ophelia about baking for Hamlet and you will see a way in which an idea suffers a sea-change into something rich and strange.

If there seem to be any number of obituaries here, those only stand testament to the variety of her interests and the network of relationships that she sustained. She was friends with so many of the people who made our city, hers and mine and Satyadev Dubey's and Vijay Tendulkar's and Ashok Ranade's and Arun Kolatkar's and Pandit Jal Balaporia's what it has always been—a city of rich, eclectic culture worn so lightly that it has vanished under the glare of the neon.

A final word: you will not find excerpts from many of the books mentioned here in this volume; this is because they are still in print. An anthology such as this, in my opinion, should be a taster menu. Now you should go out and buy her other books. You will then be able to enter into dialogue with the many Shanta Gokhales there are, and you will encounter one of the finest minds of our times.

Jerry Pinto
Lillehammer, Norway

NB: Unless otherwise stated, I have translated the pieces from Marathi. This was one of the pleasures of putting together the book.

On Theatre

'The third path'

Mapping Marathi Theatre Spaces

Theatre happens everywhere, but only when it announces itself publicly can we assume that it is relevant to the community at large. The means of communication could range from blackboards placed at street corners to advertisements in newspapers to messages on the net. When theatre is not made visible by these or any other means, when one does not even get a call from a friend to say there's a play on at such and such a place which must be seen, it is clear one is in a place where theatre is not a vital cultural expression of the community.

I use the term theatre to mean an ongoing theatre activity that we may refer to as mainstream or professional, in part because Maharashtra, where I come from, has a long tradition of such theatre. An examination of this tradition reveals relationships built over time between theatre and space, space and audience and audience and theatre that one may not have the opportunity to study elsewhere. Places where theatre is a sporadic activity driven by an individual playmaker will often produce brilliant plays. Theatre that has an unbroken history may not, because with a tradition to back the effort, theatre people can become complacent. The audience, too, may demand the comfort of the expected. A mainstream professional theatre allows its practitioners to live off it. But its very predictability often provokes others to go beyond commerce to create plays with a socio-political or aesthetic purpose. When mainstream theatre borrows whatever it finds useful from

---

This was a paper read at the 'Not-the-Drama Seminar' at Ninasam, Heggodu, 22–26 March 2008.

this other theatre, it recharges itself. In turn the shifts it makes towards the other theatre challenges the latter to question itself and possibly make radical departures from what it has been. Though a neat theory, this does not always translate into practice. However, it serves as a measure against which to examine what is actually happening in both theatres.

About fifteen years ago, I spent a fortnight each in Calcutta and Bangalore as part of my research for a book on Marathi theatre. During the fortnight I spent in Calcutta, I saw a play every evening at the government-run Nandan complex. During the fortnight I spent in Bangalore, I did not see a single play. It shocked me that Bangalore did not have a dedicated theatre space. The question about whether it had a dedicated theatre audience was answered on another visit when I chanced to see, by pure serendipity, a brilliant production of Mahesh Elkunchwar's *Vasansi Jeernani* (The Fraying of the Body), translated into Kannada by Girish Karnad and directed by K.M. Chaitanya. Even though the hall where it was staged was dull and characterless, the audience was keenly receptive.

The problem of a dedicated theatre space in Bangalore was resolved in 2004 with the inauguration of Ranga Shankara. Despite its inconvenient location, it has had a full schedule of plays ever since. Arundhathi Nag would not have spent ten years striving to make this happen unless she had been confident of an enthusiastic theatre community and an eager audience. Reversing the logic, one might argue that nobody has attempted to create a space like Ranga Shankara in Chennai because the city lacks a theatre culture. While Chennai has no theatre culture, Mumbai, Pune, Kolhapur and Sangli do not have a dance culture. To begin with, Maharashtra does not have its own 'classical' dance form. Further, I would like to speculate that any interest in dance that could have entered Maharashtra from neighbouring regions was scotched by those who influenced its culture. My speculation is based on a single, well-documented instance. The Raja of Sangli was impressed by a Bhagwat Mela* performance he had chanced to see. He instructed his courtier, Vishnudas Bhave, to create a similar entertainment for the Sangli court, but minus the 'vulgarity' of dance. Bhave wrote, designed and presented *Sita Swayamvar* in 1843. It was the first Marathi play to be staged in a secular setting, unconnected with any religious ritual or sacred day. It had music and action, but no dance.

As we have seen, a community which needs theatre creates and watches performances in the most inhospitable of outdoor and indoor spaces. Performers and audience alike are willing to overlook all kinds of physical discomfort in the process. The performers make do without lights, wings, curtains. The audience sits on floors or benches, craning its necks to view the action. This happened during the 1930s and '40s in Maharashtra, when the sangeet natak (musical theatre) declined and cinema took away theatre spaces. Consequently, theatre got pushed into clubs, school halls and unspecified recreation spaces. Outdoor spaces were always there to be used, but only certain kinds of theatre could be performed there. The Assamese mobile theatre is a case in point. In the 1960s Achyut Lahkar, who started the movement, saw that theatre had stagnated in Assam. His strategy to revive it was to take it to people's doorsteps. So he built a stage of bamboo and wood that could be dismantled, loaded it onto a truck and rolled out into the countryside. People thronged to see his plays. So successful was this venture that other playwrights and producers asked him for permission to copy the model. Permission was readily granted because Lahkar's purpose was to revive theatre activity in Assam. Over the last four decades, the mobile theatre has turned into a well-oiled industry, employing approximately 10,000 workers. Something like forty theatre companies take to the road each year with 150 new plays. They travel across the length and breadth of

---

* A Bhagwat Mela (literally: where the devotees gather) is a dance drama performed in Tamil Nadu.

Assam from September to March, each company doing about 200 shows in sixty centres. It is professional theatre, its aesthetics governed by its itinerant nature.

Outdoor spaces are inclusive. A mobile theatre audience comprises thousands. Consequently, plays must be loud in all respects—voice, movement, gesture and costume. It is interesting to note how the kind of space Marathi theatre inhabited over its 160-year-old history and the constitution of its audience, influenced its aesthetics. As pointed out earlier, its origins were in folk forms like the Bhagwat Mela which were performed in temple precincts. From available descriptions we know that even Bhave's plays performed in the Sangli court retained many features of a folk performance. When the Raja of Sangli died and his heir expressed his inability to support the troupe of players who had come to depend on theatre for their livelihood, Bhave shifted back into the open. But now, instead of performing in temple courtyards, his troupe performed in the courtyards of the rich. The base of patronage was thus expanded from one king and his court to many aristocrats and their courtyards. It is possible that Bhave made commensurate changes in his style of presentation to cater to this new audience.

Ten years after the performance of *Sita Swayamvar*, Bhave visited Mumbai. While there, he happened to see a play on the proscenium stage at the Grant Road Theatre. He was instantly fascinated by the possibilities of this kind of theatre space. He could not afford the theatre charge of Rs 500, but his wealthy Marathi well-wishers helped him get a booking. His first production on this stage was of a play called *Gopichand*. This was the first Marathi play to be performed on the proscenium stage, the first to be ticketed and the first to cater to a linguistically mixed audience.

The theme and presentation of the play were influenced by all these factors. From one royal patron to several aristocratic patrons, to a large gathering of the well-heeled, comprising Parsis and Muslims along with non-Marathi Hindus, all paying for themselves, Bhave had made really big strides. That these factors affected the presentation of *Gopichand* may be deduced from a line that appeared in its advertisement. It invited the audience to 'see the bundle of firewood on Machhindranath's head levitate and float in the air'. This magical effect was the precursor of the 'trick scenes' that became an integral part of popular Marathi theatre for many years to come.

By the time the sangeet natak arrived in 1880 (Annasaheb Kirloskar's *Shakuntal*), the proscenium was firmly established. Its possibilities were fully exploited for realistic effect. But paradoxically, the more realistic the production, the more magical it seemed to the audience. A scene from *Vadhupariksha* ('The Test of a Wife'), one of S.K. Kolhatkar's minor plays, probably performed in the second decade of the twentieth century, is described thus by Pu Shri Kale in his memoirs: 'When the desperate Triveni jumped into a well which itself was a breathtaking example of stage setting, not only did we hear the sound of the splash, but water actually flew up from the well. The same thing happened when Dhurandhar jumped in to save her. But the ultimate effect came when the two emerged from the well. The audience gasped in wonder because both of them were dripping wet.'*

B.V. Warerkar (Mama), the author of *Satteche Gulam* (The Slaves of Power, 1932) writes, 'We decided to think of the stage set as architecture rather than painting. The doors and windows were to be shown in their solidity. The depth, length and width of rooms were to be realistically represented to make them look real. For this Kale [the designer] was going to construct a proscenium arch.'

The proscenium and the box-set have remained Marathi mainstream theatre's chosen space and stage design ever since.

Spatially, Marathi theatre moved from general open-air performances to enclosed court performances, to exclusive open-

---

* Pu Shri Kale was a set designer of the sangeet natak stage. This is taken from his book *Lalitkalechya Sahawaasat* (In the Company of Lalitkala). Lalitkala is short for the famous theatre company Lalitkaladarsha.

air performances, to enclosed, exclusive indoor performances. For patrons it moved from a collectively paying public in temple precincts to a single royal patron to a more numerous aristocratic patronage to an even more numerous individually paying patronage. Thematically, it moved from mythology that belonged to everybody, to sangeet nataks about warrior heroes. But since music continued to be a vital attraction, the sangeet natak continued to cater to a heterogeneous audience.

Modern, realistic/melodramatic plays cut down on the number of songs used but did not abolish them altogether, thus maintaining its relationship with the traditional sangeet natak and its traditional audience. It was only after the advent of cinema that mainstream theatre became a reflection of middle-class mores. It now dealt exclusively with middle-class problems set in middle-class drawing rooms. This is the class that has kept mainstream theatre alive in Maharashtra till today. Other sections, which once patronized folk theatre, turned to the cinema in overwhelming numbers.

With cinema, theatre lost its indoor spaces. Every one of the playhouses listed in *Mumbaicha Vrittanta* (A Chronicle of Bombay, 1889) authored by Shingane and Acharya, including Gaiety, Novelty, Alfred, National, Victoria and Ripon, were transformed into cinema houses. The Grant Road Theatre where Vishnudas Bhave had performed *Gopichand* had by then been demolished to make way for a textile mill. In 1943, when the Mumbai Marathi Sahitya Sangh celebrated the centenary of the first Marathi play, it pledged itself to building an indoor auditorium; but it was only in 1964 that the pledge could be fulfilled. Till then Marathi theatre was kept alive in clubhouses and school halls.

What happened to the Sahitya Sangh Mandir within twenty years of its inauguration underlines sharply the relationship between an active theatre space and an active theatre-going community. Girgaum, where the auditorium is located, was once the stronghold of the Marathi clerk, schoolteacher, small businessman and government official. With liberalization, real-estate prices rose. The Marathi middle class saw an opportunity to make more money than it had ever dreamt of by selling its chawl rooms in Girgaum and moving into the distant suburbs. The communities which replaced them had no interest in theatre. Consequently, by the 1990s the Sahitya Sangh auditorium had become a dead space. Simultaneously, municipal auditoria sprang up in every suburb to which the Marathi middle class had relocated, and began to buzz with daily activity.

Till the early 1990s, mainstream theatre offered scope for cautious shifts in theme and form as long as play endings were happy and the plays contained a few fine speeches. Thereafter, coinciding with the economic boom, theatre became not just conventional but often positively regressive. A shining example of mainstream success was the late Vasant Kanetkar, who had begun his career writing off-mainstream plays. Expounding on his theory of *kalatmak tartamya* (artistic propriety) in a series of lectures delivered at the Mumbai Marathi Sahitya Sangh in 1974, he asserted that the duty of theatre was to give the audience an opportunity to experience rasa. The *bibhatsa rasa* (disgust) was inappropriate on stage. Kanetkar roundly condemned the scene in Vijay Tendulkar's *Gidhade* (Vultures) where Manik runs out of the house with blood stains on her sari indicating a miscarriage. He also vigorously argued against showing dinner scenes and scenes of lovemaking on stage because he thought they released the audience's baser appetites. He also believed, taking Rangayan's production of Ionesco's *Chairs* as an example, that plays should not be difficult for the audience to understand. In his opinion Jaywant Dalvi's play *Sandhyachhaya* (Evening shadows), dealt with 'the same subject' as *Chairs*, namely an aged couple's loneliness. But whereas Dalvi had handled the subject in a way that made it accessible to the audience, Ionesco had made his play opaque and inaccessible.

Let us now return to that neat little theory about off-mainstream theatre pushing the mainstream towards new forms, new themes and new acting styles. While the mainstream stage was held by Kanetkar and his colleagues, Rangayan and Theatre Unit in Mumbai and Theatre Academy in Pune were staging plays by Vijay Tendulkar, Satish Alekar, Mahesh Elkunchwar, G.P. Deshpande, et al. There was absolutely no give and take between these two streams till Tendulkar and Shreeram Lagoo, who began their careers off mainstream, moved to the mainstream with realistic plays and a low-key, naturalistic acting style that was new to it. Both made good on the mainstream stage, proving its flexibility. But Tendulkar was acceptable only as long as he did not offend the audience with the *bibhatsa rasa* or sexually explicit scenes. In this sense the mainstream actually co-opted the off-mainstream.

What subverted the Shivaji Mandir stage—that iconic middle-class theatre space—albeit unintentionally, was a three-day festival of Dalit plays held there in 2007. The six plays featured in the festival were uneven in terms of craft and presentation. But for those three days, this 'sacred' theatre space resounded to voices that had never before been heard there.

Theatre is thus a constant see-saw in Maharashtra between these two. The mainstream is not doing too well at the moment, but things are happening off mainstream in Pune and Mumbai. New intimate spaces have sprung up around which new writers, directors, actors and a new audience have gathered. This theatre is by no means radical or revolutionary, but it is young and it is fresh. So the tradition continues.

On Satyadev Dubey
Playwright, Director, Friend

It is not possible to encompass in one go, the enormous and unique contribution to theatre Satyadev Dubey made during his hyperactive, all-consuming career of fifty years. He lived, breathed, talked theatre non-stop from the day he discovered its power to seduce an audience into attentive silence with the voice and body of the actor. He saw it when he returned to the auditorium of St Xavier's College as the first show of the first play he had ever directed, ended, and he heard the applause.

He experienced the other side of theatre, the risk of stepping onto a stage and speaking without conviction, when he played Haemon* in Alkazi's production of Anouilh's *Antigone.* The character made no sense to him at all. A whole half century later, Dubey cut Haemon right out of his own production of *Antigone*, still believing him to be superfluous in a play that was truly and only about Antigone, the individual, against Creon, the State.

It was in 1952 that the young Satyadev Dubey first came to Mumbai from his native Bilaspur in Madhya Pradesh, to do his

---

This article has been collated from several pieces Shanta Gokhale wrote. If we were to include them all, they would have been repetitive, but to exclude some would be to lose valuable insights into Satyadev Dubey. Hence the editorial decision to fold these into each other. The pieces include 'Satyadev Dubey: Director of Words and Ideas' for *Economic & Political Weekly*, Vol. 48, Issue No. 36, 7 September 2013; 'A Tribute to Satyadev Dubey' for Indian Theatre Forum's E-rang, http://theatreforum.in/m/e-rang/?tab=issues&object_id=8 accessed on 31 July 2018 at 13:57 p.m.; and her column in *Mumbai Mirror*.

* Haemon is the son of Creon and Antigone's fiancé.

Bachelors in English and Hindi from St Xavier's College. He had lost his parents at a young age and was, to all intents and purposes, homeless. As things turned out, he adopted Mumbai as his home, becoming, in his own words, an honorary Maharashtrian.

He was a keen cricketer and somewhere in his young mind was a flickering ambition to become a cricketer. He even got selected on the college team but only as the thirteenth man. When he realized he was never going to be good enough, he ended his cricketing days before they had begun.

Meanwhile he met Vijay Anand, Dev Anand's younger brother, by chance in the college corridor. Anand led the college dramatic activity and coaxed Dubey to join.

It was by a series of similar chance encounters that he met other theatre enthusiasts and soon became immersed in this new activity. Theatre gave him a community that he could belong to in Mumbai, where he had no other roots. Gradually, he realized two things—that he had an innate sense of theatre, and that it was a perfect outlet for his creative energies.

Partly to be with his friends and partly to give himself some formal training in theatre, he joined Ebrahim Alkazi's drama school. Alkazi, who had trained in the Royal Academy of Dramatic Art, London, headed a group called the Theatre Unit in Mumbai. When in the early 1960s he left the city for Delhi, to take over as the first director of the National School of Drama, Dubey took over the reins of Theatre Unit and turned it into the most productive theatre group anywhere in the country. In the next fifty years, he did an average of two plays a year, his last being as recently as 2009.

Dubey was a terrible force in the lives of the actors he worked with. He distrusted actors who worked mentally on their roles. Clarity of thought destroyed instinct, which, he believed, had to be the prime mover for the actor. He once said to me, 'Sulabha Deshpande could be a finer actor than she is. But she thinks too much.' He also said Amrish Puri became a giant of an actor because he did not think; he let his instinct lead him. At a rehearsal that I was watching once, an actor could not move from point A to point B as Dubey wanted without understanding the motivation behind the move. 'Forget the motivation. Just move,' Dubey thundered, 'because that's what you need to do here.'

There were two Dubeys at rehearsals. One was all there, invisible cane in hand, ready to strike those who erred. The other was the absent one. For months two girls rehearsed their lines in the sitting room of his flat in Bandra while he slept, or appeared to be sleeping, inside. This went on for months till work called one of the girls away. The play was never staged. The ease with which he let go of it instead of replacing the absent girl amazed me because, from the moment he had returned after one of his visits to the National School of Drama, he had been talking about writing this play. And when it was written, about doing it. Perhaps, as he lay in his bedroom listening to the girls rehearsing the play, he heard flaws which he could not be bothered to iron out with yet another draft. Perhaps it had grown stale on him. Most importantly, other plays were pressing down on him, waiting to be done.

But that was Dubey, often described as the *enfant terrible* of theatre. Leafing through some old issues of *Facts & News*, a journal that used to be published (for private circulation only) by the now-defunct Theatre Development Project (TDP) of the National Centre for the Performing Arts (NCPA), I was not one bit surprised to see that Dubey was absent from its pages. His absence was most conspicuous in the issue devoted to actor training. For if there was one thing Dubey had done consistently for five decades, along with direction, acting, writing for films and helping playwrights to shape their plays, it was to train actors. 'Dubey is a brutal taskmaster,' Deepa Shriram once told me. 'His training is an ordeal by fire. But he has given Marathi and Gujarati theatre some of its finest performers; and I myself will never forget the debt I owe him as an actress.' Dozens of other actors have echoed similar sentiments.

Yet Dubey wasn't featured as a teacher in *Facts & News*.

Nor was he featured as a director in the TDP's 1989 edition of *Rang-Antarang* which contained interviews with writers and directors of some of the most significant Marathi plays of the time. G.P. Deshpande's *Andharyatra* (Journey in the Dark) was one of them. Dubey's production of it had stunned the audience with its power and beauty. Yet he had not been interviewed along with Deshpande.

Such negligence could not have happened by oversight. Nor could the NCPA have planned to ignore him. It is more likely that Dubey had fought with one or all of the editors and/or adamantly refused to be interviewed for some volatile reasons of his own. God knows he'd fought with practically every woman and man that he had ever called friend and with every theatre/institution where he had staged his plays. That includes Prithvi Theatre even when it was busy planning its annual festival as a tribute to him.

There are other reasons why he and his work have not been more widely documented. Chief amongst them is his stubborn resistance to the idea. He has always had better things to do than being put on record. Theatre for example. The other reason was his unpredictability. He has not acquired the gravitas of contemporaries like Shyam Benegal and Govind Nihalani. Being mercurial gave him greater freedom to be what he wanted to be at any given point of time. There was a time when he put prospective interviewers off by demanding money for interviews. Perhaps he still does. And till 1983, when his admirers in Aurangabad organized a festival of his plays and asked for his bio-data, he did not have one. He had never bothered to put one together. It took Sunil Shanbag days to persuade him to part with details of his life and work.

Dubey has consistently undercut all public attempts at taking him seriously by cloaking his achievements under mock self-deprecatory or mock-hyperbolic statements. His play *Khuda ke Liye Mat Dekhna* (For God's Sake, Don't Watch This One) does so in the title itself. Nobody can accuse him of scattering carefully chiselled gems of thought that could be stored away in shrines.

If he were to say one thing today that you thought you should remember forever, he would say the exact opposite the next. What has driven all his public statements is the desire to give the ground under people's feet a little shake. That's the method and purpose of theatre too. And so he states, 'There can be only three motivations for doing theatre—money, fame and women. I must admit, mine are fame and women.'

~

Mine was one of the many lives Satyadev Dubey touched in the fifty years he spent in, with and for theatre. I met Dubey in 1962; the place, outside Chitra cinema, Dadar, where a French New Wave film (or was it a Satyajit Ray film?) was to be screened. Such things happened in those halcyon days of film madness.

So there I was, waiting for a friend to arrive when I accidentally dropped my ticket. Before I could retrieve it, a swift hand shot out of nowhere and handed it to me. The man behind the hand said, 'I'm Satyadev Dubey. You are Shanta Gokhale. Will you act in my play?'

I did not act in his play but I became used to his directness. There was always work to be done and directness took less time. In 1971 I got a two-line letter from him when I was living temporarily in Vishakhapatnam. 'What are you doing vegetating out there? Use your time to translate this.' 'This' turned out to be C.T. Khanolkar's play *Avadhya* (The Invincible), in which four men in a seedy hotel room watch a young couple making love on the other side through a hole in the wall. It had been staged not too long before Dubey sent me the script, and had created a storm of shocked comment in newspapers and magazines. But the eminent critic, Madhav Manohar, had called it 'the first adult Marathi play'.

Avadhya was my first attempt at translating a play. I was nervous as I worked on it and even more nervous as I read it to myself. But Dubey thought I had caught the spirit of the play and sent it off to his friend Rajinder Paul in Delhi. Paul was a friend because he, too, was afflicted with theatre madness. Being mad about theatre was an important qualification for Dubey to even look at you. Paul owned a printing press and published a theatre magazine called *Enact*, primarily to cross-fertilize plays written in the Indian languages. *Avadhya* was published in *Enact*, and set me off on a lifetime's pursuit of the difficult art of translation.

Cross-fertilization was happening all over the country in the seventies, presided over by Dubey in Mumbai, Rajinder Paul in Delhi and Shyamanand Jalan in Kolkata. Vijay Tendulkar was translating, Amol Palekar was translating, Girish Karnad was translating, Vasant Dev was translating, and Paul was publishing. It was like a multi-dynamo factory at work. The atmosphere was electric with ideas, debates, discussions. It was as though our very lives depended on how fresh/stale, honest/dishonest, ideologically trammelled/untrammelled the new plays were. In Pune in 1973, Dubey brought together a large community of theatre practitioners to thrash out plays that promising new playwrights had written.

At the centre of the new theatre activity in Mumbai was Awishkar, the mother of all Marathi theatre groups in Mumbai, housed in the hall of Chhabildas Boys' High School, up three flights of dilapidated stairs in Dadar, which was then a suburb but has now graduated to becoming part of Central Mumbai. The collections at a Dubey play were initially made in a jholi that was held out to the audience as it trickled out of a show. Then a desk was set up at the entrance downstairs where five-rupee tickets (that gradually went up to thirty) were sold. Dubey's rehearsals were always open to friends. They told you the story behind what you saw on stage on opening day. It was a story of raving, ranting, abusing and tears that finally produced those rigorously rehearsed performances at the end. Chhabildas Hall was the venue for some of Dubey's plays in the 1980s. This is where I saw his production of my play *Avinash*.

Thereby hangs a complicated tale, which begins with Dubey's constant efforts to help friends get breaks. He made use of his friendship and professional association with film-makers like Shyam Benegal and Girish Karnad to recommend actors who had trained under him for roles in their films. Ganesh Yadav, Kishore Kadam, Sonali Kulkarni benefitted by the breaks that he made possible. I was not a struggling actor, but in the course of a conversation I had said to Dubey that I would love to experience all aspects of film-making, including facing the camera. He remembered this, and suggested to Govind Nihalani that he should ask me for the small role of the social worker who makes a speech against police atrocities in *Ardh Satya*. Govind asked me. Totally stunned, I said yes, because Govind, too, was a friend.

Apropos something we were saying, I described a scene from a play I had written. What are you doing with your play? Govind asked. I wasn't doing anything, I said. The next day Dubey was at my house, angry that I had written a play and not shown it to him. He took it away and within six weeks it was on stage in its original language, Marathi. This was my first and only experience of being one of Dubey's writers and I must confess he did not change a thing in *Avinash*. The only thing he did do was give it a time, 1974, and a location, Shivaji Park. I had not located the play in any particular time or place because I was convinced it could happen anywhere and at any time in India. But Dubey did not care for ambiguities. Which is why he also asked me to close the open end of the play with a strong speech that would remove all ambiguity.*

If he took me into his growing fold of admirers and friends, it was because I loved theatre. If he dropped me for many years from this fold, it was because I had 'allowed' my daughter to do a television serial. She had danced as one of half-a-dozen crows in black robes in his prelude to Shafaat Khan's satirical play, *Bambai ke Kauwwe* (The Crows of Bombay). It was her introduction to theatre and Dubey had expected her to remain loyal to it. Since she was betraying theatre, he had nothing to say to her or her mother.

~

* 'Did you?' I asked Shanta. 'I wrote it for his Marathi production and that's what got translated into Sunil Shanbhag's Hindi production. But I ended the play the way I had written it in the translation published by Seagull.'

Theatre consumed Dubey body, mind and soul for more than half a century. He was possessive about his actors, but never about plays. The discovery of a good play was the most exciting event of his life, and he could not rest till he had shared it with all his friends. This happened when he discovered Dharamvir Bharati's *Andha Yug.** The play had been written for radio; but when Dubey read it, he was blown by its theatrical potential. He staged it in 1962, on the seventh-floor terrace of a building on Bhulabhai Desai Road. The production was quintessentially what came to be known later as 'environmental theatre'. But Dubey did it as naturally as his 1960s plays on Tejpal's proscenium stage and his 1970s and 1980s plays on the bare floor of the hall in Chhabildas School. No labels. No pretensions. No theories.

It wasn't enough for him to do *Andha Yug*, a play he placed among the ten best in the world. More people had to see it. So he sent the script to friends all over the country. That included Ebrahim Alkazi at the National School of Drama. It was Alkazi's production of *Andha Yug* against the backdrop of the dilapidated Ferozeshah Kotla, that created an aura around it, and the play was hailed as a modern classic.

Dharamvir Bharati saw Dubey's production as 'the first sign of life shattering the sepulchral silence that had fallen over Hindi theatre in the previous fifty years'. Many who had been sceptical about how this radio play would work on stage, came away with a sense of having experienced something extraordinary, revealing to them the terror and beauty that theatre was capable of creating.

Dharamvir's Ashwatthama was to become one of Dubey's most cherished characters. The other was Badal Sircar's Indrajit. The pain of the mythological man and the frustrations of the modern man, both found an echo in Dubey's life. Later Sarveshwar, the hero of his autobiographical play *Inshallah* (God willing), became the utterance that defined more clearly how he saw himself. He saw himself as

---

* *Andha Yug, The Age of the Blind*, is available in English translation by Alok Bhalla (Oxford University Press; 2010).

an artist embroiled in a battle against falseness, violence, injustice, deadly routine and the commercialization of the human soul.

When Girish Karnad informed him hesitantly that he had written a play, *Yayati*, which he would be happy if Dubey would take a look at, Dubey dismissed the idea peremptorily saying you must have written it in English. English theatre was anathema to him in the nationalistic project in which he saw himself engaged. The idea was to challenge the borrowed sophistication of English theatre, supported by the moneybags of the advertising world, with an Indian-language theatre, financially less endowed but rich with original writing and ideas rooted in the Indian experience. When Karnad said his play was in Kannada, Dubey was all ears. Soon he was directing the Hindi version of it and went on to admit that it was amongst his most successful plays.

Dubey has responded in similar manner, and with equal conviction to plays written by young writers of every new generation. He conducted two playwrights' workshops, the first in 1973 at the Film Institute, Pune, and the second, some fifteen years later in his own home in Bandra. The participants in the workshops—amongst them G.P. Deshpande, Satish Alekar and Mahesh Elkunchwar in the first, and Chetan Datar, Rajeev Naik and Shafaat Khan in the second—went on to become the finest playwrights of Marathi experimental theatre. Dubey had seen the truth at the heart of their raw scripts and had helped them develop them into full-blooded plays.

It was during a theatre festival at the Academy of Dramatic Arts, Mumbai University, that he sent somebody running after me as I was walking out of the auditorium. 'I have to make a film on this play,' he said. We had just seen Chandrashekhar Phansalkar's *Ram Naam Satya Hai* (The name of Rama embodies truth; also one of the traditional Hindu chants when a corpse sets out on its last journey) directed by the late Chetan Datar, one of Dubey's most devoted disciples. 'I just need three crores to make it,' he said. 'Why don't you put an appeal at the end of one of your columns, yaar?

Who knows? The money might come.' The money never came; but he had enough admirers willing to lend their services for free, to allow him to shoot it.

Lack of money never stopped Dubey; for fifty years he did theatre without money. On the only occasion when a play of his became unbelievably popular and put money in his pocket, he was deeply embarrassed. 'I must have done something desperately wrong,' he said unhappily, looking around for ways to get rid of the burden.

His economics were simple. Don't bother about the trappings of theatre. Fancy sets, music, costumes are fine if you have the money. But when you don't, concentrate on speech. In the actors' training workshops which he conducted, he spent a major amount of time giving participants speech exercises, which included speaking with pencils held horizontally in their mouths. As far as he was concerned, all that was needed for the play to take off was an interesting script and actors who spoke with an intelligent understanding of what their lines were saying and of how to use their voices to get their meaning across. Then you have to rehearse your actors till they collapse with mental, emotional and physical stress. Get them to speak their lines with clarity and conviction. The last man in the audience must hear what they are saying and understand every nuance of the import. And don't let them drop their voices at the end of their lines. They must keep their breath till they get there, and use it. That's theatre.

Today's audiences have only the vaguest notion of why Dubey commands such awe amongst writers and actors who have worked with him or been mentored by him. They have heard of his legendary temper (and he could be truly vicious when he applied himself to breaking down and trampling all over an actor's ego). But they do not know how effective the method has been in forcing actors to think for themselves, to lose their inhibitions and give their all to theatre. He calls it samarpan (surrender). The word appears repeatedly in *Khuda ke Liye Mat Dekho*.

This play, like some of the others he has written in recent years, revolves around his own problems and dilemmas. The play is not particularly well-written or crafted or structured. But it is energetic and fun. His best work happened from the mid-1950s to the mid-1980s, during which time he was single-handedly responsible for cross-pollinating plays from the four corners of the country and beyond. He directed the Kannada plays of Adya Rangacharya, Girish Karnad and Chandrasekhar Kambar in Hindi and Marathi translations. He did Badal Sircar's Bengali plays *Evam Indrajit* (And Indrajit) and *Pagla Ghoda* (Mad Horse) in Hindi, Mohan Rakesh's *Aadhe Adhure* (Incomplete), Tendulkar's *Shantata! Court Chalu Ahe* (*Silence! The Court Is in Session*) * besides plays by Sartre, Camus, Chekhov, Pirandello, Ugo Betti, Ibsen, Pinter, Mrozek. He was like an immense, ever-sizzling crucible out of which flowed ideas, ideologies and philosophies that actors and theatre-lovers would never have been otherwise exposed to. Just as an example, Sulabha Deshpande found out what lesbianism meant while playing Inez in Dubey's *Band Darwaaze* (Sartre's *No Exit*). Though she was shocked at the discovery, she dealt with it and continued to play her role with conviction.

Though Dubey came from Madhya Pradesh, he was perfectly comfortable directing plays in both Marathi and Gujarati. Nor did Marathi-Gujarati accents in his Hindi productions bother him. If Hindi is a national language, it cannot be spoken in the same way everywhere, he argued. English was once anathema but eventually, surrounded by young people whose sole language of communication was English, he accepted it as an Indian language and directed and even wrote plays in it.

Perhaps he was right in rejecting English when he did. The received English of post-colonial times would have been culturally

---

* *Evam Indrajit* has been translated by Girish Karnad (Oxford University Press; 1975); Mohan Rakesh's *Adhe Adhure* is available as *Halfway House*, translated by Bindu Batra (Worldview Publications; 1999); Tendulkar's play has been translated by Priya Adarkar (Oxford University Press; 1979).

inadequate for Dubey's plays which always walked the thin line between realism and melodrama. That they did was perhaps the reason why his audience connected with them so well. He refracted Western theatrical modes through the prism of his deeply rooted Indian sensibility, and blended the modern with the traditional in a way that was unique to him. He was also the first and arguably the only theatre director who used film songs in his plays. To him film songs are urban folk music.

The genuine eclecticism of his work was reflected in the plays he liked. Liked? That's putting it mildly. 'Went gaga over' might be more accurate. His choice ranged from the poetic *Tu* (You) to the farcical *Sahi re Sahi* (Just Right), which hit the Marathi mainstream years ago and continues to fill houses and its producer's coffers to bursting even today. You may look askance at the choice but his admiration was as intense and serious as his dislikes.

His friends ribbed him about his own playwriting. *Sambhog Se Sanyas Tak* (From Sex to Celibacy) had been a hit, a rambunctious comedy of errors on which all his students had cut their theatre teeth. *Inshallah* was critically acclaimed. But nothing that he wrote thereafter stood up to these two plays. The carping of critics didn't faze him one bit. As a matter of fact, he felt a little sorry for critics. He once told my critical-writing class at Xavier Institute of Communications, 'Take my advice. Don't become critics. It'll stop you from enjoying plays. When you grow old and have no hair and teeth left, you won't even have pleasant memories of theatre left.'

By the nineties, Dubey was somewhat defeated by the changes in the circumstances of living in Mumbai. Actors' priorities had changed, distances had grown, and he himself had become older. He no longer had the energy to chase new playwrights and help them develop their scripts and then to direct them. It was easier for him to write his own plays. These were often unstructured, self-indulgent, repetitive and autobiographical. When friends asked him why he wrote continuously about himself, he said playwriting was an extremely difficult activity. It called for an understanding of others. He no longer understood others. He barely understood himself. That is why he found himself the most appropriate subject to explore and try to understand.

But the actors' training workshops continued. He charged no fees for his workshops out of a general distrust of money, which he held to be a corrupting influence. Young actors flocked to them, lured by his aura as the presiding guru of theatre. Once there, they came to understand how he had earned his reputation. If they showed a genuine interest in theatre, (and in Dubey's view interest had to verge on madness), he would give them their first roles in his plays. But that was not the whole story. When you saw him surrounded by bright young actors whatever his own age, you realized that he had found a way of living in an eternal spring.

Satyadev Dubey lived his life on his own terms, but the terms of his death were given to him. He believed in destiny. This was his. It's such an irony that a man who couldn't be still for a moment except when he was sleeping, should have been immobilized for two months by a brain stroke that left him in a coma. No noise, no swan song. Unless the film he'd been making for the last two years, still incomplete, could be called that.

At his funeral, mourners from age eighty to eighteen were present, each with his or her own memories of time spent with him, perhaps the most valuable of their lives. He has left behind a sharp and specific sorrow in each of our hearts. And in the Prithvi café, where he held his addas, an absent centre.

(Satyadev Dubey died on 25 December 2012.)

Who's Afraid of Vijay Tendulkar?

In the gloom cast by Vijay Tendulkar simply ceasing to exist, there appears a luminous caravan of characters he has left behind for us. Created to explore questions that troubled him, situations that horrified him, conventional ideas that did not convince him, he allowed them the freedom to be themselves. They grew into believable flesh-and-blood human beings who inhabit our world today as reference points. Here's looking at a life that was devoted to diverse forms of writing from plays and fiction to film scripts and columns.

~

Tendulkar was born in Kandewadi, a lower-middle-class neighbourhood in Girgaum, Central Mumbai, immortalized by the opening lines of B.S. Mardhekar's poem:

> Where Kandewadi, with a little kick
> Turns off from Thakurdwar
> Where the rumbling tram, bent at the waist,
> Licks the overhead wires...

He grew up, the middle one of five siblings, in a chawl—one room, one kitchen, common verandah, common toilet. Living cheek-

---

This is another collation of articles. These include 'Unflinching Gaze' for Sruti, http://www.sruti.com/index.php?route=archives/article_details&artId=124http://www.sruti.com/index.php?route=archives/article_details&artId=124 accessed on 31 July 2018; 'Silence! Tendulkar Is Still Writing', *Man's World*, August 2002; 'Luminous Presence', *The Hindu*, 25 May 2008. Vijay Tendulkar died on 19 May 2008.

by-jowl with a rich variety of the human species, he had ample opportunities to observe people. Observing and listening to people came to be Tendulkar's lifelong passion.

His father was a head clerk in a publishing house, and a playwright-director-actor in his spare time. He often took young Vijay with him to watch rehearsals. This was Tendulkar's first introduction to the magic of theatre. A world where, as he describes it, real people became imaginary people, and men in trousers and shirts, became convincing women with a quick change of voice, walk and manner. Men were still playing women's roles then.

The cramped confines of the Tendulkar house were crammed with books by the most eminent writers of the time. Young Vijay burrowed through them voraciously without necessarily understanding what he was reading. Their house was also a sort of adda for his father's literary friends. Thus the young boy became a participant in all the literary debates of the time. It is no wonder then that he began writing odds and ends at the age of six, and that he wrote, directed and acted in his first play at the age of eleven.

Films were another passion with Tendulkar—English films which he didn't understand, but which fascinated him nonetheless. He has confessed that he often even bunked school to see them when he was old enough to do so. This intense viewing of films would have given him an early insight into their making, laying the foundation for the scripts he later did for Marathi and Hindi films.

At sixteen, he left school without completing his matriculation. He moped around the house, feeling alone and alienated. Out of this internal agony were born poems, stories and even screenplays, written entirely for himself, as a test perhaps of his own capacities. They were also a way of talking to himself; for he was convinced nobody else around would understand the thoughts and feelings churning within him.

It was a time of great anxiety for his family. How would he turn out, this sensitive boy so brimming with literary talent? It could have gone either way. Fortunately for Marathi and Indian theatre, he pulled himself together somewhere along the line, and went to work as an apprentice in a bookshop. From there he graduated to working in a press and from there he went into journalism. His years as associate editor of three Marathi mainline dailies and editor of a literary magazine, put him in touch with the political events and issues of the day, possibly helping him to crystallize his own ideology.

His first play *Grihast* (Householder) flopped badly. He has given a delightful, self-mocking account of this in his 1997 Sri Ram Memorial Lectures. However, his position vis-à-vis society was established in his second play *Shrimant* (Wealthy), written in 1955 when he was about twenty-four. In this play, Tendulkar exposed the sham and hypocrisy of men of wealth and social standing. Mathura, the daughter of a rich industrialist, Dadasaheb, gets pregnant and refuses to divulge the identity of the father. In a desperate attempt to protect the good name of the family, Dadasaheb agrees to a plan to 'buy' her a husband, who will quietly recede into the background after the wedding. But the chosen man does not fall in with the plan. He doesn't wish to be bought. Penury will not make his spine bend. He digs his heels in and challenges every one of Dadasaheb's values and pretences. In the end, in this battle between crude money power and human dignity and decency, the latter wins.

Shrimant was the first time in Marathi theatre that unromanticized poverty, unwashed and hungry, entered a rich man's drawing room and settled on his sofa. *Manus Navacha Bait* (An Island Called Man), Tendulkar's next play, was the first time that the anxieties of lower middle-class, jobless, shelterless youth, trying to get a foothold in society, were given centre-stage. Else, from the mid-1950s on, Bal Kolhatkar had been riding in triumph over the Marathi mainstream, flying pennants of Motherhood, Patriotism and other sentimental claptrap to the weeping delight of the middle-class audience.

In the 1960s and 1970s, theatre the world over had turned into a major experimental movement. Tendulkar was one of four playwrights in India who were acknowledged as the pioneers of the movement here. There was Mohan Rakesh in Delhi, with no tradition of Hindi theatre to take off from, energetically hacking out his own path; Badal Sircar in Calcutta, rejecting the proscenium stage on which he had earned so much success to find a form and space that more suited his political purpose; Girish Karnad writing in Kannada, looking to history, mythology and folk literature for narrative material that would serve as metaphor for the big issues of human life; and Tendulkar in Mumbai, rebelling against the falseness, mushiness, piousness, and hyperbole of the Marathi mainstream, to create a truly realistic theatre through which to examine life and human relationships in all their subtle variety.

Human relationships and the power structures governing them continued to be at the centre of Tendulkar's work. Even when the first germ of a play was an idea, it wasn't the idea that drove him to conceive the play. It was characters. It was through them, once he could see them moving, speaking and interacting, that the idea shaped itself into a play. That was why he wrote in such a variety of forms, never patenting one that would declare a play as Tendulkar's. The characteristics of a Tendulkar play are to be found in his perceptive, sympathetic treatment of people, particularly women. Also in his language, which ranges from the delicately nuanced, crisp and ironic to the powerfully poetic, rhythmic, discursive and rhetorical.

Controversy was part of Tendulkar's playwriting career from the beginning. He was charged with plagiarism in some of his plays, and in others, with obscenity, needless violence, crude exhibition of sexuality, anti-Brahminism and distortion of history. *Shrimant* was supposed to have been lifted from Pirandello's *Pleasures of Honesty*, *Shantata! Court Chalu Ahe* from Friedrich Durrenmatt's *A Dangerous Game* and *Ashi Pakhare Yeti* (This Is How the Birds Arrive) from Richard Nash's *The Rainmaker*. In these and other cases he admitted to having been inspired by the basic ideas from those sources, but insisted that beyond that, the plays were entirely his creations.

His three most controversial plays, *Sakharam Binder*, *Gidhade* (Vultures) and *Ghashiram Kotwal*, all produced in the 1970s, invited censor trouble. They had to be defended in courts of law and gave rise to stormy public protests asking for their banning. *Sakharam Binder* offended because it stood against the institution of marriage, referred too openly to sexual gratification, showed a woman beating her husband with a chappal, getting drunk, and at one point, changing her sari on stage.

Gidhade, which portrayed the vulture-like behaviour of a family of father, two sons and daughter, offended because of its obscene language and extreme acts of verbal and physical violence. One particular scene attracted the sharpest cut from the censor's scissors. It showed the pregnant daughter's miscarriage after being kicked by her brothers, when she runs screaming onto the stage with a large blood stain on her sari. Because the censor objected to the stain, it was made blue and producer Satyadev Dubey took great delight in announcing before the play began that blue in this case was to be seen as red.

Ghashiram Kotwal was taken to be a distortion of history, aimed at maligning the Pune Brahmins by depicting Nanasahib Phadnavis, the Peshwa Chamberlain, as a lecherous old man with no other quality to his credit. The Shiv Sena led the agitation in Mumbai, headed by Mr Pramod Navalkar. *Ghashiram Kotwal* is the only play in which the dramatic focus was not people but politics. To have written realistically about the current political situation which was disturbing him, would have been to make the issues too specific, leaving no space for universalization. One day, however, he came across the story of Ghashiram and immediately saw in it the potential for allegory. And yet the play could not be written till a suitable form was found. This happened by accident, in a folk performance he chanced to see as he passed by. It was by these stages that *Ghashiram Kotwal*, one of the classics of modern Indian theatre, got written. Never after that did Tendulkar feel the need to return to history or myth for his narrative, nor to use music and dance to say what he wanted to say.*

* See Tendulkar's comment about Bhaskar Chandavarkar's music in the obituary for the latter on page 187.

Kanyadaan created another kind of controversy. This time the Dalits were up in arms protesting against the depiction of a Dalit poet in the play as a manipulative drunkard and wife-beater. Each one of these controversies caused Tendulkar deep anguish. Even today, many people think of him as a playwright who enjoyed sensationalizing issues for publicity or commercial gain.

Much of Tendulkar's work, including his scripts for films like *Aakrosh* (1980, Govind Nihalani) and *Ardh Satya* (1983, Govind Nihalani), demonstrated his preoccupation with violence. It was a serious concern with him. He had even undertaken a full-scale study of violence during his Nehru Fellowship. Seeing it as an integral part of the human make-up, he treated even his most violent characters with a degree of compassion that is rare in our moralistic culture.

It is out of his insatiable interest in the human species and his compulsion to write at all times of day and night, in all kinds of situations, conducive and not so conducive, that he produced such an enormous body of work. In his fifty years of writing, he has given us thirty-two full-length and seven collections of one-act plays for adults; five collections of plays for children; four collections of essays; four translations; one novel and eighteen scripts for Marathi and Hindi films. He tells us how he could produce so much quantity and variety of writing in the opening remarks to the Sri Ram Memorial Lectures. 'More than a playwright, I consider myself to be a writer—meaning, I love the physical process of writing. Give me a piece of paper, any paper, and a pen and I shall write as naturally as a bird flies or a fish swims.'

That is why his last months must have been miserable. In the early days in hospital, he was at his laptop every day, writing feverishly as he had always done. But later, it became increasingly difficult to do so. It might not be wrong to say that Tendulkar died the day he knew he could write no more.

~

When Tendulkar delivered the keynote address for the biannual all-America convention of Marathi speakers, he spoke not about literature, drama or cinema but about the virtues of charity, generosity and kindness. He argued that more often than not, charity was motivated by self-interest. When the giver gave his name to his gift, he was telling the world, look how charitable I am. The same was true of those who did favours to others expecting them to be obliged forever. Such charity and such favours were better not done. It was a profoundly purist viewpoint which did not go down too well with many of his listeners. Some people suggested snidely that the speaker was likely not to be a practitioner of what he preached.

The fact is that Tendulkar was not preaching. He was merely making some observations. He was not preaching because it was not his practice to preach. A preacher, by the very act of preaching, puts himself above those to whom he is preaching. Tendulkar never did that. He always counted himself as one amongst many. He observed himself as he observed others. His autobiographical writings are evidence of his total honesty and candour in speaking about himself.

Tendulkar was a quiet man. He did not believe in public display of emotions. One of the most poignant sights I recall was after his daughter Priya's untimely death. During a condolence meeting organized by her friends and admirers, he sat quietly, stoically beside her framed photograph while people paid their respects to her, shook his hand and went away. His own funeral was marked by the same quietness. In keeping with his wishes, the media had been requested not to photograph him or the funeral. Even the State's wish to give him a funeral that befitted his status as Maharashtra's leading, often controversial litterateur, one whose work had put India on the world map, was turned down. There were no rituals, no weeping, no speeches. Just a solemn and dignified farewell.

I mention all this because, to be a great playwright is one thing; but to be a man who lives by his principles till his last breath in our corrupt times is quite another. There was no disparity between what Tendulkar believed and what he practised. The seamlessness of belief and practice extended to his work. Not in fifty years of writing did he write a single word that did not represent his honest beliefs, his impartial observations, his understanding of and compassion for all human beings, including criminals and other wrong-doers.

If one is to answer the question, what did Tendulkar give to the world of Indian theatre, the answer would be: plays that looked at life straight in the face without flinching. If one is to answer the question what did he give Marathi theatre, it would occupy volumes. But putting it in a nutshell, I would say, he gave Marathi audiences their first experience of realism. He created men and women of flesh and blood. He gave them a language that belonged uniquely to them. He gave actors the chance to enrich their idiom. Actors who were trained to project their voices, assume dramatic postures and declaim were totally lost when speaking his lines. There was no drama there, no flamboyant flourishes, no heightened emotions or hyperbole. His dialogue was understated. But the spaces that he created between words and lines carried more dramatic tension than the words themselves.

A pause in drama is as pregnant as a held note in music. Just as a held note gradually releases a multitude of shrutis, a pause in a play releases unexpected shades of meaning. It also contributes to the rhythm of the whole. Unless actors catch this rhythm, Tendulkar's lines are likely to sound quite banal. Satish Alekar, whose plays *Mahanirvan** and *Begum Barve* are modern classics in the same bracket as Tendulkar's *Shantata! Court Chalu Ahe*, *Sakharam Binder* and *Ghashiram Kotwal*, was selected to play the male lead in Tendulkar's one-act play *Olakh* (Getting acquainted) when he was at college. Alekar says, 'I found it very difficult to enter the character of the man I was playing. I found the dialogue very boring. I did not find anything dramatic in the play. There were pauses all over the place. The director would tell me, "If you enter deeply into the

* *Mahanirvan* is available in English as *The Dread Departure*, translated by Gauri Deshpande (Seagull Books; 2007).

character you will find that the pauses get automatically filled with your expressions and body language at the time." But what I actually did was to fill the pauses by counting numbers in my mind.'

Gradually over time, actors learned how to make Tendulkar's silences speak.

Music is expected to elevate the listener. Realistic drama should bring the audience down to earth. The kind of mainstream drama that Tendulkar and his colleagues opposed at the beginning of their careers was full of conventional notions and sentimental cliches of middle-class thinking. It flattered the middle class by covering up its hypocrisies and endorsing all its values. Tendulkar did the opposite. He posed questions. Do you think we are peace-loving, civilized and non-violent, he asked? Then here is *Shanatata! Court Chalu Ahe*. Here is a woman who has been made pregnant by a colleague and abandoned. So what do we, her other colleagues, do? We put her in the dock and peck at her viciously till she collapses from the sheer fatigue of defending herself. That is how we can be.

Tendulkar was many things to many people. To his contemporaries, like Vijaya Mehta and Dr Shreeram Lagoo, he was the articulator of some of the most urgent questions of their generation. To his immediate successors, like Mahesh Elkunchwar, he was the great reference point by which to assess their own work. To today's playwrights he was like a place of pilgrimage. They could put their offerings in his hands, certain that they would be read with all seriousness and a wide open mind and praised or commented on as he thought fit.

To many others he was like a red rag to a bull. They believed he was born to offend, insult and scandalize them. His plays often made them paw the ground, snort and charge. Their intention was to gore him so badly that he would not stand up again. But he always did; more than a little surprised at the attack, he dusted his trousers, picked up his pen and wrote another play.

For he looked about him and saw a less than perfect society. He saw ruthless political power play, he saw violence in all its forms, he saw gender inequality, he saw crass commercialism and shameless hypocrisy. He was not the one to say, how does it all concern me? Let me see how I can profit by the situation and keep my mouth shut.

Keeping his mouth shut was not on his public agenda. He was too passionately involved with the world to let things go. He was outspoken to a fault in his public life, but he said very little in private. The idea was to let others speak so that he could understand how their minds worked. His social concerns gave him the subjects for many of his plays while his understanding of the human mind gave him the ability to create believable characters.

He was not, as the late P.L. Deshpande had been, a darling of the people. He wasn't interested in chucking them under the chin and cooing, 'Aren't we a quaint but warm-hearted lot!' He was too troubled a man for that. His plays are for those who have the strength and honesty to see the world without rose-tinted glasses on. There is nobody on the horizon just yet to replace him as a passionate observer and commentator on the state of our world.*

Ashis Nandy puts succinctly what Tendulkar did to his audiences. Towards the end of his preface to Tendulkar's filmscript *The Last Days of Sardar Patel*,† he says, 'Tendulkar...never fails to make you feel that you have entered a dentist's chamber with an undiagnosed abscess in the molars.' People are afraid of dentists. Many were afraid of Tendulkar.

---

* Is this still true? I asked Shanta. 'I would say it is. The only other playwright who approaches him in prolificity, quality of craft and use of different forms of theatre depending on the theme, is Mahesh Elkunchwar. But he does not have the engagement Tendulkar does with social or political issues.'

† The film was called *Sardar* (1993, Ketan Mehta). The script was published by Popular Prakashan in 1993.

On Habib Tanvir

Habib Tanvir is identified so completely with a theatre that used Chhattisgarhi actors, dialect and narrative material that it is difficult to believe he chose to train at the Royal Academy of Dramatic Arts in London. But it was just as well that he did. Halfway through the course he saw how irrelevant the training was to his idea of theatre. He quit and returned to India after writing and singing his way across Europe with the ultimate aim of meeting Bertolt Brecht, whose theatre he admired. Unfortunately, Brecht had died before he arrived in Berlin, but Tanvir stayed on to see his plays. It is not by accident that songs have told as much of the story as speech in Tanvir's plays. In part at least, this was a Brechtian legacy.

When Tanvir returned to India, it was with a dream he had nurtured all through his travels in Europe. He was obsessed with doing Shudraka's *Mricchakatika* (The Little Clay Cart). Its modernism and free-flowing form challenged him. His mind was sparking with ideas contrary to what pundits claimed Sanskrit theatre had been. In Delhi, Begum Qudsia Zaidi's Hindustani Theatre was willing to back him. Begum Zaidi even translated the play into Hindi for him. Then serendipity took over. Born in Raipur, Tanvir had grown up with local folk-theatre forms like Nacha and Pandavani. On a visit home, he watched an all-night Nacha performance and his mind was blown by the superb acting skills of the five actors before him. On an impulse he asked them if they would go to Delhi to act in *Mitti ki Gaadi*. They happily

---

This article was first published in *The Hindu* on 14 June 2009 as 'Habib Was Theatre', a week after Habib Tanvir's death.

agreed. This led to horror for Begum Zaidi ('Habib, theatre demands young handsome faces, not these strange creatures.') but laid the foundation of Naya Theatre, Tanvir's karmabhoomi.

Madan Lal, Thakur Ram, Shiv Dayal, Bhulwa Ram, Jagmohan and Lalu Ram became the backbones of Naya Theatre along with Tanvir's wife and professional partner, Moneeka Misra. Together they tried, failed, tried again to meld the skills, spontaneous energy and instinctive feeling for movement and song of the Chhattisgarhi actors with Tanvir's sense of narrative flow and overall structure.

'It took me years to discover the simple thing that I should give my artists autonomy, that I should give them their mother tongue,' Tanvir has said in an interview with Prithvi theatre. 'I knew the sweetness of the dialect but I was totally unaware of its communicability to non-Chhattisgarhi people. That is what held me back. And I got bad versions of Hindi and feeble actors because of their self-consciousness. Finally I said let's try this and after three years of failure I got the breakthrough with *Gaon ka Naam Sasural, Mor Naam Damaad** and then *Charandas Chor*.' The trick was to use the Chhattisgarhi dialect, allow the actors to improvise and, when their movements matched his ideas, freeze them.

The 1974 play, *Charandas Chor* became a hit in India and abroad. If earlier his 1954 hit, *Agra Bazaar*, which could so easily have been a miss, had revealed to him the possibility of bringing urban actors and rural non-actors together successfully on the same stage, *Charandas Chor* established a way of bringing together the sophistication of modern urban theatre with the vitality of folk artists. The method served him well in all his future plays.

Doing plays with Chhattisgarhi actors was not part of the 'back to the village' movement that swept in and out of social and theatre circles in India in the 1970s. Tanvir was not chasing folk forms to use as decorative elements, he said. He was chasing folk actors for the specific vitality, acting and singing skills only they could bring

---

* This delightful play has an almost untranslatable name. Literally, it means: My village is my parents-in-law's home, my name is son-in-law.

to his plays. He wanted to be part of their great cultural traditions and, in the process, help those traditions and the actors to survive. The actors were paid a salary of five to six thousand rupees a month, while Tanvir received ten thousand. No written contracts were required to seal the agreement. The actors stayed with Naya Theatre till they retired or died because it allowed them to live off their art with dignity. In the village, they were the lowest of the low. On the Naya Theatre stage, they were kings and queens.

Habib Tanvir did not believe government schemes could help folk arts. 'Government schemes are survey, budget, report on result. Art is not like drought where you can count how many died,' he once said to this writer in an interview. If folk theatre were to survive, it needed hard work from within, not 'uplift' from outside, he asserted.

Tanvir combined a passion for theatre with an uncompromising belief in secular-liberal values and a lifelong engagement with social problems. His most overtly political play *Hirma ki Amar Kahani** had appeared to some critics to be an argument in favour of feudalism against democracy. But Tanvir pointed out that democracy was not all-white. It could be used for a fascistic agenda as had happened in Gujarat. Similarly feudalism was not all black. It had encouraged the arts. In telling the story of Hirma, he was only provoking people to see both sides of the story and come to their own conclusions.

Standing up for your convictions, countering lies, fighting parochialism meant running personal risks. Habib Tanvir did that when his play *Ponga Pundit* (The Fake Priest) was attacked by the Hindu right for being supposedly anti-Hindu. Mikes and stones were thrown at him and his actors. But he stood his ground and continued to perform the seventy-year-old folk play.

Habib Tanvir was theatre in every sense of the word. His going orphans the art.

---

* *Hirma ki Amar Kahani* is available as *The Living Tale of Hirma*, translated by Anjum Katyal and Prabha Katyal (Seagull Books; 2005).

Hooked on Theatre

Ever heard of a place called Jambsamartha? It's a village of 2,000 homes, 80 kilometres from Jalna. Jalna, like our own Ulhasnagar, is a prolific producer of fake goods. It also smelts what might appear like the entire world's scrap, to produce iron rods. These twin industries have made it a wealthy city. However, nobody in Jalna sings, dances, paints, writes or acts. They are politicians.

Jambsamartha has electric poles and humming wires overhead, but little power. It gets power for only two hours a day, and that too from two to four in the morning. Time to go to the fields! But when power fails for even those two precious hours, Jambsamarth has no choice but to steal electricity. It does so with aakdas (hooks). It's a dangerous game that has taken lives. But when it works, there's power for the pumps.

This situation provided Rajendra Tangade, a local youth, with the narrative material for his play, *Aakda*. He entered the play for the State Drama Competition some four years ago and it knocked the jury cold. *Aakda* was enacted in total darkness to replicate the conditions in which the people of Jambsamartha lived. Nandu Madhav (Dadasaheb Phalke in *Harishchandrachi Factory**) was so horrified by the story, that he made a short film based on the play, so it could reach more people.

Last year Tangade invited Pune-based director Atul Pethe to do a play with them. Pethe is fiercely committed to developmental work and equally so to theatre. He accepted Tangade's invitation as

---

This article was first published in *Mumbai Mirror* on 17 February 2010.

* *Harishchandrachi Factory* is a 2009 Marathi film directed by Paresh Mokashi.

a challenge. When he arrived in Jambsamartha, he discovered how serious the challenge was. How was he to do theatre in a place that had no books, where newspapers came two days late and remained largely unread, where the drinking water was indigestible, where it took villagers nearly four hours to cover the 80 kilometres to Jalna because the road was so bad and no other mode of transport but their tractors was available, and where, horror of horrors, there were no latrines?

Unfazed, Pethe dug his heels in and Rangamala Natak Mandali's *Dalpatsingh Ale Gava* (Dalpatsingh Comes to the Village) was the result.

Pethe's six-month journey—from the shock he suffered on arrival to the tenth show of the play in Mumbai—must await full documentation. All I can say here is that we, sitting in the Yeshwant Natya Sankul in Matunga on 2 February 2010, could never have guessed that the actors performing before us with so much energy, conviction and talent, led such deprived lives back home.

Dalpatsingh Ale Gava is Pethe's dramatization of a filmscript by Makarand Sathe. It deals with the corrupt cartel of landlords, government officials and police that keeps villagers ignorant of their rights. Alka, a member of an NGO, enlightens the villagers on who exploits them and how. She holds *jana sunwais* (public hearings) to prime them to rise and fight. The fire spreads. Governments feel the heat, and the Right to Information Act is born. But the fight is not over. Wrongdoers will hit back. RTI activist Satish Shetty is murdered in Talegaon-Dabhade.

The play, cast in tamasha form, is peppered with lusty songs and sprightly exchanges. The ensemble, some on stage for the first time in their lives, acts with robust energy. Veena Jamkar, that fine actor from *Gabhricha Paus**, plays an inspired and inspiring Alka. She turned down two film roles to live in Jalna for six weeks and rehearse for the role.

---

* *Gabhricha Paus* (The Damned Rain) is a 2009 Marathi film directed by Satish Manwar.

To return to Jambsmartha—it is the birthplace of Ramdas Swami, Shivaji's mentor. We revere the man but do nothing for his birthplace. Of course, Jambsamarth boasts of a temple in his name and a pilgrims' dormitory that once housed the only latrine in the village. But now Atul Pethe has helped the Tangades build one in their home and other villagers have followed suit. Will their next play be *Sandas Ale Gava* (The Latrines Have Come)?

A Return to Gaiety

Ved Segan is not a publicly celebrated architect. He is a quiet man, but also a quietly determined man. You can see those qualities in his work like the Prithvi Theatre, for example. In today's environment, where architecture shouts for attention, this theatre is a warm space that welcomes people and enables actors and audiences to participate in a dialogue.

The late Jennifer Kapoor* was the spirit behind Prithvi Theatre. Segan saw her as the ideal client. She knew precisely what she wanted, was able to communicate her vision lucidly to him and then leave him to get on with the job.

Her passionate involvement with theatre did not end with the creation of Prithvi. She wanted to see the 100-year-old Gaiety Theatre in Simla restored. She had performed there with her family, the Kendals, and the terrible state of disrepair into which it had fallen, saddened her. Unfortunately she died before the project could be planned. But Shashi Kapoor was determined to make it happen. With INTACH† as collaborator and Ved Segan as the architect, it has finally happened, although the project has taken twenty-four years—from the time the proposal was submitted to the Himachal Pradesh government in 1985 to completion.

Gaiety Theatre, built in 1887, is set atop a hillock between the Ridge and the Mall. Those who know their Simla would know what an iconic position it occupies. When Ved Segan saw it in

---

This extract was taken from *Prithvi Theatre Notes*, August 2014.

* Jennifer Kapoor née Kendal (1933–84), one of India's finest actors.

† The Indian National Trust for Art and Cultural Heritage, a non-profit, see www.intach.org

1985, he instantly sensed that the building was incomplete. He soon discovered he was right. What stood before him as Gaiety Theatre was only part of a much larger structure that had, at one time, housed the Town Hall. As it stood now, it was not a fully integrated building, but one that had lost a large part of itself. Restoring it meant giving it a character that was independent, yet in keeping with its neighbours while adding its own beauty to Simla's skyline.

Before we move into the nitty-gritty of how this project was executed, I must quote Ved Segan on what it took to do it, for we are talking about a twenty-four-year journey, which began when the word 'restoration' had not even entered the public lexicon. He says only two faculties are required to do any job well—commonsense and sensitivity. But by the time he had told me half the Gaiety story, I had realized how inadequate those two faculties by themselves would have been to see him through. For, over and above the challenging problems that the restoration project itself presented, he had to fight Public Works Department greed and cunning, deal with political change and party egos, and even stand in a court of law to defend his belief in his project.

The long and arduous journey ended when the restored Gaiety Theatre was inaugurated with much pomp and show in 2009.

Of the two qualities that Ved upholds, I would like to put sensitivity before commonsense. Commonsense ensures that solutions to problems of stone and mortar are objective and practical in their planning and implementation. Sensitivity, on the other hand, responds not to the material form but to its spirit, helping the architect to keep faith with the original while planning for its renewal. I have before me the full text of Ved's report entitled *Proposed Conservation and Restoration: Gaiety and Environs*; and the way it begins reflects the sensitivity of the architect:

> 'Historical buildings say a lot, but a lot remains unsaid. They also have a capacity to suffer in silence the neglect and atrocities committed on them. In order to restore their dignity and glory, first

> you have to make them forget the indignities forced upon them. Next let them narrate their stories.'

Ved went to considerable trouble to unearth these stories so that he would understand the building he hoped to restore. He discovered that the Amateur Dramatic Club (ADC), formed in 1837 by British officials stationed in Simla, used to hire whatever space they could for their performances during the season, which started in April and ended in October. They were so prolific that people said they were actors by profession who took up government employ as a pastime. When the Town Hall, with the Gaiety Theatre occupying its lower floors, was built in 1887, the ADC instantly hired it as their permanent home at an annual rental of Rs 3,000. The first play they performed on the boards of the new theatre on 30 May 1887 was prophetically entitled, *Time Will Tell.*

Time began to tell rather early in the life of the theatre. Within a few years of its being built, the ADC complained to the municipality that rainwater was leaking into parts of it and damaging the property. Over the next twenty-five years the complaints multiplied, the structure springing cracks and leaks all over the place. Many surveys and reports later, it was decided that no amount of repair work would put right what was wrong with the building. In 1911, the entire edifice of the Town Hall housing the Gaiety Theatre was condemned with a recommendation that it should be completely dismantled and rebuilt.

Perhaps the habitual tardiness of municipalities ensured that these radical measures were not implemented promptly. Demolition did begin, but stopped at the floor above the theatre. There was a ballroom here with a floor of Burma teak specially transported from Kolkata. Whatever the reason for demolition work to stop here (it could even have been the First World War), the building that Ved Segan saw in 1985 was the truncated remnant of a once glorious edifice.

Grand spaces become grand dumps very rapidly in the hands of Indian municipalities. One of the biggest shocks Ved received during his inspection of the building was the tons of municipal junk stored and forgotten under the leaky roof. When carted away, it filled 350 trucks! Any building that had taken this load cheerfully for decades without sinking under the burden, had to be strong. The structural engineers appointed to report on its condition, confirmed the strength of the building, but questioned its durability. They pointed out that the stone used for the structure was of inferior quality. Reporting on the quality of material back in 1911, Mr D. Macfarlane, Resident Engineer of the Simla Municipal Committee, had also remarked on the poor quality of the stone, adding that perhaps the best stone had been used for the Viceregal Lodge, which was being built at the same time!

Reinforcing the stone was therefore one of Ved's most urgent tasks. The chemical he used to bind it had to be put through the most rigorous tests before it was approved. The crumbling columns were another concern. Ved had them wrapped in carbon fibre and replastered. Carbon fibre is a material used in the building of space ships, no less. The old leaky roof went. In its place came a structure that was designed to float above the old building like an umbrella, without putting strain on the external walls which were weak.

With the floating roof in place, another unexpected space presented itself for use: the old ballroom. This has now been converted into a modern theatre! A third theatre space has been created outside for open-air performances. Enthusiastic locals are already putting it to good use. The old auditorium has been restructured and renovated to ensure clear sight lines and rational seating. Its plush interior, old-style galleries and scalloped velvet curtain will hopefully inspire equally dramatic theatre. The entrance to the theatre, which used to be rather narrow, has been shifted to make it wider and more welcoming. In addition to the three theatre spaces, the new building houses an art gallery to be managed by the Lalit Kala Akademi.

Prithvi Theatre's interest in Gaiety extends beyond having it restored. It proposes to hold an annual festival in the complex during March, April, May and June. The proposal it has submitted to the government of Himachal Pradesh in this context, also puts the onus for ensuring that the complex is used 'for the goal of promoting the performing and visual arts of Himachal Pradesh in particular and India in general' on the State government. Further, it warns the ADC (no longer the old Amateur Dramatic Club, but the culturally suspect Army Dramatic Club, which plays cards and drinks in parts of the premises) that 'the theatre should not be used for marriages, Hindi film shows, fashion shows or any other such forms of ostensibly cultural activities'.

There is an incipient anxiety here which Ved Segan has also anticipated in the summing up of his project proposal: 'A building, even when architecturally harmonious [with its environs] to start with, can create disharmony simply due to the nature of the usage it is put to.' True. Imagine dancing baratis streaming into the impeccable Gaiety Theatre!

The Stage Is Empty

If a column could be written in tears, it would be this. I mourn the passing away on Sunday of a beloved and irreplaceable friend, Veenapani Chawla; but in this public space, I mourn the sudden extinction of a life that had been a rare and quietly influential presence in a larger world than mine, the world of theatre.

Although Veenapani began her theatrical career in Mumbai, her spiritual centre lay in Puducherry. There she went bag and baggage, in 1991, to design and develop a most extraordinary campus for the learning, teaching and practising of theatre. This was the Adishakti Laboratory for Theatre Art Research that she had dreamt of. Spread over a large tract of land near Auroville—donated to her by an admirer of her work—it was at first no more than red earth sparsely dotted with scrub and bush. But soon she had transformed it into a lushly verdant environment with living and rehearsal spaces that allowed her to do the kind of theatre she believed in.

Veenapani's theatre was tough, time-consuming. It began with a skeletal script which gradually evolved in tandem with improvisations and arduous rehearsals into the final performance piece. But final was always the wrong word to use. The staged production was only the beginning of more rehearsals in the course of which the play was tightened, fine-tuned, even rewritten in parts, till Veenapani and her actors Vinay Kumar, Arvind Rane, Nimmy Raphel, and Suresh Kaliyath were fully satisfied. Even otherwise, the actors followed a daily regime of exercise that enabled them

---

This article was first published in *Mumbai Mirror* on 3 December 2014, four days after the death of Veenapani Chawla.

to go beyond themselves when required. Veenapani believed that inspiration wasn't something that came from outside, but from within; from a potential of ourselves that we were not conscious of, but which would come into play if we worked hard enough to reach it.

Veenapani's theatre was pluralistic; or, to use her favourite word, hybrid. She saw it as a reflection of a society that was itself hybrid. When Independence gave this country the opportunity to define itself, theatre faced three divergent paths. The first was modern theatre as defined by the West and inherited by us through the colonial presence; the second was a throwback to a supposedly pure and unadulterated past; and the third was modern in so far as it incorporated all that India had experienced, thought and created through its long history, while using textual sources and forms of expression that were native to us. Veenapani chose, or rather broke, the third path, turning to Kerala, the great repository of traditional performance arts, for the means to evolve her language of theatre.

This language was a rich blend of sparse speech, rigorously choreographed movement based largely on kalaripayattu, percussion that took its inspiration from koodiyattam, and visual elements that came from both yesterday and today. Yesterday broke into Veenapani's *The Hare and the Tortoise* with shadow puppets, which the actors had learned to manipulate from an old village practitioner who had been invited to live on the campus. The contemporary entered Vinay Kumar's *The Tenth Head* with Ravana's heads projected on screens in computerized animation.

Equally heterogeneous were the sources from which Veenapani drew her references—the epics, Shakespeare, physics and mathematics—all anchored in Sri Aurobindo's philosophy of engagement with, not detachment from life. Theatrical hierarchies were happily dismantled as actors slid from the formal stylization of natyadharmi to the relaxed storytelling of lokadharmi. Humour, visual, verbal, and ribald, brought laughter, but also added other perspectives from which to view the theme of the play. Willy-nilly the audience was shaken out of its customary expectations of single narratives and pure forms to respond to this theatre that unsettled them all.

Veenapani's contribution to theatre was publicly acknowledged when she received the Sangeet Natak Akademi award three years ago. But the citation said nothing about how deeply she had touched the lives of those she had worked and collaborated with, those she had shared her ideas for future scripts with, those she had looked to for constructive suggestions and those in her ever-widening circle of friends who had been drawn by her gentleness, generous love, infectious laughter, deeply ingrained spirit of democracy and unfailing optimism in the face of odds. Sadly, many came her way, financial and otherwise.

Impossible as it has been to accept Veenapani's going away, it is a solace to know that she has left behind a committed group of actors at Adishakti, ready to take her vision forward.

On Mumbai

'Vital organ missing'

Lalit Estates, No. 5

That's what our house is called. Lalit Estates No. 5. Presumably there are or were at least four other Lalit Estates belonging to the actress, Shanta Apte, our one-time landlady. My mother used to tell us there was one in Lallubhai Park in Andheri. She thought it was No. 4. Maybe it was; maybe not. But this house is No. 5 and because we aren't sure of the existence of the other numbers, we have stopped including No. 5 in our postal address.

The house is fifty-eight years old and I am fifty-seven. So we've kind of grown up together. With intermediate absences, I have spent all of forty-two years in it and have seen every phase of its life except one. The years of the lovebirds. I was away in England then, trying to equip myself with a university degree. The lovebirds, Nilu, Sonu and company, and their doings occupied much space in the long, chatty letters I received from home every week. By the time I returned, they had all passed on.

My relationship with the house has been formed by memories from my growing-up years. I have never felt imprisoned by its walls, perhaps because the house is more doors than walls. As a child, whenever I wanted solitude, the house offered me the two corners of its verandah to hide in. And when I wanted company, there was always plenty to choose from. My parents, when they were alive, made this house a home for many. It was never free of the comings and goings of relatives and friends. Its spaces, even now, echo with the voices of those who came, stayed and went their way.

This was first published in the 1996 Diwali Special Issue of *Ruturang*. It has been translated from the Marathi by Shanta Gokhale.

'Gondya, get up you lazy lump!'

That was Hari Kaka every morning, and the one barely stirring at the sound of that loving call was our Konkani live-in domestic, Govind Ramji Chavan. When the simple opening of eyes in the morning was such an acute problem, actually rising and getting down to the day's work was beyond Govind. The family would be hurrying through their morning chores before leaving for school and work, when Hari Kaka, who worked with the Railways and left home late, began his wake-up calls. He did not dislike the task. As a matter of fact, he applied himself to it with great gusto. Most Gokhale men were blessed with stentorian voices. So Hari Kaka's 'lazy lump' carried a special weight that even Govind could not ignore for long. Reluctantly then he would hoist himself up, stumble into the kitchen and make himself his first cup of tea. It was only after a few swallows of that sweet-milky beverage that his eyes actually opened. Then, looking around sheepishly, he would say to whoever was in the vicinity, 'Without tea I feel ekdum sarbareet.' Sarbareet is anything that's halfway between solid and liquid. Like sludge. It was a pretty accurate description of his pre-tea condition.

The verandah of this house has heard and stored so many different voices, that it is difficult to separate one from the other. And yet there are two that rise above the rest of the babble. One belongs to my six-foot tall, barrel-chested, pink-skinned grandfather who stood here every morning at 4.30 and sang '*Jaago Mohan Pyaare*' to the world before proceeding for his walk on the beach. The other belonged to his wife, my four-foot six-inch, coffee-skinned, green-eyed grandmother, muttering '*Jai Ram, Shri Ram, Jai Jai Ram*' nonstop, even when spying on my mother to make sure she wasn't wasting my father's hard-earned money. What amused us sisters most was how she managed to stick angry comments about relatives and events in between Ram and Jai Jai, without losing her rhythm.

The verandah was also where grandmother told us colourful tales from mythology. Her favourite, or so we thought because she told it so often, was about Krishna hiding the gopis' clothes while they swam. At the point where she demonstrated how the gopis tried to hide whatever they could of their bodies with their hands, her face broke into a toothless grin which had more to do with pleasures unknown to us than with the simple joys of storytelling.

Ajji was devoted to our little white Bush radio which stood in the verandah. Come keertan time in the evening, she would ask one of us to turn on the 'raidoba', her fond corruption of 'radio' to give it a divine status alongside Vithoba and Khandoba. She stuck her comparatively good ear right up against it so she could hear the keertankar's sermon at normal volume. But conversations with her had to be carried out at full volume. Even then she sometimes misinterpreted what we were saying and broke into a delighted laugh when she realized her mistake.

Although my parents were very happy with having two daughters and never yearned for a son, my father did compensate for this lacuna by calling my sister Nirmal, 'Balya', a boy's pet name. My grandfather compensated similarly by calling me Shantaram. Those two names are part of my aural memory of the house.

Since I'm talking about the verandah, let me describe it briefly. I believe it is unique. There's not another one like it in the whole of Mumbai. When my mother directed people to the house, she made the verandah her final trump card, describing it as resembling the deck of a ship. This made little sense to those who had never seen a ship's deck, or those whose vision of it didn't match hers. So let me describe it more specifically. Its length, I would say, is about twenty feet. It has a large ten-foot bulge in the middle—like an expansive beer belly—flanked by two corners about four feet across. It seems a little far-fetched then to claim that it looks like a ship's deck. Why, it doesn't even look like a verandah.

When my grandparents came to stay with us and my father decided they required a room to themselves, he restructured the spaces of the house, creating a bedroom out of the living room and converting the verandah into a living room. Fact is that large and spacious as this house is, it has, in effect, only three rooms—a living room, a large singularly shaped bedroom and a spacious kitchen-cum-dining room. And of course the verandah, where we sisters slept. When uncles, aunts and cousins from Dahanu, Nashik and Nagpur came to spend their summer vacations with us, we all slept in a row down the length of the verandah. Even in high May, a lovely breeze wafted over us from the sea, rustling the fronds and leaves of the coconut palms and jackfruit trees that filled the wadi across the road from the house.

Even little Vasant found the temptation of sleeping in the verandah irresistible. His parents, my Mama-Mami, lived behind the house. Every time they came up for a post-dinner chat, Vasant would cross his chubby legs on the mattresses laid out in the verandah and declare, '*Mi ithe jhopan.*'(I'm going to sleep here). Jhopan was how he pronounced jhopnaar, or will sleep. Like Govind's sarbareet, this word has also crept into the family dictionary and been passed down to my children. The one who still uses it occasionally for fun is my daughter.

The two ends of the verandah were our special play spaces. Here we were afforded the secrecy we craved. In one of the corners stood our doll's cot and cradle and two tiny cupboards to store our toys in. Our mother had had them made in Dahanu where her father had a rice-mill manufacturing plant and the carpenters were obliging. This corner was our house within the house. We used the other corner when friends came to play. Here we could set up an umbrella and drape my mother's sari over it to make a house. These corners, so filled with joy, were also where we were made to stand as punishment.

It was in this verandah, too, that my father's literary, academic and journalist friends would meet on Saturdays. Present on these occasions were Professors Kangle and Mahishi; Professor Tongaonkar and his young French lecturer wife Vijaya; Professor Rajadhyaksha and his young Marathi lecturer wife, also Vijaya; Purushottam and Vimalabai Chitre, publisher-editors of *Abhiruchi*; G.R. Kamat, screenplay writer. Once in a while, writers Vyankatesh

Madgulkar and P.L. Deshpande would drop in and in the early years, Marathi literature's first modernist poet, B.S. Mardhekar. Saturday evenings were full of debate and discussion about the latest books and plays, experiments in music and painting, anecdotes kind and unkind and imitations of people known to the circle. And while the friends talked and laughed, delicious aromas wafted out of the kitchen promising spicy tongue-ticklers.

Of the several skills my mother was mistress of, one was the culinary art. Ours was one of the few houses blessed with piped gas, courtesy the Bombay Gas Company. Some of the credit for my mother being able to study for and pass her matriculation and later go to college must go to this invaluable facility. There was no way she could have cooked on a kerosene stove for the many mouths that ate at her table and still caught the 9.30 local to her college at Marine Lines.

For years we have stood at this cooking platform watching spellbound as she turned out her soft ghadichya polya* and her delicately flavoured dishes. There was a rhythm in all she did, whether it was rolling out polya, moulding modaks or coaxing the mille-feuilles of chirote to blossom in the kadhai. When her glossy, elegant modaks, precisely fluted with seven pleats pinched to a sharp nose, slid onto our plates straight out of the modak pan, we wondered for a moment, but only for a moment, if we dared eat the works of art.

Here on the red koba of the kitchen floor, we have sat with my mother, rolling out papads. We did not do this merely as our filial duty towards a hard-working mother. There was another incentive. After every five papads rolled out to the right size and thinness, we were rewarded with one ball of dough dripping with oil. There is no point even attempting to describe to those who have never touched, smelt or tasted these spicy balls, the tiny explosions they caused in our mouths.

---

* Rotis folded and oiled and rolled again and then fried.

After the kitchen, the large, odd-shaped bedroom, the only one in the house. In this room with more doors than walls, a curved frontage which reduces one corner to an acute angle and the other to an obtuse, are gathered sounds of years of music and dance. This is where Ashtaikar guruji taught my mother bandishes in Yaman, Jaijaiwanti and Ramkali to prepare her for her BA paper in music. This is where my father decided to test his gruff voice out with Tilak guruji's help. He had an innate sense of rhythm and was note-perfect. But what could he do with a voice that could not, by any stretch of imagination, be described as melodious? He gave up, but Tilak guruji remained a family friend till his death. It was in this room, too, that Parab guruji taught my mother the sitar, and Tendulkar guruji taught Nirmal the violin. This is where Guru Ravi Bellary taught me Bharatanatyam; and this is where my older aunt Nalini and younger aunt Sindhu, when they came to stay for their respective college educations, sang popular bhavgeets of the day for us.

Perhaps the sound of music embedded in these walls is responsible for bringing alive any musical performance that happens here. For many years, we marked our mother's death anniversary with music. Sharadchandra Arolkar, Jal Balaporia, Dinkar Kaikini, Padma Talwalkar, Sarla Bhide, Yeshwantbuwa Joshi, they all sang here and every one of those concerts exuded a special something that made them uniquely memorable.

When Ajji-Ajoba left our house to stay with my eldest uncle in Nashik, their room became our room, my sister's and mine. The long curtain that had partitioned this space from the living room, was replaced by a floor-to-ceiling twin book-case facing outwards. This was my piece of heaven on earth. My supreme pleasure was to name, register in the catalogue and arrange by category, the books my father splurged on once a month. The smell of new books was pure intoxication. To sit on the cool floor in front of the book-case during summer vacations, browsing and reading, was to forget time. Evening seemed to fall suddenly, out of the blue.

At night, my father would settle with a book and I would offer to do what he loved: massage his head. Again the motive went beyond filial love. Standing behind him, I could look over his shoulder and read what he was reading.

The door of this house was always open to friends and relatives who needed a temporary home. A friend of my father's lost his young wife suddenly. Her death depressed him so much that he was on the point of going to pieces when my father coaxed him out of his dark, despondent flat into ours. Here he stayed for two years while he mended. When young uncles and aunts fought with their elders, this is where they arrived, bag in hand. Two battered wives stayed here till my mother found them work and permanent homes, sending them off with a pair of saris, blouses, bath soap and hair oil. Relatives came to Mumbai for operations and recuperated here. An aunt came for her delivery and stayed for three months. Our special pleasure in having aunts deliver their babies in the hospital next door, lay in the special laddoos my mother made for them: one lot to help labour and the other to help lactation. Our downstairs neighbour John Pereira married Effie and had no place for the wedding lunch and dance. This is where he invited his guests and they danced to a four-piece band.

It is nearly thirty years since my father died and ten since my mother. After their going, I have not changed a single thing in this house. I have retained the original madness of its spaces intact. For my mother, the house was a living entity. On the rare occasions that the whole family had to be away, she left a light on to give it company. I have followed this practice in the full knowledge that it is not a rational thing to do. Houses don't get lonely. But this bit of sentimentality is a way to keep alive my link with the history and culture of this home.

Maxi-mum Story

It is 11 a.m. The market is in full bloom. On feet that seek a firm footing among the abandoned peelings and leavings, their eyes scanning the fruit and vegetables for the best produce, intent on finding bargains and securing these at the lowest possible price, two women move from shop to shop, both wearing maxis.

While choosing tomatoes, a third woman says, as if to herself, but in a voice designed to be audible: 'How can one wear home clothes and come to the market?' She is looking at me out of the corner of her eye. I return the glance without speaking. And as I look at her, I begin to wonder about the origin and development of the maxi. When did Marathi women begin to wear this and from where did it come? How do new fashions take root here? For the maxi that we wear and the floor-length dresses that were the height of fashion at one time in the West are very different indeed.

In the West, there is a system by which high fashion reaches the common woman. Every season, designers have two kinds of showings of their new lines, each for a very different set of clients. One is for the super-rich who choose the clothes they like and have them made to measure. As these are originals, they pay extravagantly for them. There is no greater social disgrace in high society, we are told, than for two women to turn up at the same party, wearing the same 'original'. At the next level is the buyer who is at the opposite end of the spectrum. These are the representatives of the big chain stores. They have an almost infallible instinct about which designs will work on the high street, an instinct honed by

---

This article was first published in Marathi in *Loksatta* on 14 May 1998.

years of experience. They do not buy clothes, they buy the designs that they believe will work with the mass market and those that can be mass produced. This means, in turn, that high fashion has some effect on the clothes that the woman on the street is wearing. This relationship rests on an important assumption: that ready-to-wear clothes are practically the norm. Western countries do not have a tailor on every other street corner. Most middle-class people buy their clothes off the rack.

When there are changes in women's fashions, it is the colours, the fabrics and textures, and the lengths of the hemlines that change. In the 1960s, the mini-skirt had become the rage. The words 'midi' and 'maxi' came thereafter, each for a different length. We did not take to the mini. Few had the guts—or the legs—to carry it off. And the mini was certainly not for married women. The midi was welcomed by young women. The knee-length skirts could look fashionable and met with parental approval too. Once we take to something, we take to it and we stay put. We treat the new with faint suspicion because it is new. Which is why it is still possible to spot a few midi frocks in some places. The story of the maxi is different.

When the maxi burst on to the Indian fashion scene, it was what girls wore to college or to hang out with their friends. But the maxi was uncomfortable to walk around in. It flapped around your feet. After a couple of years, the fashion died and the maxi was relegated to the back of the wardrobe. But in the dark of the night, it changed shape and became a nightie. It ballooned and acquired a frill over the shoulders. Its sleeves puffed out. By around 1980, huge piles of maxis spilled out of the shops and on to the streets. The maxi began to spread to smaller cities and towns. The maxi revolution came about because it served a need.

At this point it might be good to take a look at men's behaviour and clothes. When a man comes home, the first thing he does is to change his clothes. He takes off his trousers and shirt and puts on the comfort clothes of his choice: pyjamas and a banian with pockets perhaps, or a lungi and banian, whatever. When a woman returns home, she takes off her 'out-going' sari and puts on a 'homewear' sari. When she steps into the kitchen, she must deal with her pallu, generally tucking it into the fold at her waist. At some point, it must have seemed easier and more comfortable to wear a maxi in the kitchen. And so a working woman would come home and slip into her maxi. Once she began to do that, the unemployed women and the homemaker began to wear them too. And just as men take their evening strolls or go to the fish market on Sunday wearing their home clothes—striped pyjamas, most often—women began to step out in their 'home' maxis.

When women in societies like Japan and China began to work outside the home, they abandoned traditional dress and took to Western clothes. Traditional clothes began to be restricted to festival days and special occasions. The Indian woman, however, continued to wear saris, neatly pleated and tucked in, the pallu attached to the blouse with a pin. Her second shift begins when she gets home. If at this time, she pays attention only to her comfort, surely she has the right?

I want to tell the tomato-buying woman who sneered at her maxi-wearing sisters that the maxi has the right to break the barrier between the home and the world outside. It has this freedom because of its very nature. It covers everything, from shoulder to toe. It conceals every flaw of the physique whether you're bulging or your bones are poking through your skin. And the most important thing: wherever it came from, it is now as much ours as a play on the Kamani Auditorium stage, a Marathi novel or a modern painting. And so wherever it shows up, it has every right to be there.

The Heart of the Matter Is Missing

Every so often, grave doubts are expressed in the media about the existence of Mumbai's heart. Somebody dies somewhere, is discovered two years later, and out go journalists with their stethoscopes, ready to find Mumbai's vital organ missing. They forget that they had celebrated its existence only a while ago when the city opened its purse wide to help a citizen in distress. Or when it rolled up its sleeves to assist in rescue operations at an accident site. Such a heart doesn't suddenly up and leave. It reacts to different situations in different ways. Our ancient text on the performing arts has codified human emotions, of which we believe the heart to be the repository, into nine rasas or sentiments. The positive ones are sringar (love), hasya (joy), karuna (compassion), adbhuta (wonderment) and shanta (tranquillity). The negative ones are bhaya (fear), krodha (anger) and bibhatsa (disgust).

The ancients would have listed the ninth rasa, veera (heroism), also amongst the positive ones. But we aren't so sure today. Some images of war persuade us that the heart could do without it. We are not convinced that heroism practised at the cost of innocent lives is a good thing. So, there it is. A list of nine sentiments, each of which at various times dominates the human heart and either propels it to action or freezes it in inaction. But the complexities of human life don't make for reader-friendly copy. It's easier for journalists to declare Mumbai heartless and then return to other times when things were different. When people lived in chawls, for instance.

This article was first published in *Mid-Day* on 20 May 2003.

Those, it appears, were the times, and those the homes that defined love, goodwill and generous neighbourliness. Such is the nostalgia that grips some erstwhile chawl-dwellers when they speak about that long-ago life (theirs through sheer economic necessity, not by choice), that they romanticize even toilet queues. That is where love happened, they say!! Wow! Who needed the rocks at Bandra or the Marine Drive parapet when you had your very own toilet queue to exchange stolen glances and brush hands surreptitiously in?

But which chawls are these anyway? The ones in Worli where quarrels break out every day at the water tap? The kind that the late poet Shanta Shelke lived in where—so a shocked visitor reports—the common toilet was permanently lightless and its walls crawled with cockroaches? No. It's the prissy upper-caste chawls in and around Girgaum that they go misty-eyed over. Then why did they leave if they were such a sublime joy to live in?

Because chawls lacked that precious commodity of urban life: privacy. No wonder Raja Thakur's 1970 film, *Mumbaicha Jawai* (Mumbai's Stay-at-home Son-in-law), became such a hit. Remade a year later as *Piya ka Ghar* (The House of My Lover) by Basu Chatterjee, it depicted the frustrations of a young couple yearning for a place of their own where they could feel free to be themselves and live their own lives.

It is certainly shocking that forty-six-year-old Vivian Peter Almeida's death was discovered two years after he had died. But it wasn't because Mumbai is 'callous' and 'apathetic', but because it allows people to live their lives as they choose. Clearly Almeida had a problem if he communicated with only one of the eighty residents of his housing society and if none of his three brothers had been in touch with him for years!

The same goes for Dr Rebello whose body was discovered last year, a year after his death. He had wished to live as a recluse, and his neighbours had granted him the freedom to do so. If either of these men had looked for company and support, they'd have certainly found it next door. So let's not get nostalgic about toilet queues.

Who Owns the City?

Since the ownership of Mumbai is once again being claimed exclusively for the sons of the soil, let me translate a few passages from Govind Narayan Madgaonkar's book, *Mumbaichay Varnan** (Describing Mumbai) published in 1863, to define once and for all who these sons of the soil might be.

First a descripion of the city as it was before the British took over:

> The city that has ascended to such magnificence today was, in 1530, when it passed from the Muslims to the Portuguese, no more than a wild and deserted place that comprised about 400 households and a population of roughly 5,000 all told. These people belonged to the Koli, Bhandari and Panch-kalashi castes. The revenue that accrued to the government from their lands amounted to approximately Rs 350.

It is only these 5,000 inhabitants and their descendants who can be named sons of the soil in the strictest sense of the term. Everybody who came after was an 'outsider'.

The city's progress in the following 300 years was such that by 1863, according to Madgaonkar, its treasury boasted of three crore, twelve lakh, fifty thousand rupees, contributed by the labour of 'outsiders'. By 1861 the population of the island had leapt from the original 5,000 to five lakh. And at the time Madgaonkar was writing, that is by 1863, it had risen from five lakh to seventy lakh!

This article was first published in *Mid-Day* on 6 May 2003.

* This is now available in English as *Govind Narayan's Mumbai: An Urban Biography from 1863*, translated by Murali Ranganathan (Anthem Press; 2008).

The writer now proudly claims the following distinction for the city:

> Just look! Today whatever kind of person comes to Mumbai, be he poor or weak, lame or blind, deaf or dumb, good or bad, gentleman or thief, innocent or crooked, conman or fraud, the city does not kill him for lack of food and shelter. All he needs to do is work hard and the city will turn him from a zero to a hero.

Madgaonkar knew it then and we know it now. The only mantra that works in Mumbai is hard work. The lesson for the sons of the soil is simple. If people from far-off places can come here, struggle, find a foothold and make good, so can they. So what's the problem?

There has been much introspection amongst thinkers in Maharashtra over this question. A couple of years ago, a Marathi periodical devoted an entire issue to inquire into the psyche of the Marathi manus. Is he doing badly? Does he have a genuine grievance? Or does he simply lack the ambition and drive required to survive and thrive in the city?

In this context, I recall an incident that said more than any survey finding could. It was very late at night. We were passing through an area where a number of incidents had occurred recently of cabs being held up by armed thieves for the day's takings. As we entered the area, our cabbie, a migrant from Karnataka, pulled out a white cap from his pocket and placed it carefully on his head.

'What's that in aid of?' we asked.

He grinned broadly and said, 'I want to be mistaken for a Marathi man.'

'Why?'

'A Marathi man still out on the street at this hour means he doesn't have even fifty rupees in his pocket. If he had that much, he'd be at home fast asleep!'

The other day, I was reading about a good samaritan from a Konkan village determined to find the unemployed young men of his gaon jobs in the city. He himself had started out poor, scrubbing floors. Today he is an influential man. Of the ten men he brought to the city, nine went home, because the jobs he'd found them didn't come up to their 'level'. The same jobs were later snapped up by 'outsiders'. Whose Mumbai is it then?

Bharat Mata on Veer Savarkar Marg

A painting of Bharat Mata has come up recently on the façade of the Swatantrya Veer Savarkar Smarak near Shivaji Park. Towering behind a statue of Savarkar, the goddess embodies his dream of a Hindu Rashtra.

The statue itself is something of a puzzle. As a revolutionary, you would expect Savarkar to be represented standing upright. But he is seated rather meekly on a chair. Countering the effect of this, his right arm is raised, and his forefinger points at the sky. The gesture could mean the sky is the limit once my dream is fulfilled. But taken along with the left hand, which holds an umbrella, it might suggest an inappropriate preoccupation with the weather.

Graphically, the two hands make excellent sense. The upward thrust of the right hand is exactly balanced by the downward thrust of the left. But where do we go from there? What sense does a black cloth umbrella make in the hands of a revolutionary? I'm not saying it doesn't have its uses as a weapon in real life. I can never forget the summer evening sixty years ago, when an aunt of mine thrashed the daylights out of a man with just such an umbrella on Dadar Bridge because he had dared to touch her. But Savarkar is not my aunt. The only explanation I can offer then for the lugubrious prop is based on guesswork. Perhaps Savarkar was given to carrying an umbrella. Perhaps the sculptor was stuck for what to do with the subject's left hand. So bingo! He gave him his favourite accessory. Nice bit of realism.

The image of Bharat Mata behind Veer Savarkar presents only one puzzle—the conflagration in the background. Behind the map

This article was first published in *Mumbai Mirror* on 18 July 2007.

of Bharat on which the four-armed goddess is superimposed, leap angry flames. Try as I might, I am unable to figure out what they stand for or even decide whether they constitute a cleansing or a consuming fire. Otherwise, the goddess is an easy read.

She is yet another variation on the goddess images that calendar artists churned out once Raja Ravi Varma had decided what they should look like. They were to be fair-skinned, voluptuous, encased in a nine-yard sari and crowned. After travelling all over India looking for an appropriate dress for his goddess-women, Ravi Varma had settled on the Marathi woman's nine-yard sari as the best choice because it revealed the female form to greatest advantage.

Before Ravi Varma's goddesses came to adorn the walls of middle-class homes across the country, artists had felt free to imagine their own Bharat Matas. One of the earliest was Abanindranath Tagore's well-known image. Though this image has four arms, she hardly looks like a goddess. Slim as a reed, she wears a saffron robe that looks like a Coorgi-style sari, and no ornaments to speak of. She carries a book, a mala, a sheaf of wheat and a white cloth in her hands, symbolizing knowledge, spiritual search, food and dress. Her face is peaceful, her look serene.

The Bharat Mata on the Veer Savarkar Smarak is exactly the opposite. Here we have a political figure with a one-point agenda. She carries an orange pennant, an agnikund and a trishul in each of her three hands while the right lower hand is raised in an abhay mudra. Do not fear, it says. You are safe.

But another Bharat Mata, painted by an unknown artist, sits like a grieving Madonna with the slain Gandhi in her lap. And yet another is imaged in the bitter poetry of the Dalits. Jyoti Lanjewar asks, 'How did we ever get to this place, / this land that was never mother to us?' L.S. Rokade puts the same question another way. 'Is this land yours, mother, because you were born here? / Is it mine because I was born to you?'

The fair-skinned goddess has been unfair to many.

A Parsi Wedding

When I go away from Mumbai for a few days, I begin to miss two things: the sea and my Parsi friends. In a way the vast and eternal Arabian Sea and the Parsi community, which is gradually dwindling, share an ancient bond. Eleven hundred years ago, the ancestors of the present-day Parsis were hounded out of their homeland, Persia, when its Muslim rulers imposed the predatory jizya tax on people of the Zoroastrian faith. Better the wild ocean than the tax they decided, and flung themselves on the mercy of the waters. There were times on that long journey when the sea grew merciless; but they persisted through high waves and tempests till they finally landed on the coast of Gujarat. They had lost home and land, but not their faith for which they had abandoned them. They had brought with them what mattered most, the sacred fire and the three simple tenets of Zoroastrianism—humata, hukhta, hvarshta (good thoughts, good words, good deeds). In time, these three tenets combined with hard work, skills, astuteness and an undying spirit of charity, earned the community wealth and a good name.

When the Parsis landed in Gujarat, they adopted the local language, dress and customs. When they moved to Bombay, they took to the language, dress and customs of the ruling British. They were pragmatic enough to know that, for a small community like theirs to survive, the wisest course would be to emulate the chameleon and camouflage themselves in local colours. Today, whether the Bombay Parsi dresses in a dagli and pugdee or in a three-piece suit, his culture remains the unique blend of customs

---

This article was first published in Marathi in *Saptahik Sakal* on 12 July 2003.

that evolved over time in Gujarat and then in British Bombay. One thing the Parsis never did through all their wanderings was to confuse religion with culture. They absorbed local customs and lifestyles without hesitation, but guarded the sacred fire with their lives.

The Parsi bhonu or wedding dinner reflects the distilled essence of this mixed culture. My first experience of it came in the mid-1970s when I was invited to a Parsi friend's wedding. I was teaching at H.R. College then. It was examination time and I was invigilating with a Parsi colleague. At some point during that hot and tedious afternoon, I whispered to her that I was anxious to know what kind of present I might be expected to give my friend.

'Why anxious?' she asked, surprised. 'Give money.'

'She's a very close friend,' I demurred. 'Giving money doesn't sound right.'

'This must be your first Parsi wedding then,' she said. 'Money is what we give. The amount depends on how many of you are going for the wedding. Remember, you are paying for your dinner. The current rate per head is Rs 75.* Multiply that by the number of people, put the amount in an envelope and that's your present.'

Seeing the expression on my face, she laughed and said, 'The first Parsi wedding is always a shock for people like you. But whichever of our forefathers thought up this custom, we should be eternally grateful to him. Otherwise we, too, would have received six lemonade sets, four steam irons, a bunch of wall clocks and ugly *objets d'art* for our weddings.'

My friend's wedding was in an agyari (fire temple) in Colaba. At the centre of its spacious grounds, stood a small stage for the bride and groom. In front of it, tables had been set up for guests. Behind it, partly blocked by a screen, were a dozen or so long tables for dinner. The agyari building itself was painted white and decorated with

---

* The current rate in Rs 1001 (The one is for good luck). Thanks are due to Meher Marfatia for this.

simple strings of fairy lights. White, not multi-coloured. On one side, a band played English tunes which included a Parsi wedding favourite, the Birdie Song, to which little children did the birdie dance. The men were dressed in daglis and pugdees and looked impressively traditional; but it was the women who arrested and held our attention. My friend's upper-crust mother, who otherwise dressed in smart pants and well-cut tops, was wearing a brilliant purple China silk sari that evening. It was a traditional Parsi gara, covered in intricately embroidered flowers, creepers and birds. The gara had its roots in China. When Parsi merchants started trading in opium and cotton with the Chinese in the nineteenth century, they brought back heavily embroidered lengths of Chinese silk for their wives. In time the locals mastered this style of embroidery and created saris with borders and pallus, which soon became the high-point of Parsi couture.

My friend's wedding sari, a tanchoi, also had a similar history. Amongst the merchants who traded with China were the three Chhoi brothers (*tran* Chhoi) who learned the Chinese art of weaving brocade and introduced it back home as material for saris. Unlike the flamboyant garas which came in jewel colours, tanchois, like the one my friend was wearing, shimmered in delicate pastel hues.

While we were busy gawking at the women's garas and tanchois and chamois silks and georgettes and chiffons, all worn with sleeveless and backless blouses, we became aware of a sudden movement in our vicinity. Our neighbours had risen en masse, like birds at the sound of a gunshot, and were flying to the tables behind the stage. We looked around in alarm trying to figure out what this meant, when one of our group said, 'What is Arnavaz doing?' Following the speaker's gaze, we noticed that our newly married friend was flapping her arms hysterically at us like a duck in distress. At a loss to understand what she was trying to say, we continued sitting around the table like toads at a tea party, our eyes popping. In despair, Arnavaz rushed to our table and said, 'If you sit around like this, there will be no dinner for you.' She grabbed a passing aunt by the arm and told her to do what needed to be done with us.

The aunt sat at our table laughing and talking convivially. Everything appeared normal except that she turned once in a while to look at the diners behind the stage. Then, at some signal that we had neither heard nor seen, she too sprang from her seat as if a firecracker had gone off under it. Grabbing us, she set sail. She sliced through the crowd like some enormous cargo ship with us in tow till we reached the nearest long table. Here she dropped anchor.

The table was fully occupied with not a single seat free. That apparently was as it should be. She placed the four of us behind four chairs with instructions to slip into them as soon as the occupants rose. Wasn't that rude, we were wondering till we noticed that all the chairs at all the tables now had lines of hopeful diners behind them, waiting for their turn at the trough. The diners dined, undeterred by the pressure that had built up behind them. The hopefuls chatted with the insouciance that came from years of Parsi wedding practice. But the minute the diners had finished eating and even before we could say lagan nu custard, the aunt had shoved us into the barely vacated chairs in a smooth operation.

The waiters now went into action, placing banana leaves before us. Next, two chapattis, a sweet mango chutney and sago crispies fell on them from the air. What you ate with what was entirely your decision as was the choice between Duke's Lemonade and Ginger to wash down the food. *Saas ni machhi*, pieces of pomfret swimming in a tart white sauce, was the next course to be shovelled on to your banana leaf. Vegetarians like me were overlooked. I had already had my chapattis and mango chutney. What else could a vegetarian want? I was told by my neighbour that in the old days vegetarians, being freaks, were given a separate table. But now they were allowed to sit with normal people. The food they were served, however, was neither Parsi nor recognizably anything else.

As I ate it with good grace, I realized it was best to keep my eyes fixed on my banana leaf if I wanted to avoid the pitying stares I was getting from my normal neighbours. My immediate neighbour gallantly overcame his pity and said to me, 'The Parsi loves his food. Zoroaster taught us the three tenets: good thoughts, good words, good deeds. But he didn't see the need to teach us the fourth one, good food. That is part of our DNA.' So saying, he laughed uproariously and fell to his fish.

As soon as the *saas ni machhi* was polished off, it was time for chicken farcha—plump spicy chicken legs dipped in egg, rolled in breadcrumbs and fried. The fish and the chicken were eaten neat, so to say, with no accompaniment like bread, rice or roti. The repast ended with the famous *lagan nu custard*, which seamlessly combines culinary elements from the British, Gujarati and Maharashtrian cuisines.

In times when other communities had begun to abandon their traditional sit-down wedding dinners, preferring the much less cumbersome buffet, it was a very special experience to be at a wedding dinner that still adhered to tradition.

Right now a debate is raging in this hard-working, joyous, generous community. Seven Parsi priests have issued a fatwa. Anybody who marries outside the community is to be excommunicated. Young Parsis have launched a strong protest against it. The fatwa is out of sync with the times and with reality, they say. When the Parsi population is dwindling, does it make sense to hold on to racial purity? Would it not be wiser to merge with the larger community and survive? There is much sense in this viewpoint. In their earliest years in this country, Parsis were wise enough not to confuse religion with culture. Now when times have changed, one hopes they will not confuse religion with race.

On Feminism

'Grab a bride, push her out'

The Impossibility of Being Nora's Sisters in Marathi Theatre

Till the 1970s, Nora was simply Ibsen's best-known female character. She belonged in a play that had been refined by its maker into a consummate work of realistic drama. As such it had had a worldwide impact. Around the beginning of the twentieth century, this world of Ibsen admirers came to include university-educated young people in Mumbai, to whom the acquisition of the English tongue had opened doors to Western literature and drama.

In the 1970s, at the height of the women's movement, Nora was removed from the context of her play *A Doll's House* and turned into a feminist icon. Simultaneously, the door that she had walked out of became a symbol of women's liberation. The woman and the door told women that they no longer needed to look upon marriage as a sacred bond and the husband as the unquestioned lord and master of their lives. Both could be questioned and rejected. In short, the door that let them into their husbands' homes could also let them out.

It is with this background in mind that I would like to ask the question, did a real kinship exist between Ibsenian drama and Marathi drama, and between Nora and the female characters of Marathi drama, either in the first phase of the discovery of *A Doll's House* or later when Nora became a feminist icon? I am not even considering Ibsen's other female characters, except to say that the Indian view of women (or human beings at large) being moralistic, we have no audio-visual representation of a

---

This was a paper presented at a one-day seminar 'Nora's Sisters' held at Symbiosis College, Pune, on 18 January 2008.

character like Hedda Gabler whose behaviour cannot be praised, condemned or justified.

The first discovery of Ibsen in Mumbai happened when the reformist movement was well underway. At the centre of the reforms was the woman question. Most of the social evils that the reformists fought against were focused on women. Plays had already been written and staged on some of them. G.B. Deval's *Sharada*, staged in the last year of the nineteenth century, questioned the practice of marrying young girls who had not even attained puberty to rich old men. The question of women's education was brought to the stage from the conservative side of theatre with Narayan Bapuji Kanitkar's *Taruni Shikshan Natika Athva Aadhunik Shikshan va Stree Swatantrya Yaanche Bhavishyakathan* (The Education of Women or a Prophecy on Modern Education and Women's Freedom; Shri Shivaji Press, Pune; 1896) whose exaggerated satire was meant to show the harm that would befall society if women were given education. Novels, too, were being written on every aspect of the position of women in society. Therefore, when Western-educated young men discovered *A Doll's House*, they discovered two things simultaneously. First, they discovered a play that made the position of women in marriage a central concern, questioning the nature of marriage and the attitude of fathers and husbands towards their daughters and wives. Second, they discovered a play that discarded the old device of asides and soliloquies as a means of revealing the workings of a character's mind, and relied entirely on dialogue and that specific sequence of situations to reveal them before the very eyes of the audience as it were. Events led from one point to the next without the writer's hand being visible and when the end came, it seemed completely inevitable.

Many young people were thrilled with Ibsen's drama on the page. But only one group decided to put it on the stage. This was Natyamanwantar, which roughly translates as theatre for change. One of the group members, Anant Kanekar, even translated *A Doll's House* as *Gharkul* (Little home). The translation was ready; but the group members were not. They balked at the idea of actually performing *Gharkul*. No historian of Marathi drama has been able to put a finger on exactly why this happened. But perhaps one can hazard a guess. Natyamanwantar wanted to change Marathi theatre. The music drama which had held sway over it for fifty years was on its last legs. Younger audiences no longer had the patience to sit through hours of drama lengthened by songs that went on for ever. Nor did their modern outlook allow them to accept men playing the roles of women.

The problem was that though Natyamanwantar wanted to change things, it also wanted to do business. The patronage of young people alone would not have given them sufficient returns. In this light, *A Doll's House* in faithful translation must have struck them as too bold for the times. Consequently, they made a compromise. They presented an adaptation of Bjornson's *The Gauntlet* as their first production. One of their members, S.V. Vartak, adapted it as *Andhalyanchi Shala* (School for the Blind), making it more palatable for the regular play-going audience. *The Gauntlet*, we are told, is about the double standards practised in patriarchy—one standard for men and quite the opposite for women. *Andhalyanchi Shala* evades this point. Instead it proposes that human beings are made up of shades of grey. Nobody is pure white or pure black. We have to understand this and be compassionate. It just so happens that the wrongdoers are men, and the compassion is shown by the women who forgive them their misdeeds. The big revolution in *Andhalyanchi Shala* did not lie in questioning patriarchy. It lay in the fact that the play was urban, modern as against mythological.

With Ibsen's drama having been reduced to taking a woman-centred problem, putting it into a one-act-one-scene structure (earlier plays followed the Shakespearean mode of multiple scenes to an act) minus asides and soliloquies with some attempt at realistic dialogue, many imitations of *A Doll's House* were spawned. These are best described in the words of the well-known critic, the late Madhav Manohar. He says, 'Dramatists without the vaguest clue to why it was inevitable for Nora to leave her home, took to pulling wives out of their homes simply to be with the times. It became a kind of craze—grab a bride, push her out. A wholly new kind of drama was thus inaugurated.'

The attempt to transplant Ibsenian drama in soil whose properties were too different for the new plant to take root, failed on two counts. The playwrights and producers were not bold enough to take on the subjects that made them sit up in Ibsen's plays. For, though the impetus for a new social order was in place, it affected only the veneer of society. The larger majority of the theatre-going public was simply not willing to have such radically new ideas thrust down its throat. Second, the general comprehension of the Ibsenian form of drama was superficial and, in a peculiar sense, innocent.

Soon Natyamanwantar fizzled out and finally closed shop. Of the plays imitating *A Doll's House* that came in the following decade, particular mention must be made of M.G. Rangnekar's *Kulavadhu* (A well-born wife). Compared to Nora, the wife in this play is in a position of strength. She becomes a film actress after her husband loses his job. She does very well in the profession and begins to earn high fees. This becomes a thorn in her husband's side. His male ego is hurt. He becomes possessive and jealous. Unable to bear his tantrums much longer, she decides to leave the house, but not for the big, bad, uncertain world outside. She decides to live with her in-laws in the country where she can continue to be a good daughter-in-law.

Despite this sop, two gentlemen, who had seen the first show of the play, lay in wait for Rangnekar to return home to ask him whether the woman would in time return to her husband. It was not a point on which Rangnekar could reassure them because it lay outside the purview of his play. However, seeing how agitated they were, he gave them permission to believe that she might very well return if circumstances allowed it. This satisfied them enough for them to leave.

~

I move on now to the seventies when the women's movement was in full force and one could have expected the birth of some sisters for Nora. By which I do not mean the feminist version of women going out in search of self-fulfillment; but confused conventional women who become gradually aware of the trap that conventional society has laid for them and desperately search for a way out. And succeed.

I will return for a moment here to the late Madhav Manohar who wrote a series of essays under the general title, 'Why Is Marathi Drama Deficient?' In dealing with the influence of Ibsen, he argues that it harmed rather than helped the growth of Marathi theatre because Marathi theatre people never really understood its essence. This led to a false start from which it took nearly three-and-a-half decades for the theatre to recover. Manohar sees a silver lining in the 1970s. He says, 'There is only one playwright today who has absorbed Ibsen in his totality. His name is Vijay Tendulkar. I have already said that anybody who decides to follow in Ibsen's footsteps must be willing to undergo an ordeal by fire. This young, highly talented playwright is going to be the first victim of that ordeal.'

But when you look at Tendulkar's female characters, you realize that nowhere in his plays has he created a woman who takes hold of her own life as Nora does, knowing it is going to be difficult, but also knowing as surely as anything, that it is the only way to 'become a human being'. Let us look at Sarita, the protagonist of *Kamala,* who comes close in a way to the situation in which Nora finds herself. Having taken her position in her husband's life for granted, Sarita is suddenly woken up by a question Kamala asks her. Kamala has been 'bought' by Sarita's investigative reporter husband to show at a press conference as proof that women are being sold like cattle in certain parts of the country. Taking in the general situation in this middle-class home, Kamala asks Sarita, 'And how much did our owner pay for you?' It is a moment of revelation. She sees her life with her husband in a new perspective. And yet, at the end, when she seems to be on the point of deciding to leave (they do not even have children to complicate the issue), she looks at her husband lying on the sofa with his shoes on. He has lost his job and has got drunk. She takes off his shoes and stays where she is.

When questioned about this end, which most people thought was not true to where the play was leading, Tendulkar said, middle-class women don't leave their homes so easily.

Dr Rajeev Naik has written a small play in answer to the question that is often asked about Nora: 'Where did she go when she closed the door of her home behind her?' His protagonist has left before the play begins. At the beginning of the play, she has come crawling back. It transpires that despite having a job and a place to stay (in themselves the biggest hurdles to women trying to make a life of their own), she finds it difficult to continue by herself. It is never clear why. But when she returns, it is to a relationship where the power equation is now entirely in her husband's favour. Both husband and wife pretend that this is not so. She pretends it is her love for him, the fact that she was missing him that has brought her back. He pretends to believe her and 'forgives' her. But their brief asides tell us that they are both waiting for their chance to get at each other—he to show his power and she to leave once again.

These are but two examples of the many other women who fail the Nora test. Which is why I call this paper 'The Impossibility of Being Nora's Sister in Marathi Theatre'.

Her Mother's Name

Just when things were looking as bleak as ever for my gender, with news of grown men having used their authority to molest young girls and hound them out of school, home and life; and when a downturn in the rise of crimes against us was not even a distant hope, *Mumbai Mirror* carried a piece of stunning news on its front page on the second day of the new year—schoolchildren will soon have the benefit of using their mother's names as their middle and last names.

Innumerable women are going to thank that unnamed woman from Jalgaon for this. They may not understand exactly what she did when she 'sought government directions' for allowing her school-going children to use her name as their middle name rather than that of her husband's; but the outcome of that action is something they have fought for, for years. The same innumerable women will also thank, from the bottomless depths of their hearts, the unnamed State Lokayukta (is he a man or a committee?) 'which nudged the government into taking a decision on the issue'.

If a loud cheer goes to each of these two entities, there are more for three others—a lusty cheer for School Education Minister Balasaheb Thorat; another to whichever body or bodies have the power to veto his move for not using that power; and the third to the readers of this newspaper for not flooding the letters to the editor column with vitriolic warnings about what will come to pass if women are allowed to give their names to their children.

This article was first published in *Mumbai Mirror* on 6 January 2010.

If the idea is indeed implemented, if we actually live to see the day when a school-application form carries that incredible slash after 'father's name' to accommodate 'mother's name', one of our most-cherished notions of the male child as the kuladeepak, the shining light of the family name, might suffer some damage. It will shake up the hoary tradition of putting only heirs to the family name on a family tree. Daughters anyway don't have a place in those large tomes that trace family histories back to the year dot. But if a male child, heir to something like the proud Dahibhatkar name suddenly becomes a Dudhbhatkar, the family tree will be shaken to its very roots.

These are but distant musings. I have given rein to them here only to indicate the ramifications of the new rule that, taken to its logical end, will go far beyond school-admission forms.

Returning to the here and now, I'd like to add one more category of women to the list that this newspaper cites as prospective beneficiaries of the proposed new rule. To women in live-in relationships, women with adopted children, divorcees, women separated from their partners and widows, I will add women who are traditionally exploited by men—commercial sex-workers and devdasis.

Narayan Surve has one of them deal with the question of names in what is arguably his most-loved poem. This woman wants to enroll her son in a school. Presumably, the teacher has asked her what he should write under father's name. The poem is her response to the question:

Write your name sir,
Write yours.

Don't give him a god's name
Give him a man's.
Give him yours.
My caste?
Don't ask me that.

Are we one man's women?
Are we cosy home women?
Such luck is not ours.

Bend child
Bend.
Touch his feet.
Please sir, do it.
Write your name.

But the woman also says something else that begs the question, how many women will claim the right that the proposed new rule offers them? She says,

The soil may be ready
But will anything grow
Without the plough,
Without the seed?
How can I give him my name
In place of his father's?
So please sir,
Give him yours.

Kanakabai
'I'm Still a Student'

For a long time, I have been hearing about Kanaka Murthy. She is one of the last traditional Indian sculptors, renowned for her stone statues of gods and goddesses and busts. Once in every while, when I visited Bangalore, I would resolve that this time I would try and meet her but somehow it never did work out. Finally, last week, I did manage an encounter, even if it was a cinematic one. On 14 November, I saw a documentary film on her at the National Centre for the Performing Arts' Little Theatre. It was one of a collection of films shown by the Sound and Picture Archives for Research on Women (SPARROW), all based on women artists' lives.

The very first shot of this film administered a powerful but pleasant shock to the system. A stout lady, with spectacles perched on her nose, every muscle of her face speaking of her concentration, sits on a modha, her legs apart, at work on a goddess' crown. She is chipping away industriously. It's obviously fine work now, for which she deploys a little hammer and chisel. We have never seen an image of a woman sculptor at work like this and had her father had his way, we would not have seen it even now. But three things intervened: her mother who stood by her, a pillar of strength; a teacher of almost god-like grace; and what she herself calls 'a kindness done to her by nature'.

It would be best to hear of his kindness in her own words for they bring back the puckish sense of humour demonstrated by

This article was first published in Marathi in *Loksatta* on 19 November 1998.

Lakshimibai Tilak in her autobiography, *Smritichitre.** Kanaka's father was an orthodox man. He only sent her to Bangalore for higher studies on her mother's insistence. But no sooner did she acquire her degree than he yanked her back to the family village near Hoysala. There was nothing to do there and nowhere to go but no doing or going was expected of her. She was to be married off and she was simply to wait for marriage to happen. She might learn singing, of course.

'My mother was a singer. My siblings also sang. I lived in a music-rich world but wanted no part of it,' Kanaka says. 'I wanted no part of this orchestra. Nor was my voice at my command, refusing to cooperate in bringing the song in my mind out of my mouth. I wanted to do something different.'

Perhaps she knew that there was more art in her hands than in her throat. But her father thought the visual arts were worthless. He had even stopped his own wife from painting. 'My father was hell-bent on getting me married. The only problem'—and here a hint of mischief shows—'was that nature had done me a kindness. She had made me dark.'

Taking advantage of this, Kanakabai made her father an offer he couldn't refuse. Her younger siblings were now studying in Bangalore. Instead of just sitting at home, could she not go to Bangalore and take care of them, make sure they got good home-cooked meals? Such affection for one's younger siblings fitted in well with her father's beliefs about how a young Indian woman should behave. She got permission to go to Bangalore. Having escaped her father's eye, she now had some room to think about her own artistic aspirations. She would stand for hours outside the Kalamandir Chitrashala, watching the students at work. Seeing the young woman standing there every day, a teacher called Mr Subbarao invited her in. He was a Gandhian whose experience had

* Available in English as *Smritichitre: The Memoirs of a Spirited Wife*, translated by Shanta Gokhale (Speaking Tiger; 2017). This is the first time the book appears in its entirety in an English translation.

taught him that if you teach a man, you teach only a man, but if you teach a woman she would educate the next generation as well.

With her father blissfully unaware of what his maverick daughter was up to, Kanaka began to study art. There was no question of her taking formal admission; but when Subbarao heard that she did not have the money to buy art materials, he paid for them out of his own pocket although he was not in the best of financial health. And so began the art school years.

Even as she was studying, one day, a famous traditional sculptor by the name of Vadiraj came over to meet her brother. Kanaka was hard at work over her drawing. Vadiraj must have seen something different in her work for he immediately invited her to learn sculpture with him. At this point, Kanakabai acknowledges that she owes her career to the support her brother offered her at this critical juncture. It was also good fortune that Vadiraj did not belong to one of the traditional families of sculptors. 'It would never have occurred to them to let me learn simply because I was a woman. Imagine, they don't even educate their own daughters because they say they're afraid they might act too big for their boots when they go to their in-laws' homes.' In other words, she just got lucky. At each step, several factors had to come into play so that she could take the next step.

When she discovered her special calling for sculpture, Kanaka got up the courage to tell her father what she had been up to. She also informed him that now that she had a career, she had certain clear ideas about what she wanted out of a husband. He didn't have to be an engineer or a doctor. He could be a hamaal so long as he lived in Bangalore and did not object to her continuing to work. Her luck held: she got that kind of husband. Not just that, she adds with a twinkle, but one without encumbrances. In other words, she did not have a mother-in-law to contend with.

Kanakabai worked under Vadiraj for the next twenty-five years. At that time, most artists believed that women were not able—physically—to make sculpture. Finally, Kanakabai took up the challenge and made a clay statue of a journalist who was present at a public demonstration of her prowess.

'He was very jowly, so I had to keep slapping the clay on to the lower part of the face. When it wouldn't hold, they giggled a bit but when I was finished, I silenced them all.'

As she says this, there is no trace of anger on her face. She has achieved what she set out to achieve. And so she seems to be content.

From accepting the colour of her skin as a blessing to using her position as a woman to subvert patriarchal values to her advantage, Kanakabai has never betrayed her art. She is now accepted as India's best-known traditional sculptor. When her guru died suddenly, she took over his incomplete works and single-handedly finished them before starting her own independent practice. Even today, she is positive she can feel his presence, as clearly as if he is standing behind her. But when she is asked how many students she has, her answer is unequivocal: 'Not even one. They come as students for a few months and they leave again. You can't be a student of anything for that short a period. Look at me: I'm still studying.'

The Real Joy of Cooking

Mr Pramod Navalkar has a weekly column in *Mid-Day*. Since he is the minister for culture and I have had some association with culture, what with one thing and another, I sometimes read his column for the pleasure and instruction it affords. Well, the instruction at any rate.

Take his column of 2 February, in which I discovered some important information: In 1970, there were only 1,013 restaurants and boarding houses in Mumbai. Today that figure is closer to 9,887. This makes Navalkar very uncomfortable. He says: 'There can be no objection to my saying that in the past twenty years, this profound change has meant that our kitchens now lie deserted.'

I do not want to contest something that is so obviously wrong. That is not the issue here. We should seek out the real roots of Navalkar's discomfort. We do not have far to look; those roots are visible in the sentence that follows: 'The stove is the repository of culture of every home. It is the magnet that holds the family together. It is the arena in which the housewife proves herself and the fountainhead of all homely happiness.'

These women who should be disporting themselves in the kitchen are now to be found in control of the remote. And what happens? 'As soon as she is mistress of the remote control, she finds no time to cook for her family, and so she orders in food from the closest restaurant. This is now almost a daily habit.'

Navalkar is deeply pained: 'What is the meaning of the word "home"? It is not just a construction. A home is built of a husband, a

---

This article was first published in Marathi in *Loksatta* on 5 February 1998.

wife, children, grandparents, relatives. It has a hall, a bedroom and a kitchen. The kitchen is the temple at which the housewife worships. If that goes, the life of the home goes. To cook up different dishes and to watch her family eat them with relish is her greatest pleasure.'

Navalkar is horrified at the sight of these women cutting off their noses to spite their faces. The spectacle of these women enjoying themselves fills him with foreboding: 'The day that the kitchen is destroyed will be the day when the housewife loses her role. If every house becomes a "two-bedroom-hall-no-kitchen" it will foretell the ruin of our society. A wife will become only a companion.'

Darkness, all is darkness, in front of Navalkar's eyes. I do not have the courage to consider this apocalyptic scenario. A wife as only a companion to a man? None of that, please. But all is not lost. We can still turn back the clock, retrace our steps and recover lost joys—all by turning the kitchen into a temple again. But to do this we will have to recover the ideals of those 'wives of olden times'.

If we read the *Mahabharata* or the *Ramayana*, we do not find a single description of Sita or Draupadi cooking up a delicacy or two for their husbands. Not one single description. In defence, it might be said: how could you find such a description? The two great epics were written by men. How could they know the joy women experience while cooking? Only a woman would understand.

Perhaps we should turn to women's accounts of their own lives and joys.

First let us consider Lakshmibai Tilak (1885–1936). Unfortunately, she turns out to be a flighty sort. If Navalkar had met her, he would have seen signs of the malaise even in her time. In place of Navalkar, Lakshmibai had an aunt and an elder sister. She speaks of the taunts they threw at her: 'If I began to tell a story, they would say: these stories are the legs on which a woman abandons her home. If I sang a song, they would say that I was singing about the outside world where it was obvious I wanted to be. If I played with dolls, the world was nothing but a playhouse for me. But these words had no effect on me.'

If Lakshmibai were alive today, she would have told those carping women: 'Where have all those meals you cooked gone? But today people are still reading my *Smritichitre*.' And even if she did not say something like this, what her female relatives predicted did not come true. She remained by her husband Vamanrao's side through thick and thin.

Let's look at another ordinary woman, one who had no time for the folderol of dolls. Let us ignore for a moment the fact that we know that Bahinabai Chaudhuri's (1880–1951) mind would not stay focused as she ground the corn; it flitted here and there. But what of 'the fountainhead of all homely happiness'? A poet like her, a poetess like her, perhaps I should say, would surely have mentioned it? She has, but not in the way one might have expected.

There is a single poem set in the kitchen and that too is a complaint. Bahinabai is to be found here, puffing on the bellows until her eyes are red.

> 'And then a gasp of relief,
> A brief breather;
> Then it's back to the grind:
> The tava back on the stove.'

So what is to be done with these women? How will Kamal Desai talk of the joys of the kitchen? In her stories, the women wear hats! And as for Gauri Deshpande, she probably has her own hat.

I turn from literature to the visual arts. I have a Mughal miniature in my kitchen. In it, a woman in immaculate white, sits in a kitchen. She's stirring something in a pot. Around her, there's a cutting board, a rolling pin, a potholder, et cetera. I stare at her face closely to see if I can spot some trace of happiness. Instead it seems as if her face is filled with sadness. Why should that be? We see that this Radha has been kept in the kitchen by Krishna, while he, her lord and master, disports with some other woman. Since miniatures do not bother themselves with reality and perspective, we can see him at it on the verandah.

We're back to square one. Because I couldn't find the perfect housewife anywhere, I turned on the television. This was not so that I could watch a soap opera before calling for a meal. It was to experience the real joy of cooking. On television, the person who represents this joy is Sanjeev Kapoor on his show, *Khaana Khazaana*. There he is now, his face flushed with happiness as he cooks up a storm every week. All we have to do is sit back and say, 'Mr Kapoor, may your tribe increase.' Atlas shrugged and it is now up to Hercules to bear the burden of the true delight of cooking.

Colour-coordinated Babies

When I read the story of a dark-skinned Indian woman married into a fair-skinned family looking for a white man's sperm to produce a child that would colour-match the family, I laughed my head off. Designing babies isn't that simple. Suppose some distant foremother of the sperm-donor had cohabited with a black man? The nurse might then hand over to the mother a dark bundle of grief instead of the white bundle of joy she had so longed for. Also, a white man's sperm, like any other, is a package deal. You can't order a white skin without running some risk of its coming with, say, carrot-coloured hair. Finally, closer to home, what about the danger of the mother's colour leaking into the embryo?

The news brought back a silly little story I'd heard in my student days in London about a Japanese man who takes his wife around Kew Gardens, explaining how each tree is the natural result of the seed that was planted. At the end of his patient botanical lesson, he turns to his wife and asks mildly, 'So how I put in seed and you get blond, blue-eyed baby?'

In Shivaji Park, the heart of colour-consciousness, we grew up winning Maharashtra's favourite consolation prize hands down. We were 'dark but smart'. That phrase has been one of the two most frequently used currencies in the Marathi marriage market, the other being, 'dark but sharp-featured'. Then there's the third, gahuvarni or wheat-coloured.

In the old days, the Indian Railways used to have four classes of carriage—first, second, intermediate and third. If one were to

---

This article was first published in *Mumbai Mirror* on 31 July 2013.

classify women according to that categorization, the 'dark but smart' would be the intermediate class. The fair would be the unquestioned first. And the wheat-coloured the second. Surprisingly we, who make such fine distinctions between the various shades of a woman's skin, are never called upon, in the last case, to identify precisely which species of wheat we are referring to. Is it Punjab Pisi, Gujarat Pisi or Sihor?

Once in a while, however, the marriage market throws up a true aesthete, endowed with sublimely refined tastes. When an acquaintance of my mother's, the fair-skinned, fat and ever-frowning Mrs Kirkire, was on a girl-seeing spree, she confessed that a girl the whole family had liked, had one unfortunate drawback—a father who was the wrong colour. 'Black as coal! Imagine how he'd look in our drawing-room,' she sighed. She had a point. Put a wrongly coloured human being on a carefully selected settee and your entire décor goes for a toss, doesn't it?

With such high stakes placed on colour, one is not in the least bit surprised at the haul that companies manufacturing fairness creams are making. Their ever-expanding market stands on a long tradition of abject hope. Once turmeric was supposed to work magic overnight. It gave birth instead to a discouraging Marathi proverb which warned people looking for a quick fix that '*pi halad, ho gori*' (drink turmeric and become fair) never worked. Later there was (perhaps still is?) Afghan Snow which men and women applied liberally to make their faces shine with snow-like radiance.

It is against this tough, all-pervasive, deathless tradition, this society-induced sense of inferiority in dark women that Nandita Das has taken up arms, and all power to her. I have had to face only once, as a vulnerable seventeen-year-old, what she has faced repeatedly during her long and impressive career. I was playing Geeta in an amateur production of Pu La Deshpande's play *Tujhe Ahe Tuja Pashi* (You Are What You Are). The make-up man, as much an amateur as any of us, had been instructed to make my skin lighter and my nose sharper. At the end of his two-hour operation, my skin looked like a circus clown's and my nose like a turnip. Disgusted, the director ordered the goo off and I walked proudly onto the stage with my natural skin and nose intact.

Good people, however, have always felt disturbed by our colour consciousness. Scholar-playwright Adya Rangacharya tells us that the sixteenth-century saint-poet Kanakadasa once wrote a play called *Rama-dhanya-nataka* (Rama and the Cereals, a play). In this play a bunch of fair-skinned cereals argue with the dark-skinned ragi, claiming superiority over it. Finally Lord Rama is called in to settle the dispute. He asks the cereals to bury themselves in the ground for two years. At the end of that period all the cereals except ragi have rotted.

A bit of reverse snobbery there. But why not?

On This Grand Nation

'An imagined past'

Between 'No, I Couldn't Possibly' and 'You've Eaten Nothing'

Last week, I met a European friend who has travelled the length and breadth of Maharashtra. She is an old hand at Marathi, speaking it fluently and idiomatically. She has made it her business to study the people and the culture of the state. We had a long conversation during the course of which, she asked me a question: 'Why are all of you so forceful in matters of eating and drinking?' She said it ought to be a given that every person would eat as much as s/he wanted. Did I not think that insisting a guest eat more was an imposition on their liberty? My friend said that when she refused more food, it was because she had had enough. Some people would recognize this eventually. But many others would not get it and would place her in an awkward position. To refuse would be to give offence, to accept would be to be forced into eating food she did not want. What did I do in such circumstances, she wanted to know.

She put me in a quandary with these four simple questions about a common social practice. The first question: why do we use unwarranted force when we offer guests food? It sounds like a simple question but like most simple questions, it is difficult to answer unless you're willing to risk solipsism. Why is the earth round? Because it is round. We insist on people eating more because it is our culture to insist in such a manner. What would an inquiring mind make of such an answer? I cast around for excuses and realize that it is never easy to think up answers to questions about customs

---

This article was first published in Marathi in *Loksatta* on 23 July 1998.

that are so much a part of our everyday lives that we never discuss them amongst ourselves. So I thought I should reverse the question to demonstrate to her the difficulty of answering questions about the quotidian.

She seemed to see the question—why do you never insist—coming before I asked it and began to answer. 'In Europe, we do not insist on people having more food because it seems an imposition on the personal liberty of one's guests.' I remarked that such an attitude must presuppose that each person would eat as much as s/he wanted. How much to eat or not to eat is then a personal decision. When a guest refuses to take any more, the hosts do not see it as a test of their hospitality. However, in Maharashtra, to refuse a request that issues from the person whose hospitality we are enjoying is the mark of the uncivilized. It would not do. This is not a matter of personal freedom but of cultural custom.

Her explanation also foregrounded two axioms of hospitality. In her culture, most people, by and large, live their lives in accordance with their own personal wishes and desires. In ours, we base our decisions, more or less, on the wishes of others. In her culture, marriage is a personal decision. In ours, it is a decision taken *en famille* and if you dig a little further, it is based on caste. The bride does not marry the groom; she takes on his entire family. To choose a spouse, one does not only examine the personality of the person concerned; one puts the entire family under the scanner. Once the woman is married, it is assumed that she is now at the beck and call of her new family. Only when she has paid her dues to them, may she use the rest of her time as she chooses. In such a situation, eating one more laddoo when one's stomach is full is not really difficult.

The explanation offered by my friend with the inquiring mind yielded a second axiom: each person eats as much as s/he wants. If you give this a little thought, this should hold true for any adult of any culture. Even a babe in arms knows to turn its head away from the breast when its tummy is full. My friend could asseverate this with certainty about the people of her culture; why did I not feel that I could say the same of the adult Indian? Where's the catch?

The answer surfaces again in tradition. Eating in another person's home is not an easy thing. Let us see how this unease arises. Let us assume that a mother is taking her daughter to her friend's home in some European country, say Norway or France. When they arrive, their host serves a snack. A plate of biscuits is set before the child. Her mother asks her: 'Would you like a biscuit?' The child says yes or no and eats or does not eat, accordingly.

Now when one of our children goes with her mother on a similar visit, she is schooled in how she must behave. She is not to ask her auntie for anything. She is not to eat anything. Thus when her auntie sets a plate of biscuits in front of her, she, obedient to her mother's commands, refuses them and looks at her mother for approval. Meanwhile, her auntie is saying, 'Go on, have a biscuit. Don't look at your Mum. She won't scold.' Still the little one refuses, even if her eyes are filled with a childish longing. Auntie stuffs a biscuit into her hand with a spritely, 'There you go.' Once again, the little one's eyes turn to her mother. At this point her mother relents. 'Go on then, since Auntie insists,' she says and the little one heaves a sigh of relief and falls to.

This is where the war of 'No, no, I couldn't possibly eat another bite' and 'Go on, go on, you've eaten nothing' begins. The guest has only two options. First, she can serve herself a little less than she usually eats so that she can give in to her host's insistence. Or she can let her stomach stretch infinitely. If you prefer the second option, you will have to practise and you risk losing your health. If you prefer the first option, it might hurt your host a little.

As to her third question—how do I refuse without giving offence?—I told her that I always ate only as much as I wanted. When the insistence begins, I help myself to just a little more and then I place my hands over my plate and refuse to move them until the serving is over and the dinner things are cleared away.

My host's wife says, 'Now, don't tell me you're on a diet. Nothing wrong with your figure. You can afford to have some more shrikhand.' I smile and keep my hands where they are. My host tries a devious move. 'She must not have liked our food. Don't force her.' My smile is unchanged, my hands stay in position. His mother says, 'We'll be stuck with these leftovers. Who's going to eat all this?' Smile unchanged, hands unmoved. Finally everyone gets it. I have eaten my fill. That is all they wanted to be sure of. Now that they have this assurance, they can abuse me affectionately and release me from the prison of the dining table.

'*Nachaiyye-gavaiyye*'

The culture of a political party that swears by culture is somewhat suspect. In recent years it has turned out to be no more than fatwas delivering a series of no-nos. Don't eat this, don't eat so much of that; don't drink this, don't drink it there; don't touch a person of the opposite sex in public, don't touch a person of the same sex even at home; don't question the country's top honcho—in fact, rid yourself of the bad habit of questioning altogether—and don't dare breathe the K-word unless it is to say we are right (as we always are) and they are wrong (as they always are). That's the sum and substance of what's generally thrown around as culture. Music and dance figure occasionally, only as objects of contempt.

On Dr B.R. Ambedkar's 126th birth anniversary on Friday, the BJP MP from Sagar, Laxmi Narayan Yadav, put all his seventy-two years of culture on display when he said that before the V.P. Singh government awarded Dr Ambedkar the Bharat Ratna in 1990, it was only '*nachaiyye-gavaiyye*' who had run off with the honour. Suspecting that the terms he had used for musicians and dancers weren't in themselves suggestive enough of contempt, he added, '*Jo jitna badmash tha woh utna jaldi le gaya*.' (The bigger the scoundrel the sooner he got it). In 2003, the late Pramod Mahajan had similarly dismissed musicians as '*gaanewale-bajaanewale*'. His audience had found the remark very funny. Yadav's audience, too, must have laughed.

Perhaps the honourable Shri Yadav's disrespect for dance and music comes from a deep prejudice against them internalized

---

This article was first published in *Mumbai Mirror* on 20 April 2017.

from colonial times when the British–Brahmin combine, under the influence of missionaries, crushed the devadasis of the south and the tawaifs of the north, forcing them into prostitution as the only means of survival. Before that, in eighteenth-century India, tawaifs had been highly respected as embodiments of refinement and culture. It is an irony that some of what goes by the name of ancient culture today is in fact of colonial vintage.

Let us return then to the pre-1990 Bharat Ratnas, termed badmashes by Yadav. Although a majority of them were politicians who had been part of India's freedom struggle, there were also exceptions like P.V. Kane, author of the five-volume *History of Dharmashastra*; the Nobel Laureate C.V. Raman; and India's pre-eminent engineer M. Visvesvaraya. Then there was Dhondo Keshav Karve who had started a shelter and school for widows in Hingane, a village on the far outskirts of Pune to which the orthodox Brahmins of the city had pushed him. He would walk miles every day to Fergusson College where he taught mathematics and then all over Pune to collect paltry sums of money from progressives as donations for his life's work.

So Yadav got his post-Independence history wrong when he claimed blithely that it was practitioners of dance and music who received Bharat Ratnas before 1990. Not so. Musicians got them after 1999; and no dancer has got it to date. The list of musicians is short but dazzling. The first was M.S. Subbulakshmi, with regard to whom Jawaharlal Nehru is reported to have said, 'Who am I, a mere Prime Minister before a Queen, a Queen of Music.' After her came Pandit Ravi Shankar, Lata Mangeshkar, Bismillah Khan and Pandit Bhimsen Joshi.

If Shri Yadav and his ilk were to look back at our performing arts before the faux colonial variety of culture took over, they might stumble on this description of the first dance: 'Seating Gauri, the mother of the three worlds, on a gem-decked golden throne on the rocky surface of Kailasa, the trident-bearer Shiva, performs his dance at eventide, when all the celestials surround him. Saraswati holds the lute, Indra the flute, the lotus-born Brahma has his hands engaged in rhythmic beat, the goddess Sri pours forth music, Vishnu dexterously beats the noble drum, as all the celestials stand around respectfully at sunset.'

Even if one doesn't take this mythical evocation of Shiva's heavenly performance at face value, one must remember that it is in the nature of myths to paint larger-than-life pictures of existing beliefs, customs and rituals. Contemporary society must have held dance and music in very high regard for this myth of their divine origin to take root. But Yadavji thinks it's smart to disrespect them publicly, forgetting that silence is the best way to conceal ignorance. Do occasionally try silence, Yadavji.

The English Language and Its Damages

'The English language has caused a great loss to the country. We are losing our language, our culture, as there are hardly any people who speak Sanskrit now.' Thus spake Shri Rajnath Singh in the capital last week. I think this statement needs looking at. Clearly Singh's perception has suffered a slippage between our present and an imagined past. Putting aside the losses and gains of the English language that history has bestowed on us willy-nilly, let us examine the causal link Singh proposes between the alleged loss of our culture and the paucity of people speaking Sanskrit today. It is a formulation that is deeply offensive when seen in the context of our thriving cultural practices like music, dance and theatre that are governed by language. Hindustani and Carnatic musicians have never sung in Sanskrit except when the ancient dhrupad form was more alive than it is today. They have sung in Prakrit languages like Telugu and Braj. The compositions that accompany our classical dance forms like Bharatanatyam, Kathak, Kathakali, Mohiniyattam, Kuchipudi, Manipuri and now, Sattriya of Assam, which was accepted into the classical canon as recently as 2000, are again largely in local Prakrit languages like Telugu, Malayalam, Braj, Bengali and Brajawali. The exception is Odissi which is danced exclusively to songs from Jayadeva's *Geet Govinda*, written in the lyrical Sanskrit of the twelfth century.

Modern theatre is of course a lost cause, done in all sorts of uncultured tongues, including gibberish. But ancient drama? If that's the past Rajnath Singh is looking back to nostalgically, then here's the lowdown on its socio-cultural-linguistic ethos. The *Natyasastra*, Bharata Muni's revered treatise, explains the origins of Sanskrit

---

This article was first published in *Mumbai Mirror* on 25 July 2013.

drama thus: 'When the Tretayuga arrived, people became victims of lust and covetousness. They were overwhelmed by jealousy and deluded by wrath, and were engaged in rustic rites and activities.' To correct this, an edifying entertainment had to be devised which would be accessible for 'those of the sudra caste' who were 'prohibited from Vedic discussion and practice.'

So contemporary values upset the cultural pundits of those Sanskrit-dominated times as much as they do Rajnath Singh today, although English was nowhere in sight; and the entire bahujan samaj, farmers, weavers, potters and craftsmen, who formed the base of the population, was excluded from learning Sanskrit. Add to this women who were similarly deprived, and you have, in that golden age of our culture, not more than a thin layer of the population, upper-caste men, mainly Brahmins, being allowed to learn Sanskrit. This is why Kalidasa, the master of Sanskrit drama, who knew how his society and its culture functioned, put Prakrit lines and songs in the mouths of his sudra and female characters, while his kings, ministers and priests spoke in sacred Sanskrit.

Fortunately for our culture, the divisiveness of society could not prevent people from expressing themselves. Women and sudras, unperturbed by their exclusion from Sanskrit, wrote and sang in the myriad colourful, melodious bhashas that this great country was blessed with. Buddhist nuns wrote passionately in Pali, speaking of the equality Buddhism offered them. This was in the sixth century BC when the English, destined later to impose their language on us, were still running around tattooed with woad and being called *picti*, or 'the painted ones' by the Romans. Writing exultantly about freedom, the Buddhist nun Mutta says,

> So free am I, so gloriously free.
> Free from three petty things—
> From mortar, from pestle and from my twisted lord.*

* Translated by Uma Chakravarti and Kumkum Roy; from *Women's Writing in India: 600 BC to the Early 20th Century*, edited by Susie J. Tharu and K. Lalitha (Oxford University Press; 1997).

Apparently Mutta's husband was a hunchback! Five centuries later, women poets flowered in the south in classical Tamil. Free to love and free to write about love, Velli Vitiyar speculates about a missing lover, 'He will not dig up the earth and enter it. / He will not climb into the sky. / He will not walk across the dark sea. / If we search every country / every village / can your lover escape us?'*

In brief, Shri Rajnath Singh, culture is a dynamic, flowing thing. Our culture is what it is because of what it was. But, as Heraclitus says, you can't step into the same river twice.

* ibid; translated by George L. Hart III

Guests of Chandigarh

There is an American who lives in Mumbai and loves India deeply, a love affair that has lasted thirty-six years. It began in 1962 when he came to India for the first time as a Peace Corps volunteer to work in a little village deep in Uttar Pradesh. He learned Hindi and Urdu there and lived as the people of the village did, transforming his life in every way to merge with theirs.

When his term ended, he returned to America to complete his education but he wanted to return to India as soon as he could. On graduating, he chose to work in a cultural organization that had many branches in India. In this way, he was assured of being deputed to India at some point in time. And so it came to pass that he was deputed to India, not once, but three times. The third time, he was posted to Mumbai.

He enjoyed the city. The free atmosphere, the people's zest for life, the energy, the differences in cuisine and culture among all the various castes and communities in the city—once reputed to have as many as eighteen different ways of wearing a turban in order that each might tell the other apart—and above all, the overflowing hospitality. Eventually, he decided to make his home in the city. When he told me this, I felt a glow of pride about my city. It was as if some seemingly immutable rule had been reversed. Indians generally go to the United States of America in order to earn money but what drew him to us was the pull of emotion. I've heard many descriptions of how wonderfully hospitable a city Mumbai can be. But this is the case only when the guest is white-skinned. Folks of other flesh tones have other stories.

This article was first published in Marathi in *Loksatta* on 16 July 1998.

About three weeks ago—or was it a month?—some time ago, anyway, I heard a story. Two South African women were denied entry into the permit room at Café Leopold. This was published in a newspaper and for the next week or so, there were any number of articles and editorials about the matter. Some of the regulars were so outraged that they swore never to go back. Those African students who have lived in Bombay and have experienced the behaviour that we reserve for those with black skins must not have been surprised.

Two students from Sudan who had come here to study in college told their stories. They said: 'The picture we were painted of India is very different from reality. We were told this was the nation that gave us Gandhi, Nehru and *Mother India*. We were told it was a country of equality, great beauty, love and warm hospitality. But when we got here, we discovered that all this was reserved for those whose skins were white. We have seen a very different face of India. Whenever we go out, we hear abuse: "Hey Kaalu" or "Hey Kaalya" (both variations of Hey Blackie). In all these years, none of the students in our colleges have tried to make friends with us. When a couple of them did try, they were treated so badly by their friends that we thought it best to stay away from them. One of them invited us over for Diwali but his family was outraged and he was caught in the middle.'

When I hear stories like this, I feel like going to every African student who has ever been insulted in my city and apologizing. For I have borne the exact equivalent in insults when I was a student in London. I had had the opportunity to live there for a while and was looking for a flat. I would consult the advertisements and choose a flat. I would call and the owners would ask me to come over and take a look. As soon as I got there, the owners would take one look at me and say something to the effect that they were so sorry but the flat had just been taken. When this happened two or three times, I began to realize what was happening. The fifth time, I announced that I was an Indian, a black, and that saved me a lot of comings and goings. Finally, I did get a flat, a lovely one that was rented to me by a white South African woman who had no problem with the colour of my skin. This despite the fact that her country was then run and riven by apartheid.

This prejudice against black skin expresses itself in different ways in many places all over the world. But perhaps we are the only society where most people are black but look down on those with black skin and reserve a god-like status for those with white skins. One can understand why a white homeowner might be reluctant to rent out a living space to a black girl but what of the brown-skinned Indian woman who refused to rent to a West Indian—whose skin was a couple of shades fairer than hers? I heard this from a West Indian friend, a true account of our racial prejudice.

Leaving their own countries, going to another country to study, or to live in another country, blacks still find it difficult to live with respect or to settle down legally, though the Scandinavian nations and Holland seem to be better behaved. But never mind other countries, we need to look to ourselves. There must be many people who try to behave with humanity. Why don't such people try to change the situation? Even if it's just a smile offered to these strangers who have left their families and their countries to live among us.

Once, a Nigerian student named Chris came to eat with us. He was talking about Chandigarh with much love. Finally, we asked, 'Why do you like Chandigarh so much?' That's when he told us his Chandigarh story. He was studying in a Chandigarh college with three of his friends. He would often feel lonely. Once, he went to a wedding with his friends, assuming that no one would ask who they were. And so it happened. They had dinner, they danced and when they were on their way out, an old Sardarji asked them, 'Why were you here? Tell me the truth.' They did and he said, 'Don't do it again. Instead, come every week to have lunch with us. You are guests of Chandigarh.'

Thereafter the four of them went every week to meet with him. And so Chandigarh seemed to them the most beautiful city of India, just because of one man's open-hearted generosity.

Kisses That Cross Lines

To kiss or not to kiss and if to kiss whom to kiss and when are all culture-specific matters. But they are simultaneously intensely personal decisions and so any attempt, on the part of any government, to make laws about the kissing of others would be to reveal an immaturity of culture and a lack of understanding of what constitutes the basic principles of democracy. Although my sister and I may have known that our parents cared for each other and we for them, we never witnessed any kissing. It just wasn't part of our culture. In fact, if someone were to kiss in our family, it would immediately raise some doubts about the real-ness of their love. This was true of some of the families we knew but not of others. In some families, to offer another cultural meme, it was common for the youngsters to touch the feet of their elders as they came and went. To those who shared our attitudes, this smacked of hypocrisy, specially since the same youngsters spoke disrespectfully of their elders behind their backs. One of my close friends has a family that just can't get enough kissing in. From the grandparents down to the uncles and aunts, the cousins and the in-laws, everyone falls into each other's arms and lavishes kisses upon each other. They extend this courtesy to visitors such as me. Whenever I go over, my face is carpet-bombed with kisses. But all this seems so natural with them that I never notice that I have crossed some cultural boundary and entered another zone. I feel no embarrassment as the kisses fly.

Perhaps I should make some things clear about this family of

This article was first published in Marathi in *Loksatta* on 11 June 1998.

kissing cousins. They are solidly middle-class, moderately educated, with very few traces of Westernization. They are the kind of people who bring Ganpati home every year, installing him and worshipping him with every sign of belief and devotion. They do not, however, make a big thing about their Hinduism—never dream of putting it to political use, for instance. That kind of simple, ordinary Marathi family, risen from Marathi soil.

Some time ago, the front pages of several newspapers, once reserved for the leaders of the nation, carried stories about a kiss that caused much hissing. On a stage somewhere, a man by the name of Mark Robinson asked a woman by the name of Sophiya Haque whether he might kiss her. Sophiyabai was well over the age of consent. Both Sophiyabai and Markrao and all the youth gathered in front of the stage shared the same cultural coordinates. So it might be safely assumed that Sophiyabai was aware that kissing someone by way of greeting had nothing to with matters of gender and would arouse no sense of indecorum. And so she proffered her cheek to Markrao.

But in the gathering there were people who were from another culture. No sooner had Markrao's lips touched Sophiyabai's cheeks than they erupted. From their cultural coordinates, this seemed like a sign of the apocalypse. We parse everything we encounter—words, acts—from our understanding of culture. When we try to apply our own standards to the behaviour of people from other cultures, things fall apart, the culture cannot hold.

Bombay's film world brings together people from all cultures and conditions. A premiere attracts crowds of film people and journalists. Some shake hands, some smile, some wave and some stick jujube kisses on each other's cheeks as greeting. On just such an evening, a reviewer who writes for a Hindi monthly film magazine, now defunct, is slouched in one corner of the room, drinking steadily. He is silent except for the small talk he makes with those who approach him. Then a journalist of his acquaintance comes into the room. She smiles at some people. Others get a wave or a nod or both. Some she shakes by the hand. And then seeing a film-maker of mature years, she bestows affectionate air kisses on his cheeks. She notices the reviewer in the corner whom she knows and smiles at him. The reviewer advances upon her. 'This won't do,' he says. 'You have to kiss me too.'

It may be something in his tone but suddenly the air-kiss takes on an entirely different meaning. The reviewer has been brought up in an entirely different culture and has never sought to leave it. His usual way of greeting people is to smile and nod. The young reviewer knows this and is embarrassed. He sees her discomfiture and gets angry. 'You've been kissing everyone here. It seems I'm the only one who doesn't make the grade,' he says and he tries to add a laugh but it fails to conceal his anger. Now the people around have begun to realize what's going on. At which point a kindly Parsi lady says, 'If it's only a kiss you're looking for, here you go,' she says and lands him a good smacking kiss. But this doesn't make up. It's not the kind of kiss he wanted. In his world kisses have sexual connotations. But how does one invest a social gesture with a sexual connotation? His demand is half-warning and half-invitation. It has not been satisfied by affection.

This is not just an Indian problem. It turns up across the globe in different cultures and in different ways. When Mikhail Gorbachov, the Premier of the Union of Soviet Socialist Republics, arrived on a state visit to The United States of America, he kissed them all: President Bush and all his men. Now in America, 'real men' don't kiss and men of power don't kiss, at least not in public. One of the most surprising things for American or European visitors must be the sight of many Indian men, strolling about hand in hand, or resting their heads on their male friends' laps.

To understand another culture and its values, we have to enter the framework of that culture. But of course, if you want to show your power, then there's nothing worse than actual understanding. In which case, 'our culture' becomes the only culture.

Blood Sport

My Dear Little Rohtaki,

We read the news of the horrific assault on your body and childhood on Sunday, Mother's Day. It told us that at ten years old you were five months into being a mother. It didn't make sense to us. Forget all the sentimental crap about how you should have been going to school and playing on swings and slides. What we kept imagining was the physical agony of having a grown-up man thrust himself on you for who knows how long. The idea of what that must have done to your ten-year-old body was so repugnant, it made us throw up. All we wanted to do was gather you up in our arms and let you feel the comfort of a good human touch. We desperately hope you will get the understanding, warmth and protection you will need to help you overcome the trauma.

If there is a silver lining at all in this, it is that you didn't have to face a police officer's disbelief. He would have asked you then if you hadn't imagined the whole thing. They do that, you know. For wasn't it unbelievable that your stepfather, who is also your paternal uncle, assaulted instead of protecting you? But the tragic fact is that over 300 of the 2,267 rapes recorded in a single year in a single state in our great nation are instances of incest. Fathers, uncles and brothers do rape their daughters, nieces and sisters. Even when this is known to neighbours and relatives, they will not help, because these are after all private family affairs. See how badly trapped we are?

That is why we say you are fortunate not to have had to face

In May 2017, a ten-year-old girl from Rohtak was found to be five months pregnant. She had been raped by her stepfather. This piece was first published in *Mumbai Mirror* on 18 May 2017.

disbelief from the police. The proof of what was done to you was stirring in your body. You were also fortunate that, being so young, you couldn't be accused of asking for it because of the way you dressed. Even our society, vicious as it is, would have found it difficult to claim you were a siren who had led a hapless male up the garden path. You were fortunate too not to be old enough for men to desire you, as one man did your twenty-year-old fellow Rohtaki. He proposed marriage to her. She thought she had the right to say no; so she did. And see what happened to her. Raped by seven men, private parts slit with a sharp weapon, head smashed in with bricks, run-over to destroy her body so completely she became unrecognizable. To say no to a man is to challenge his ego and his sense of entitlement. That is dangerous.

Today's news tells us that your doctors have received the court's permission to terminate your pregnancy. It will happen any time now. We'll keep our fingers crossed for you, little one. We hope you will come through safely and return to school. As you grow up, you will gradually realize that the odds are stacked high against us. Your state, for instance, regularly records the highest number of female foeticides in the country. Luckily, being from Bihar, you and your sister were allowed to be born.

There are laws against what happened to you. One was in place already when Jyoti Singh, thirteen years older than you, was raped and brutalized five years ago by five men in Delhi. We said then that enough is enough. We demanded harsher laws. Harsher laws were made to deter men like your father-uncle from thinking they were free to do what they pleased with our bodies. But while laws are necessary, they are not sufficient. Do you think those seven men who did what they did to your fellow-Rohtaki were thinking of the noose that might fall around their necks? They were not. They were enjoying a blood sport that men are brought up to believe they are entitled to play. The more players there are against a single helpless woman, the more fun the game is.

So what do we say now when enough is still not enough? Perhaps just this. When you grow up to become a happy mother, as one day we hope you will, make sure you bring up your sons to think of us as fellow human beings, not as territory to be grabbed, overrun and ravaged.

Meanwhile, we stretch out our arms to you as you undergo an operation not meant for your age.

Yours in love and grief,

Women of the world

A Selection from Woman-to-Woman

I
The Organizer

The greatest triumph would have been to get him to agree, at the end of it all, that it had been a good evening. Not good in a chaotic, fun kind of way, but good in a fairly well-organized fashion. His black book, which started as a memory aid and plays a very important role in his social life, has now become something of a tyrant. Only things that go down in that little black book get done.

My request was quite simple. 'Please come and have dinner with me tonight.'

He regarded me from his academic heights and smiled the soft smile he reserves for people who enjoy bandying words for the fun of it.

'Will you?' I pursued.

His smile became a worried frown. 'I alone, or I and the wife?' he asked.

'Naturally, both of you.'

He considered that. It appeared that I had said the right thing, because the line between his eyebrows became fainter. But it was still there.

'Well?' I said. 'What is it for?' he said.

'The dinner? Because I'd enjoy having you and your wife over.'

'Thank you. But then we could come another day, couldn't we?' and he brought out his little black book.

'Why? Are you doing something tonight?'

This article was first published in *The Evening News of India* on 29 August 1978.

'Doing something? No I don't think so.'

'Then, are you not feeling well?'

'Not at all. In fact we are both feeling remarkably well.'

'Then you'll come, won't you, for dinner?'

He fiddled unhappily with his little black book, 'I'll tell you what,' he said. 'We'll make it next Saturday. I'll put it down here in my book right away, so I won't forget.'

'You're most welcome next Saturday, but I'd like you to come tonight as well.'

'But you've just thought of it, and you've got a day's work ahead of you. When will you go home and cook?'

'I have a magic thali. You'll get your fill.'

He was embarrassed. That is not what he had meant.

'I'll have to call my wife and she may not be at home.'

'Don't worry. I'll call her every five minutes till I get her.'

'Oh all right then, we'll come if it's all right with her.'

He sounded unhappy, miserable in fact. And when he put away his little black book, he sighed audibly.

I called his wife. 'Will you have dinner with me tonight?'

'You mean me alone or with my husband?' she asked.

'Both of you, of course.'

'Not likely,' she sighed. 'He'll never come.'

'He's promised to come.'

'You mean he had you in the black book and forgot to tell me this morning?'

'No. I invited him only fifteen minutes ago.'

'Then he's not coming. But I'd like to if you don't mind my coming without him.'

'I assure you, he is coming.'

When they came on the dot of eight, he was in a fairly advanced stage of misery.

'It's quite a strain, this kind of thing,' he said. 'Things always go wrong when you act like this, on impulse.'

'Did you lose your way?' I asked.

'No,' he admitted glumly.

'Nor did our great-aunt turn up as we were leaving,' his wife said. 'Nor did the servant decide to take the night off.' She was laughing and looking as if she was really enjoying herself.

Halfway through the meal, he also relaxed and they both talked and laughed and the party wound up at midnight. When they left, I said, 'Was it good? Did it work?'

And he said, 'I don't know, I'm not sure. Do you think we could come over next Saturday? I'll put it down in my little black book straight away, so I won't forget.'

II
Down Under in Udupi

He said he had sworn, after the incident of the jumping spoon, never to take an Australian woman to an Udupi restaurant.

For a man whose attitude to life is to a great extent scientific, this seemed rather a strange resolution to come to. After all, generalizing from a particular incident and assuming that one Australian woman who put you in an embarrassing situation in one Udupi restaurant was enough reason to ban the entire race of Australian women from the entire range of Udupi restaurants was unrealistic and unscientific.

This is what had happened. They had entered the Udupi joint during one of its rush hours and were shown to a mezzanine table. Tables in Udupi restaurants are placed cheek by jowl in order that more people may partake of more idlis and more dosas in a smaller span of time. Across the table from them sat Mr Subramaniam, or possibly Mr Nageshwaran, with his fresh and beautiful doe-eyed bride.

Settling down, Don Juan and Matilda discovered that there was no place anywhere to keep their effects, and their effects were many

---

This article was first published in *The Evening News of India*. The date of publication is unknown.

and varied. For Don Juan loves reading poetry to his women and is never without a sackful of appropriate volumes, while Matilda, fascinated by our ancient country, carried her own volume on its art and its culture. The poetic sack went on the floor, while Art and Culture was carefully balanced upright between their two places in such a way as to leave enough place for the waiter to set down their order of idlis with its retinue of sambhar and chutney, without obstructing their gazing into each other's eyes and their holding hands which is sometimes more to the point than reading poetry.

Thus settled, they were ready to attack the idlis which soon came. Something in its own incongruous position on a table laden with things of the stomach must have upset Art and Culture, for, without any apparent provocation and certainly without any warning, it leaned over and crashed upon the end of Matilda's idliful spoon.

Now, said Don Juan, shuddering at the memory of what followed, an Udupi restaurant is like a nuclear reactor. Once a neutron is released a chain reaction is set up, which no power upon earth can halt. (I think I've told you that Don Juan, despite his penchant for reading poetry, has strong scientific leanings). The spoon upon which Art and Culture had crashed took flight, somersaulted and went double diving over Nageshwaran's head to disappear over the banister of the mezzanine. In its hasty trajectory, it dropped its load of idli in Nageshwaran's lap and dripped festoons of sambhar down his nose and chin.

The waiter, who had come to their table bearing a trayful of glasses containing water, got rattled and leaned back. The glasses in the tray swayed uncertainly. Some righted themselves, while others accepted their fall. One flew off the tray and emptied itself in the unsuspecting and innocent lap of a moustachioed man at the neighbouring table, whose only fault was that he sounded like an emergency generator when he was eating.

Meanwhile, Matilda had gone red in the face because Art and Culture, which was her book, had misbehaved so grossly. She sprang out of her chair, pulled a lace-edged handkerchief out of her pocket and began to dab assiduously at Subramaniam's face, clucking soothingly the while like a hen over a frightened chick. Subramaniam's doe-eyed wife, who had touched her husband's face for the first time two days ago, dilated her eyes to unbelievable dimensions and made gurgling sounds in her throat.

While this was happening upstairs, the spoon, which had disappeared over the banister of the mezzanine, had plumbed straight into the bowl of sambhar that a waiter downstairs had just placed before the head of a family of four, none of whose members measured less than 75 cms round the middle. Not accustomed to spoons coming at them like remote-controlled missiles, the head of the family assumed, with justification, that the waiter had carelessly dropped the spoon in the sambhar, unpardonably splashing the voluminous front of his own kurta and the even more voluminous front of his wife's blouse with spicy liquid.

While a battle of words which showed signs of becoming a battle of arms between the man and the waiter ensued, doe-eyed Mrs Subramaniam upstairs found her voice and said to Matilda: '*Chee oorsuthi, nee panrathai udane niruthu*,'* in a voice that would have shaken an army general. Matilda, always fearful of misunderstanding Indians, ignored the sharpness in her voice and took what she had said to mean powerful support and encouragement. So she brought more vigour and pep to bear on Subramaniam's nose and chin; while Subramaniam, realizing the full portent of his wife's admonition, leaned back, away from Matilda's ministrations, upsetting once more, a fresh trayful of water glasses that the waiter was carrying to the neighbouring table.

At this point Don Juan took a snap decision. He hauled up his sack of poetry, he hauled up Matilda who was still making sambharous passes at Subramaniam, left enough money on the

* Chee gadabout, stop what you're doing immediately. Thanks are due to Arundhathi Subramaniam for this translation.

table for compensation all round and ran down. Cutting their way through the knot of people downstairs who were still arguing heatedly about where the offending spoon had come from, they came into the great outdoors, where, under the soft light of stars and with the moon as witness, Don Juan swore he would never again take an Australian woman to an Udupi restaurant.

Most unscientific, I think.

III
Seek and Ye Might Not Find

We were looking for an important document. Because it was important it had been kept in a very special place.

The specialness of the place lay in its total safety from all forms of invasion, either by house pests, which included cockroaches and kids, or outsiders, which included petty thieves and robbers.

Now, it so happens that when we put something away in a very special place, we forget where it has been put away because there are many special places in our house and many things to be put away. So we always make a note of where we have put away what. Obviously such top-secret information has to be recorded in a top-secret notebook. And if kids or cockroaches, or termites for that matter, got at this notebook, all would be lost.

So we lock this notebook away in a drawer. The key is placed in an old beaded purse that my grandmother made when she was thirteen, and the purse is tucked away in the corner of a shelf in our large wooden cupboard, which is full of little bits and pieces of cloth left over from sewing, where no robber in his senses would think of looking for the beaded purse which contains the key to the drawer in which we keep the notebook that would give him the vital information about where the most important things in the house were kept.

When I said we were looking for an important document, I was

This article was first published in *The Evening News of India* on 19 September 1978.

not being precise. What we were looking for, to be precise, was the key in the beaded purse. It wasn't there. We turned the purse upside down and inside out, and prodded in the lining and peeped between the lining and the beads. And the key still wasn't there. The trouble with having everything so beautifully thought out is that, if one link in the think chain snaps, you are left holding the loose ends with not half an idea between the ten of you about what to do.

At such times, saying the obvious helps. My mother said it. She said, 'The key doesn't have legs. So it can't have walked out of the house.' For years this sentence has served to spur the family on to greater efforts of searching. It once led me to find my sister's missing pyjamas in the tin of atta, and my father's missing spectacles clutched protectively in his hand.

The search was on. Systematically we went through boxes and trunks and bottom drawers and ordinary drawers and we came upon many treasures. There was a box of shells which my sister and I had collected a quarter of a century ago. 'What have you kept these for?' I asked my mother. She said, 'Isn't it amazing how bright they still look? Just look at the colours.'

In one drawer, there was a box full of string neatly wound on innumerable reels. It wasn't special variety of string. It was the kind that banias tie around pockets of tur dal and common salt, and every household collects about ten yards of it in the course of a single day.

'What are you hoarding all this string for?' I asked.

My mother said, 'You never know when you'll suddenly need it. Remember the time you wanted a length of blue nylon rope and had no time to go out and buy it and I gave you just what you'd been looking for?'

I remembered. She told me she had just what I wanted and we'd spent two hours looking for it, in which length of time I could have made six trips to the local hardware store to buy some. 'Ah,' she had said when I pointed this out to her. 'But why spend time unnecessarily when you have specially put away something for just such a contingency?'

There was also a boxful of nappy pins. 'Mothers are so careless. They change their babies' nappies here and leave spare nappy pins around,' she said.

'Throw them away,' I suggested, deliberately using a verb which is considered insensitive and obscene in our house. But such obscenity is required if change is to be effected. 'Throw them away? Why?' she asked. 'They are perfectly good nappy pins. Look. They aren't even rusted.'

'Throw them away,' I said, 'because the babies to whom they belong passed their school-leaving exams last year and gave up wearing nappies fifteen years ago.'

'That doesn't mean there aren't other babies around to use them.'

Which, to my mother, was a conclusive punch line because if there's anything one can say about our country with any confidence, it is that there's never a paucity of prospective nappy pin-wearers.

Halfway through a box of old newspaper cuttings, each one of which was carefully shaken out for the missing key, my mother paused thoughtfully and said, 'Wait a minute.' While I waited, I went through the rest of the cuttings, and found that one was a piece about an old sage who lived in a mountain cave and talked animal language and another was a design for the kind of dress fashionable teenagers wore twenty years ago and another was full of recipes which called for a cup of almonds and two seers of khoya. But partly because Mother was busy thinking, and partly because it would be futile to do so, I didn't ask why the cuttings had been preserved for so many years.

Coming out of her mammoth thinking session, Mother got up briskly, walked to the big wooden cupboard, sent her fingers wriggling under the paper which covered the middle shelf and brought out a plain white envelope. Opening the envelope, she brought out, between delicately pinched thumb and forefinger, the missing key!

'But that's not grandmother's beaded bag!' I said accusingly.

'Of course it isn't,' she snapped back. 'If it had been, there wouldn't have been a problem. But don't you see, what is no problem for us is also no problem for thieves. One must never keep the same things in the same things over any length of time. It's always good policy to shift things around to put people off the scent. Now remember, the key is in this envelope there.'

'How long will it remain there?'

'How can I tell you that? Change is effective only when it us unplanned and unknown. A spur-of-the-moment decision.'

'Cheers,' I said, 'here's to a lifetime devoted to hide-and-seek.'

On Writers and Writing

'Tele and micro, both scopes'

Inextinguishable Fires
Dalit Literature in Marathi

One of celebrated Dalit poet Namdeo Dhasal's childhood reminiscences is about the time he and his young friends committed the crime of swimming in a well whose water they, as untouchables, were forbidden to 'pollute'. The boys were mercilessly stoned by the villagers for the crime. So when Dalit writers say their literature is about life, they are talking about a bitter and humiliating struggle for existence. To be denied water is to be denied life. How then are they to feel they belong to this land and its gods?

L.S. Rokade writes,

> I spit on this great civilization
> Is this land yours, mother,
> only because you were born here?
> Is it mine
> only because I was born to you?
> ....
> Sorry mother, but truth to tell,
> I must confess I wondered
> Should I be born
> Should I be born at all into this land?

Trymbak Sapkale says in a hybrid Marathi-English,

Amhi god maker	(We are god makers)
bajavato notice tujhyavar	(We serve a notice on you)

This article was first published in *The Caravan* on 1 August 2013.

negligence of dutychi	(For negligence of duty)
Your services are not required.	(Your services are not required.)

These are the angry poets of the 1970s and after. But before they arrived, there was another, Baburao Bagul, who was writing impassioned short stories that pitchforked readers out of their well-lit world into one that was dark, desperate and dangerous.

Baburao Bagul was born in a village near Nashik in a desperately poor family. At ten years old, he was sent to Mumbai to live with his maternal aunt in the Matunga Labour Camp. This was a colony built by the Bombay Municipal Corporation* for migrant Dalit labour from the interiors of Maharashtra, located on a piece of marshy, mosquito-infested land abutting Dharavi in Central Mumbai. Bagul's school education ended with matriculation, after which he did several odd jobs till he found permanent employment in the railways. The Labour Camp at that time buzzed with intellectual activity. The Communist Party held regular study circles there and Dr Babasaheb Ambedkar's Scheduled Caste Federation office was also located there. Thus Marxist and Ambedkarite ideologies came to form the foundation of Bagul's thought, and gave his writing muscle.

In 1963, ten of Bagul's stories appeared in a collection titled *Jevha Mi Jaat Chorali Hoti* (*When I Hid My Caste*†). The book created such a stir that Bagul was interviewed by *The Times of India* and *Maharashtra Times*, while the Marathi mainline dailies, *Navakal* and *Navashakti*, ran editorials about him and his work. It is often said that *Jevha Mi Jaat Chorali Hoti* gave a new momentum to Dalit writing. This does not mean that the collection suddenly galvanized Dalit writers into writing. Writers like Shankarrao Kharat and Anna Bhau Sathe were already writing stories that had won them admiration. One of the factors that must have contributed to the

---

* As it was then known. It is now the Brihanmumbai Municipal Corporation, the acronym remaining the same and the inefficiency.

† *When I Hid My Caste: Stories* by Baburao Bagul, translated by Jerry Pinto has been published by Speaking Tiger, 2018.

upsurge of Dalit writing in the 1960s is education, which gave Dalit youth a sense of self-worth. The People's Education Society, of which Dr Babasaheb Ambedkar was chairman, had founded the Siddharth College of Arts and Science in Mumbai in 1946, and the Milind Mahavidyalaya in Aurangabad in 1950, to encourage Scheduled Caste and Scheduled Tribe youth to choose education as a path to a better life. However, what Bagul's stories did do, was to give Dalit writing a public face. His work told writers that they could write about their universe of experience without worrying too much about established norms of literary construction and language.

It has been fifty years since *Jevha Mi Jaat Chorali Hoti* was published. Its eleventh edition, published in April 2013, proves that these stories continue to exercise power over the reader's imagination. Perhaps this is a good time to ask what it is about them that has made the collection such a landmark in Marathi literature; and also a good time to look at the directions in which Dalit literature has moved since then.

The impact of Bagul's stories comes from the monumental characters he creates, the live-or-die situations he places them in and the ferociously driven prose in which he describes their ordeals. Bagul's unnamed protagonist in the title story of *Jevha Mi Jaat Chorali Hoti* tries to escape cruel discrimination by concealing his caste. When his prospective landlord asks him about his caste, he replies, 'How dare you ask me my caste? Me? I am a Mumbaikar. One who fights for truth, dies for it, carries weapons on its behalf, liberates Bharat, gives it power. Do you understand? Or do you want me to repeat myself? Sing to you the ballad of our great deeds?' When his caste is finally revealed, he is beaten to within an inch of his life. Kashya, a knife-carrying Dalit worker, rescues him and asks, 'How could you have allowed those men to beat you up like this?' The protagonist replies, 'It wasn't they who beat me. It was Manu.'

Bagul's prose style is full of powerful, impassioned strokes that create unforgettable images. In 'Goonda', 'The road took rapid turns and a paan shop sprang into the angry man's eyes and got trapped there.' Later, 'He lunged forward and surged straight towards Jayantiben's shanty. Mosqitoes and grime-covered people made way for him. He placed a hand on the poverty-stricken top of the hut and thrust his massive head through the door.' Damu, the protagonist of 'Bohada' (a ritual mythological play), '...stood in the wide doorway like a statue of a towering warrior carved out of black rock.'

Girja, the prostitute, needs money desperately. A telegram has arrived with bad news about her son. She washes and makes up her face, stands outside the garden to solicit men. 'But as yet, not one of her customers had shown up. She stood chewing paan with a dry mouth, trying miserably to bring colour to her lips. She walked to the tap. Washed her face. Tried to scrub away the sadness. She smiled at the men. Used every art she knew to arouse them. But nobody would come to her. Nobody would ask her her price. Time and men passed her by.'

Jevha Mi Jaat Chorali Hoti was followed in 1969 by Bagul's second collection of stories, *Maran Swasta Hote Ahe* (Death Is Becoming Cheap), which focused on life in the slums of Mumbai. This collection consolidated his position in the literary world and brought him the Maharashtra State's Hari Narayan Apte award.

The most prominent amongst Bagul's contemporaries was Anna Bhau Sathe, the Marxist shahir, short-story writer and novelist. He, too, lived in the Matunga Labour Camp. His life experiences were no different from Bagul's. However, unlike Bagul, who wrote like an elemental force with no time to spare for embroidering descriptive details into his stories, Sathe wrote in a more conventional style. The following randomly picked passage from his story 'Sapla' (Trap) could have been written by any writer. The story is an account of a conflict between the Mahars and caste Hindus of a village over the former's refusal to haul away a dead bull, one of the traditional duties assigned to Mahars which Dr Ambedkar had exhorted them to give up. As a result, the Mahars are ostracized by the villagers. The Mahar leader Hariba is on his way to the taluka town to register a complaint against them, and Sathe writes, 'It was still dark when

Hariba left home for the taluka town. The east had just begun to brighten. A band of light had appeared between the earth and the sky. Enormous clouds drifted high above. Their forms looked fearful as they dashed softly into each other. Birds twittered in the trees lining the path.'

There was another contemporary of Bagul's, Narayan Gangaram Surve, whose long poem '*Majhe Vidyapeeth*' (My University), published in 1966, did for poetry what Bagul had done for fiction. It brought into poetry life experiences, a world view and a street language that it had not known before. Abandoned on a footpath in Mumbai as a baby, found and looked after by a mill-worker couple, Surve was to go on to win the Padma Shri and Kabir Samman awards. But '*Majhe Vidyapeeth*' was about the lessons he learned on the streets of Mumbai. Its first two lines are:

> I had neither home nor kin, just as much land as I could walk on.
> Shops offered shelter, and municipal footpaths were open, free to use.

And the last two:

> Now that I have come into this world, to wander in its harsh reality,
> I have no choice but to live, to belong, giving and taking blow for blow.

Around the mid-1950s, Dalit writers had begun to assert their different-ness from mainstream writers. Their themes, language and narrative style were unique to themselves. They were committed to writing about the socio-political issues that affected their lives. The annual Marathi literary conferences did not offer them a platform to debate these issues. The writers felt they needed a separate forum, and the first Dalit literary conference held in Bombay in 1958 was the outcome. Baburao Bagul did not attend. In an interview given to Dr Nazareth Misquita, author of a critical study of Bagul's work published in 2006, he dismissed such conferences as occasions to stand on daises and make speeches. Anna Bhau Sathe not only attended but made the inaugural speech in which he said, 'This world, this earth does not stand on the hood of Sheshanag. It stands on the palms of Dalits. The Dalit must be raised to his rightful place in society and writers must stand shoulder to shoulder with the common people to bring this about.'

One of the questions raised at the conference was how to define the term Dalit literature. After much heated discussion it was resolved that Dalit literature was literature written by Dalits or non-Dalits dealing with the life of Dalits. This definition was discussed in other fora and efforts were made by writers to sharpen it further. Collectively and individually, they identified four values which Dalit literature, in order to be called so, should uphold—rejection of the establishment, protest against injustice, rebellion against the caste system and promotion of the scientific temper. Playwright and academic Datta Bhagat went further. He categorically linked Dalit literature to the Ambedkarite movement. In his book, *Dalit Sahitya: Disha Ani Dishantar* (Dalit Literature: Directions and Departures; Abhay Prakashan, 1992), he concluded that Dalit literature could be defined as 'the expression of an intense desire, born of a complete understanding and assimilation of Dr Ambedkar's thought and world view, to know the self and the socio-political reality that surrounded the self.'

To assert that Dalit literature was distinct from upper-caste literature was simultaneously to reject the critical criteria that had evolved to assess the latter. Dalit poet and critic Keshav Meshram stated in the March–April 1970 issue of *Asmitadarsha*, 'Marathi criticism is inadequate to the task of assessing Dalit literature.' Bhagat agrees, but hastens to point out the pitfalls attached to dismissing existing critical criteria. He argues that writing about Dalit life from an Ambedkarite perspective and rejecting established critical criteria does not mean that writers forget they are, first and foremost, artists. If upper-caste critics find Dalit literature too rough and raw for their palates, that is as it should be. But at the same time, he contends, Dalit writers cannot go away with the notion that the unique moral value of their subject matter will, by itself, qualify their work as Dalit literature.

~

Although the publication of Baburao Bagul's short stories was a watershed moment in the history of Dalit literature, the short story as a literary form did not find immediate favour with young writers. Through the 1960s and 1970s, the form they largely chose to express their anger and protest through was poetry. While the literary magazines of the establishment, the prestigious *Satyakatha* and *Mouj*, had no place for their disruptive poetry, Little Magazines offered them a ready platform. Little Magazines were irregular periodicals, sometimes no more than two-page fliers, published by rebellious writers who considered the writing that appeared in *Satyakatha* and *Mouj* stuffy and without literary merit. Some twenty-three of them were published between 1955 and 1969, amongst them Namdeo Dhasal's 'Vidroha'.

Dhasal's first collection of poems, *Golpitha*, published in 1972, was the next literary landmark in Dalit literature to come after Bagul's *Jevha Mi Jaat Chorali Hoti*. Golpitha is the area in and around Kamathipura, Mumbai's oldest red-light district where Dhasal grew up. Says Dilip Chitre in his essay, 'Poetry of the Scum of the Earth' (*Namdeo Dhasal: Poet of the Underworld*, Navayana; 2007), 'As a practising poet and a reader of my contemporary Marathi poets, I was dazzled by *Golpitha*. More than three decades later, when I wrote an introduction to the book, I said that it would be a contender for as high an award as the Nobel Prize for literature.' *Golpitha* blew the roof off readers' heads, deliberately destroying every fond notion of poetry nurtured by upper-caste writers. It lies beyond my powers to do justice to any of the poems that fell from Dhasal's pen like live sparks from an unextinguishable fire. But I will attempt to translate the last part of the long poem, 'Maansaana' (Man Must). In the early part of the poem, Dhasal hammers out a stomach-churning list of sins and crimes man must commit before he can attain humanity. And then:

> Let the filth of these deeds swell like a universal boil,
> Ripen, burst and drain away.
> Then, of those who remain,
> No man shall enslave another, loot another,
> Call another black or white, brahmin, kshatriya, vaishya, sudra,
> Launch parties, build houses, forget blood relations
> Commit the crime of not recognizing mothers and sisters.
> Man shall snuggle against the sky his grandfather,
> The earth his grandmother,
> To live in peace, harmony and joy
> And do such deeds as will make the sun and moon look pale.
> Man shall crack a sesame seed to share with all,
> Compose a hymn to man.
> Man shall sing about man.

Before he wrote the poems in *Golpitha*, Dhasal had written lyrical poetry that adhered to the rules of *chhand shastra* (prosody). In an interview with poets Satish Kalsekar and Pradnya Daya Pawar that appears at the end of the first edition of *Golpitha*, he explains the shift. 'I moved from the traditional track to this track because of an incident in my life involving a girl. I suffered a terrible heart-break on account of the caste hierarchy. Even in the Praja Socialist Party in which I was a prominent worker, I realized that members who called themselves progressive were as casteist as anybody else. I raged then, went berserk, decided to throw away all shackles, including those of prosody, wrote a poem as and when it came. Sharpened my weapons. Started writing recklessly.'

A month after *Golpitha* appeared, writers J.V. Pawar, Raja Dhale, Arjun Dangle and Dhasal co-founded the Dalit Panthers, a movement for social transformation. The name of the militant movement indicated its kinship with the Black Panthers of America. The black voice demanded land, bread, housing, education, clothing, and, above all, social justice and peace. The Dalit Panthers were fighting for the same things. The founders wrote angry, provocative prose and poetry, giving the Dalit voice a sharp, aggressive edge. Raja Dhale wrote an article in the magazine *Sadhana*, deriding the national flag. Such writings brought cathartic relief to Dalit youth who had not received the benefits they had expected from the country's Independence. The politics of Maharashtra had passed into the hands of Marathas, who dominated every facet of the rural economy, including banks, marketing federations and sugar cooperatives. If rural life before this had been feudal and therefore oppressive for Dalits, the new economy dominated by cooperatives had no place for farmers with small holdings, which is all that Dalits had. One kind of exclusion had been replaced by another. In this situation, the Dalit Panthers became a rallying point for young Dalits, and 'Maharashtra was once again charged with discussions on Dalit literature and language,' as Arjun Dangle wrote.*

The Dalit Panther literary movement turned out to be no different from the faction-ridden Republican Party of India. Internal differences caused Namdeo Dhasal to be thrown out. Soon, ten years after its formation, the Dalit Panthers stood dissolved. However, while the movement was alive, it brought Dalit lives and Dalit issues to the forefront once again.

The next landmark in Dalit literature, poet Daya Pawar's autobiography *Baluta*,† was published in 1978, hitting upper-caste critics and readers alike between the eyes. 'Baluta' is a term that describes the system of traditional village duties Dalits had to perform for a share in the village produce. Unlike *Jevha Mi Jaat Chorali Hoti*, which had no followers of comparable power, *Baluta* inaugurated a stream of explosive autobiographical narratives.

It was never easy to tell these personal stories of humiliation and oppression. At one point in *Baluta*, Pawar writes, 'What I had seen

---

* 'Dalit Literature: Past, Present and Future', from *Poisoned Bread: Modern Marathi Dalit Literature* (Orient Longman; 1992).

† *Baluta* by Daya Pawar was published in 1978 in Marathi by Granthali; English translation by Jerry Pinto (Speaking Tiger; 2015).

of the life of Mahars in my childhood has cut a permanent gash in my heart. The past will never be erased. It will go only when I go. The layers of abjectness that you see on my face even today, have their source in those times. Hard as you might scrub them, all you will do is draw blood. They will not come off.' However, Pawar balances his personal pain with the thought that telling these stories is politically important. 'Some Dalits feel such stories are like digging up a garbage dump. But if a man does not know his past, he will not know which direction he must take in the future.'

Dalits, who had moved up the economic ladder into the middleclass, were the most vociferous in their criticism of *Baluta*. This class of Dalits has come to be known as 'Dalit Brahmin'. Yet Dr Narendra Jadhav, educationist, economist, policy maker, who fits the description perfectly, has himself authored an autobiography, *Aamcha Baap Aan Aamhi* (Our father and us; Granthali) which came out in 1993. As the title indicates, it tells the story of how he and his siblings grew up under the influence of their Ambedkarite father, Damodar Runjaji Jadhav. In writing this autobiography, Jadhav drew on his father's meticulous diary notes about the events of his life, keeping his father's dialect intact. Ten years later, he published an expanded version of the book in English, incorporating into it stories related by his mother. This version ends with an interesting postscript written by his sixteen-year-old daughter, Apoorva. Born in Bloomington, Indiana, she has this to say about her identity: 'I am just Apoorva, not tied down by race, religion or caste.'

And yet it is not so easy to forget, even today, that Dalits are considered outcasts by caste Hindus. Urmila Pawar, a major voice in contemporary Dalit literature, recounts in her autobiography *Aaydaan** (Basket; Granthali), published in 2003, the aftermath of her daughter Manini's birthday party to which she had invited her classmate Kishori and her older brother. On returning home, the

* Translated by Maya Pandit and published as *The Weave of My Life: A Dalit Woman's Memoirs* (Stree-Samya Books; 2007).

boy told his mother that there were portraits of Gautam Buddha and Dr Babasaheb Ambedkar in the Pawar home. The following day, the mother arrived at Urmila Pawar's house, stood outside the door and said tersely, 'Next time my daughter visits you, please don't give her anything to eat. We are Marathas and we don't allow it.'

From small incidents like this in educated, urban, middle-class Dalit homes to atrocities like the lynching of four members of the Bhotmange family in Khairlanji in September 2006, exhaustively recorded by Anand Teltumbde in his book, *Khairlanji: A Strange and Bitter Crop* (Navayana; 2008), the upper-castes continue to discriminate against and oppress Dalits. And women have come to realize that they are doubly oppressed—by upper castes and by their own men. Consequently, the Dalit feminist voice has grown increasingly stronger over the years. In *Aaydaan*, Urmila Pawar narrates the incident that sprang the first crack in her marriage. She had scored good marks in her Bachelor's examination and was planning to join the Master's programme. Her husband told her there was no need to study further. Stay at home and look after the children's studies, he said. Knowing that she was perfectly capable of balancing home, job and higher education, she replied, 'Why don't you pay some attention to the home for a change? It will help if you don't go to the bar for a drink every evening but come home and look after the children's studies yourself.'

Along with the woman question, there is another issue that has been exercising Dalit minds in recent years. Can Dalits afford to be rigidly exclusive and paint themselves into a corner? Why should politically committed writers hold so determinedly apart not only from upper-caste literature, but also from Dalits who are not politically committed but are fine writers all the same? Years ago Dr Raosaheb Kasbe, author of *Ambedkar ani Marx* (Ambedkar and Marx; Sugawa Publications, 1985), wondered whether it was not possible to, for example, examine Grace and Dhasal or Grace and Pawar together. The late poet Manik Godghate, who had assumed the pen name Grace, was born a Dalit, but wrote subjective, expressionistic poetry shorn of the socio-political context. Yet he was a very fine poet, and a recepient of the Sahitya Akademi and several other awards.

An allied question of social relations has also come to the fore in recent times. As some Dalits have moved from village to city, educated themselves and entered middle-class professions, they have encountered and grown close to members of the upper castes, inevitably leading to inter-caste relationships often ending in marriage. Sanjay Pawar's play, *Kon Mhanta Takka Dila* (Passing the blame), first performed in 1990, deals with the caste conflict arising out of an educated Dalit youth's relationship with a Brahmin girl, strictly disallowed by the caste hierarchy. Pradnya Daya Pawar's short story 'Vihar' from *Afwa Khari Tharavi Mhanoon* (So that rumour might prove true; 2010) deals with the reverse of the theme. Here a Dalit activist, Karuna, falls in love with Sagar, a Brahmin scholar and sympathizer of the Dalit cause. She belongs to a Bauddha nationalist outfit whose members are pledged to marrying only neo-Buddhists from the nomadic tribes. Karuna's decision to marry Sagar upsets the leader and her co-workers, but is supported by her Ambedkarite sister Sujata, who believes that caste rigidity will harm the larger cause of equality and a just society.

The Dalit playwright Premanand Gajvi's *Kirwant*, first performed in 1991, deals with the lives of a sub-caste of Brahmins called Kirwants, who are shunned by their caste fellows because they perform funeral rites. He maintains that they too are Dalits. When he wrote the play, some Dalit critics reproached him for 'defecting' to the other side. In this context, Gajvi articulated the dilemma of the Dalit artist in an interview with this writer in 1990. 'Can I be an artist at all or must I always be a man who was born into a particular caste? As an artist, do I have the freedom to write about any issue or subject that touches my heart and conscience, or must I always write according to a pre-set agenda?'

Gajvi asserts that Dr Ambedkar stood for progress. 'If our people converted to Buddhism in 1956, why should they continue to write about their lives before they converted?' he asks. The argument against this is that all Dalits have not converted, nor has the old life ended for many of those who have. After all, caste still remains the strongest factor in determining social relations in our society. Even Mohandas Gandhi, with all the moral force at his command, made little difference to entrenched caste attitudes. So a lot of Dalit writing even today continues to show acute awareness of caste reality as it affects Dalit lives.

Looking back over the last fifty years, it would not be wrong to say that some of the most groundbreaking poetry, fiction and autobiographical writing have come from Marathi Dalit writers. Baburao Bagul's *Jevha Mi Jaat Chorali Hoti* is still being read fifty years after it was published and five years after his death. Contemporary writers like Pradnya Daya Pawar and Dr Kumar Anil are writing interesting, inventive poetry and fiction. And Namdeo Dhasal, sixty-four, arguably the most celebrated living Marathi Dalit writer, is reported to be writing his autobiography.*

* Namdeo Dhasal died in January 2015. This autobiography seems to have remained incomplete.

Farewell to Arun

In the days, weeks and years to come, friends will fondly exchange oft-told and retold tales of Arun Kolatkar's life and times. I will tell my tale about the first time I met him. It was in the Sea Lounge. He was to design a magazine that I had been commissioned to edit. We were supposed to discuss the magazine, its thrust, its contents.

I was considerably intimidated by his reputation. He had won the Commonwealth prize for *Jejuri* (Clearing House; 1975), by then a cult book. He wore his hair long, knew Allen Ginsberg and did not give interviews to the Press.

I stepped up to him with a falsely brave smile and lowered myself into a seat. He stared into space, vaguely taking me in along the way. I shuffled my papers professionally. He said hullo and asked if I would need him to say anything more. I falsified my smile further and began, 'Well...' At this point he produced his pouch of tobacco and said, 'In that case I will...' and proceeded to place a wad of the stuff in his mouth. Thereafter I talked, and he mulled over his tobacco, remembering to nod encouragingly at me once in a while. That magazine never came out. Or else it would have surely been another example of the minimal beauty of his visual imagination.

You see the stamp of that imagination on many of his books. The large white 'S' that snakes down the unblemished black cover of *Sarpa Satra* (Pras Prakashan; 2004), turning up four red tails at the end, is his idea. So too is the hieroglyph on *Bhijki Vahi* (The Drenched Book; Pras Prakashan, 2003), ancient Egypt's sign for a

---

This article was first published in *Mid-Day* on 28 September 2004, four days after the death of Arun Kolatkar.

tear. The pale yellow bands above the titles of his *Kala Ghoda Poems* (Pras Prakashan; 2004), are also his work.

Open any of his books and you are at once in the presence of a poet whose home is the world itself. And yet a ten-by-twelve room in Prabhadevi was space enough for him to live in. Framed within the jambs of his doorway, he roamed the world, while bhajans and squabbles from the neighbouring hutments poured into the crannies between countries and cultures. From here he addressed the Isis and the Nile, journeyed back to Troy and moved, fast forward, into Vietnam.

In Vietnam he showed us nine-year-old Kim, still running down that highway in terror-stricken nakedness, her dress consumed by napalm, heading straight for Nick Ut's camera. It is a reality pic for all of us to see and…? Well, just see. That is why the poet calls upon little Kim to forget and forgive—forgive the pilot who dropped the bomb, the colonel who gave the order, history itself and finally, at the bottom of a page left evocatively blank, he asks her to forgive the poet.

Sitting in that ten-by-twelve room, Arun Kolatkar also looked back to mythical times, drawing his sad, ironic gaze away from the glittering crowns of our ancient heroes to the ruthless trampling of their clay feet. From this low-angle view, he created two brand new myths—*Dron* and *Sarpa Satra.*

Tele and micro, both scopes created his poetic world, drawn for us finely with words picked eclectically from every linguistic culture—ancient, modern, classical, folk, salon and street. He had long tapering fingers, made for picking words with care and setting them down on paper in neat lines, always mindful of the spaces in between which said so much.

Arun Kolatkar was what some might call eccentric. The root meaning of the word is off-centre, and he was certainly off-centre in many ways. If the centre is the play safe conventions of mainstream lifestyles, then he was categorically off-centre. If the centre is the self and obsession with the self, then again he was off-centre. If the centre is fads and fashions, then too he was off-centre. Yet he was an unbudgeably centred man within his world. He had his decades-old habits, haunts and friends, each with their own place and purpose in his structured life. And beside him, always, that bastion of strength and support, his wife Soonu.

Without these guarantees of everyday life, would he have had the strength I wonder to take on the inequities, sorrows and brutalities of the world as he did in *Bhijki Vahi* and *Sarpa Satra*? Without them would he have had the spirit to laugh at the ironies, absurdities and joys of the world as he did in the *Kala Ghoda Poems*? Such questions would have been too intrusive to ask him when he was alive. And now that he's gone, they don't matter.

So there it is. Arun Kolatkar has gone away. But not before friends took from him all that he had written and not had the time to publish. Arvind Krishna Mehrotra has his *Boatride* and other poems; Ashok Shahane, his long prose work on Balwantbua. Soon enough then, we shall hear from him again. Meanwhile here's his prayer addressed to the Mother of the Universe. Let all the filth and muck of human thoughts and deeds drain out of your eyes pleads the poet, till only the one pure tear is left. Preserve that, he says, for it is only that tear that will help you renew our world.

Human Visionary
On Vinda Karandikar

It is a supreme irony that Govind Vinayak (Vinda) Karandikar, prolific poet, eminent critic, sophisticated thinker and creative translator, won the Jnanpeeth award for *Ashtadarshane* (Eight Philosophies; Popular Prakashan, 2003), a collection that came twenty years after he had announced his retirement.

He had intended *Virupika* (Distortions; Popular Prakshan, 1983) to be his last collection. 'I believe I have done what little I could in the field of poetry,' he wrote in the preface. His admirers grieved but hailed it as a rare and brave decision for an artist to take. Yet, to their joy (mixed with some dismay), he came right back with *Ashtadarshane*. He called these eight poems explicating the philosophies of Descartes, Spinoza, Kant, Hegel, Schopenhauer, Nietzsche, Bergson and Charvaka an old man's game. The outcome of the game won him the country's most prestigious award.

In a sense the entire body of Vinda Karandikar's work may be seen as a grand and serious game. He played with metres, words, forms, ideas. The result was a poetry rich in colour, sound, smell, texture, thought and emotion. In one of his poems he pleads ardently for words to express the myriad shades of human life he sees around him—grey words, black words, happy, tasty, pregnant words. Words alone can marry abstract thought to concrete utterance to bring forth a sacred union.

This article was first published in *The Hindu* on 3 April 2010. It was written as a tribute to Vinda Karandikar, who died on 14 March 2010.

Vinda was a sensuous man. He believed in touch as the ultimate means of communion between man and man, man and nature. He asserted that the fullness of a flower's fragrance filled him only when he had touched its petals. To stroke a child from little hand to soft cheek was to experience ananda. He dismissed the possibility of ordinary mortals attaining the highest bliss which is known as paramananda. But there was a deeply satisfying joy that men could experience if they became one with the human world.

He was a Marxist, a non-believer. Speaking humorously about a poem in which he looks forward to the next birth to win his lady love, he explains that he wrote the poem when he was still a Hindu. It was a comforting thing to be able believe in rebirth in those days when college classes consisted, most unfairly, of 145 boys to five girls!

Many of Karandikar's earliest poems were written for and about the working class. The title of his first collection, *Svedganga* (Sacred River of Sweat; Popular Prakashan, 1949) itself reflects this preoccupation. The anger of these early poems turned mellow later, but was still capable of flaring up on occasion. There is deep disgust at the self-centredness of the middle class in lines like, 'True, I am a winner, don't you see it? / I have avoided battles, to avoid defeat'; and deep despair in lines like, 'You cannot avoid this road / These hungry, naked, shivering souls / Don't look at them / Sew up your eyes / Forget they are there / Repress your sob / Heart and mind, turn to stone!'

It is amazing but true that Vinda Karandikar, who has given the Marathi language some of its most memorable lines, has also left for children from four to fourteen poems to love and cherish. No other writer of his stature has gifted so much poetic fun to the young. 'The chair said to the stool / 'When will you learn to walk?' / Said the stool, 'Exactly when, / You learn to clap for a lark!' / Hearing this the fan laughed aloud / And legless, ran round and round.'

Karandikar lived his beliefs. On the one hand he vowed never to give away a poem free. Poetry had to be respected. It was for the principle, not for the money. Indeed money per se had never mattered to him. He had been imprisoned during the freedom struggle. When friends urged him to apply for the grant that the State gives to freedom fighters, he refused. 'Why do I need a grant when I have a job?' He also gave away all the money he won in awards to charities while he himself lived a frugal life.

He was fortunate to have married a woman like Suma, who had the education and the sensitivity to be a true partner to him. She financed his first collection of poems from her savings as a teacher. He loved carpentry and built her a shrine for her gods though he was himself an unbeliever.

Vinda and Suma, both are gone, she a few years before him. He was prepared for this to happen. 'It is but a short walk now,' he wrote. 'An easy slope to the end / You first or I first makes no difference / We will soon meet again.'

On Marathi Culture

'The local crop'

The Mascot of Maharashtriana
That Peculiar Person from Pune

To an outsider, a person from Pune looks no different from any other. He has the requisite number of limbs and features all in order, and there's neither tail nor horn to tell him apart. Yet there is something, a red Peshwa pugdee that rests unseen on his head, revealing itself only to close observers. Relic of past political power, it is the symbol today of a secret sense of superiority that every true Pune person carries in his heart.

To call a Pune person Puneite, therefore, is a semantic blunder. The weak middle of the word just doesn't describe the man. We must call him Punekar instead, with its no-nonsense 'k' and its rolling 'r'.

To identify and name attitudes and habits of the Punekar has been the amused and sometimes exasperated business of social historians, writers and humorists amongst them, such luminaries of the Marathi literary world as T.S. Shejwalkar, P.L. Deshpande, Dr Anil Avchat and S.J. Joshi. But even the casual visitor to Pune will come away with a strong impression of the place and its people.

A brief while spent in this erstwhile seat of the Peshwas, listening to its people, reading its papers, or just generally sniffing the air, is enough to tell you that censure and advice are the two modes in which the Punekar most frequently and happily expresses himself. Belligerent opinions are the local crop, grown for public good. When the mighty of the world bend their ears to the ground, it is the unminced words of the Punekar that they hear and are

---

This piece first appeared in *The Sunday Review* of *The Sunday Times of India* on 17 May 1992.

guided by. Faced with the necessity of expression of a favourable opinion, however, the Punekar's eloquence seems to forsake him and he is reduced to barely lifting a corner of his upper lip to register approval. Detractors see it as faith in the dictum: censure improves, praise corrupts.

Parsimony rules the life of the true Punekar. There's a pair of jeweller's scales located somewhere at the back of his head in which pleasantries are carefully weighed against grams and tolas before being dispensed. A smile in Pune is read as hypocrisy, bluntness as a virtue. Indeed, most traits that outsiders think of as, at best, odd and at worst, downright anti-social, are considered the high water marks of Pune culture. If others see the Punekar as miserly he sees himself as thrifty. If others think he's inhospitable ('When are you planning to leave?' is said to be the first question the Punekar asks a house guest who has just arrived), he sees himself as being practical. If others think him rude, he considers himself merely straightforward. He is impatient with the frills of social intercourse which get in the way of direct discourse.

Tryambak Shankar Shejwalkar sees in these traits of the Punekar an uncanny resemblance to the Puritans of seventeenth-century England. Comparing the quintessential Punekar of his time (the residents of the Brahman Peths—Sadashiv, Narayan and Shaniwar) to the Puritans, he says, 'The Brahmans who crossed the ghats from the Konkan strip during the Peshwa regime and took over the reins of administration were ready to do any kind of work. They were intensely industrious, unencumbered by false egos and prepared to start on the lowest rungs of office and climb gradually up. They had no addictions, were highly intelligent, shrewd and thrifty.' Compared to the Konkan Brahmans, the plateau Brahmans were lazy, self-indulgent and extravagant. As a result, they lost what they had, while the Konkan Brahmans grew in power and ultimately 'came to leave their impress, both good and bad, on the whole of Maharashtra.'

The Punekar's pride is part of this legacy. It marks all his dealings with fellow human beings of whom he seems to hold in greatest contempt those who attempt to purchase goods and services from him. The grave mistake a customer makes is to assume that the Punekar, like lesser creatures, is interested in commercial transactions.

Social activist and writer, Dr Anil Avchat, who has eaten off hand-carts and in poky little eateries in working-class Pune, where every other man has a story to tell about his having once been a champion wrestler, describes the business style of the owner of a certain well-known tea-shop which serves excellent batata vadas. 'People queue up outside his shop waiting to get in,' Avchat says. 'You'd think the owner would cash in and make more vadas. He doesn't. He reads his book and, when the vadas are over, he puts up, with great relief, a board which says "Vadas over", and returns to his book.' But the man is honest to a fault and quality conscious to boot.

A typical exchange in 'general stores' even in the Gymkhana area, inhabited by a comparatively later strain of Punekar—the retiree and the professional—might go like this:

'May I see some ball-point pens please?'

Once the specimen is placed before you: 'Price?'

A sum is stated.

'Do you have anything less expensive?'

The specimen is taken away and replaced in its tray.

'D-do y-you have anything less expensive?'

The head is shaken sideways and the lip curled in contempt. If you are lucky, a dry comment is volunteered. 'We don't keep cheap goods.' You crawl out of the shop on your stomach vowing to use reed quills.

Dr Ashok Kelkar, distinguished linguist, resident of Pune and admirer of its people, says: 'Whatever the Punekar's fault, you must admit that it is his strong individualism and concern for public good that gave birth to the reformist movement here. Just look what it's done for Pune women.'

I look. And remember the woman in a nine-yard sari, whom I saw forty years ago, jump into a crowded Tilak talao and stroke her way expertly down its length unhampered by her sari flapping and billowing around her. Another, also in nine yards, who rushed at a shuttle-cock and slammed it over the net, immobilizing an opponent thirty years her junior. I remember audiences applauding Usha, daughter of General Paranjape, thrashing the daylights out of an 'eve-tease'. I also remember the redoubtable Iravati Karve and Shakuntala Paranjape. And there are all the 'ordinary' women, whizzing about the city on their bikes and mopeds, wheel to wheel with men.

Wheels. The Punekar is born with them. Notice the two bumps of every new-born Punekar's behind? That's where they will grow, either mechanized or motorized, depending on his economic condition. According to P.L. Deshpande who takes a somewhat unkind view of Pune cycles, the vehicle is used

a) as a weapon
b) as an impediment to be carefully heaped outside the front door to stop prospective visitors from visiting and
c) as something to lean against while chatting with friends in the middle of the road.

Be that as it may, I am a great admirer of the extraordinary sangfroid with which the Punekar faces contretemps on the road which can only be described as wheels within wheels. Far from shouting, 'Get your fucking spokes out of my fucking wheel,' he allows destiny to sort out the mess. Given enough time and no pushing, destiny does.

In all this truculence, there is the subject on which the Punekar, whatever his age or station in life, waxes eloquent: 'Pune isn't what it once was,' she says with a sigh. In his book *Puneri* (Shreevidya; 1978), S.J. Joshi writes of the Deccan Gymkhana as it used to be when he was in college and what it had become by the time of his writing in the 1970s. 'As a collegian, I and a writer friend of mine would trudge over Tilak Bridge, every evening, in our flapping chappals, to the Gymkhana grounds and sit there awestruck by the dazzle of the luxurious bungalows around. It was like a dream—like sitting in the pit of the Aryan theatre gaping at the unreal beauty of Joan Crawford and Greta Garbo. My friend was busy churning out love stories by the dozen in those days. "If you want to write love stories," he would say, "you must observe the Gymkhana and its residents. Whoever heard of love in Sadashiv Peth!'" But by the 1970s, he says, the Gymkhana had lost class. 'The grandchildren of the old Raobahadurs now have jobs in Khadki or Dehu Road and carry their lunch boxes with them like anybody else. Daughters-in-law of the house do their B.Ed and teach in schools. And riff-raff like me has moved into the neighbourhood.'

Over the last ten years, a third strain has entered Pune culture. The entrepreneur and the rich farmer have arrived, bringing with them the flash of neon and the froth of beer. Whereas Joshi talks nostalgically of the one and only Lucky Restaurant, where daring Brahmin boys from conservative families tasted their first forbidden omelettes and dreamt their first forbidden dreams of romance in its 'family rooms', hundreds of restaurants have now sprouted up all over the city serving a variety of foods and drink, patronized by boys and girls who mix freely with each other. Amidst all this change, however, the core, the essential spirit of Pune, still remains virtually untouched, expressed best in its deep and genuine love for good theatre and classical music and its continuing tradition of crazy eccentrics.

Writer Arun Athalye has compiled a 200 page study of Pune's eccentrics for an enormous tome on the city which Dr Aroon Tikekar is preparing for publication next year. It took him eighteen months to research and put together a list of 121 eccentrics, past and present. One of them, a Gandhian, who was jailed during the freedom struggle, refused to wear prison clothes because he had vowed only to wear self-spun khadi. At the same time, he did not wish to break prison rules by wearing his own clothes. So he completed his jail term wearing no clothes at all. The helpless prison authorities were forced to provide him with a separate cell.

Today there's a seven-foot couple in Pune whose front door bears the declaration: *Garv se kaho hum lamboo hain.*[*]

Says Mr Athalye, 'Many of my collection of eccentrics are good for a laugh, but many prove my thesis that it was the Punekar's extreme adherence to principles that helped him change his society. The great champion of women's education, Dhondo Keshav Karve, is said to have paid his son for every meal he ate with him, but he also walked miles every day to collect at the rate of four annas per head the Rs 30,000 he needed for his destitute women's home in Hingne.'

Strong in his sense of himself, the Punekar is not one whit perturbed by the pot-shots people love taking at him. Says P.L. Deshpande about the occasion when he was invited to address Punekars on the subject of Punekars. 'It was like being asked to dance Kathak on a blistering-hot metal road. I was relieved to see a wheelchair in which one of the guests of honour had been brought in. It would serve to wheel me out, I thought, when my audience had done with me.' But the wheelchair wasn't required. P.L. walked out on waves of laughter.

* *Garv se kaho hum lamboo hai* or Say it with pride, we're tall, is a riff on the popular twin slogans: *Garv se kaho hum Hindu hai* and *Garv se kaho hum insaan hai* which are still battling for the heart of India.

How a Nineteen-Year-Old Orphan Won the Battle for Marathi

Seven hundred and ninety-two years ago, Marathi won a glorious battle against Sanskrit. It was fought by the gentle nineteen-year-old orphan Dnyaneshwar Kulkarni, whose *Dnyaneshwari* put Marathi on the world map.

Sanskrit was then the tongue of the powerful. It was the repository of all knowledge. It had a long literary history. It was the language of poetry and drama. It was the ultimate sign of human refinement. It was the lingua franca of the elites of Bharatvarsha. The north spoke to the south, the east to the west in this language of the gods. In short, Sanskrit was everything that English is today.

As far as language is concerned, Dnyaneshwar and his three brilliant siblings belonged to the magic inner circle of Sanskrit, but socially, they had been cruelly ostracized by its powerful members. Perhaps as a consequence of this, but even more importantly because he held that the divine spark resided in every living organism, Dnyaneshwar rejected the notion of knowledge as the prerogative of the chosen few. For him, the *Mahabharata*, for instance, was 'the original source of all joy, the treasure-house of ideas, and a vast ocean full of all the nine rasas.' The *Bhagwad Gita*, embedded at the centre of this sublime literary work, had to be read and understood by every human being, whatever his rank, caste or class.

And so he wrote the *Dnyaneshwari*, his commentary on the *Gita*, in everybody's language, Marathi. In doing so, he didn't for a

This article first appeared in *Mid-Day* on 12 May 2004.

moment feel that this vernacular tongue was in any way inferior to Sanskrit. 'Certainly, Marathi is the language I have chosen to write in,' he declared in the sixth chapter of his massive work, 'but so sweet are the words I use, that were they to enter into competition with nectar itself, they would emerge triumphant.' Later on he wrote, 'My listeners' ears will grow tongues to taste the sweetness of my words, and every other sense organ will fight to possess them.'

If the State of Maharashtra and sundry others who keep harping on the need for 'outsiders' to learn Marathi were to possess even a fraction of the conviction, love of language and sheer missionary zeal of the young Dnyaneshwar, they would be in a position to turn the recent Supreme Court verdict, making it a compulsory language, into a boon for students. But the State is only interested in showing who is boss. Marathi thus becomes a kind of jiziya tax to be imposed on all 'outsiders'. Some educationists also appear to view it this way. Their contention is that the State which aids them has the power to 'thrust' Marathi on them, and as 'outsiders', they must lump it.

That's a pity, because learning a language can be a supremely enriching experience, provided it is taught with that purpose in mind. But what has the record of Marathi teaching at English-medium schools been so far? Dismal. Do students come out understanding the language? Vaguely. Can they speak it? No. Do they even want to? No. Why? Because the textbooks prescribed to them are as dull as ditch-water and very often, the teachers of Marathi even duller. A young friend from a convent school was telling me the other day that they had to learn conjugation in their Marathi class. Yipes! Whatever for? Wasn't grammar as a means of learning languages given up the world over centuries ago?

Like Dnyaneshwar in his time, the State today must recognize the simple fact that there is a dominant language around that we are up against. English is attractive. English is everywhere. English is a passport to all sorts of goodies. In practical terms, Marathi has hardly any place in the lives of 'outsiders'. In Mumbai they can get by painlessly without knowing a word of it. Mumbai is not like Calcutta, nor Maharashtra like Bengal. Maharashtra's highest love has been given to a warrior king, Bengal's to a Renaissance man of letters. This has made a huge difference to the way the people of the two states look upon their respective languages.

What we need to do at this point is to forget political power play and give way to a genuine love of our language. We must look very seriously at how we are going to teach it to young people in order to share this love with them. Through grammar and texts that make no sense to young people in today's world? Or through lively, informative, with-it texts that go beyond being 'lessons', becoming, instead, a way of expanding the student's cultural horizon?

With a little less arrogance and a little more imagination, Marathi could win itself genuine followers instead of a trail of captives. But who wants followers, when captives demonstrate political power?

So there it is. The fate of Marathi at non-Marathi medium schools might remain what it has always been. Unloved and more or less useless.

Buying a Buffalo

'And don't forget to buy a buffalo,' the old women hollered at her son, in the midst of the crazy hustle and bustle of the State Transport Bus Terminal. I was instantly transported back to the day I was involved in buying a buffalo.

My father had built himself a red-tiled cottage in Talegaon, near Pune, and in violent reaction to the fumes and rat race of Bombay was now going full tilt for rusticity. And what finer fulfillment of rustic dreams than one's own buffalo mooing in the shed?

So my mother and I were dispatched to the weekly bazaar at Chakan to buy a buffalo. She herself had spent the first twenty-six years of life as a village woman grafting roses, training pumpkin creepers, swimming in wells and mixing cattle feed. I, on the other hand, was reported to have once said to my aunt, 'Do you get your milk from this cow? We get ours from our milkman.'

Along with us went Krishnabai, dignified and inscrutable, and Janabai, a substantial woman to look at and to contend with. That she had spent most of her life with buffaloes was immediately obvious from the set of her lips, the turn of her nostrils and the expression in her eyes. It was infinitely comforting to have these two women with us.

The journey to Chakan was made in the company of brightly dressed men and women who talked all at once loudly in an esoteric jargon. But the palpable excitement of people going to sell or buy was so infectious that soon we too were talking unnecessarily loudly about the bargain we hoped to make.

This version was published in the *Reader's Digest*, January 1976; where it was noted as being condensed from *Imprint*.

My first step into the lowing black mass of bovinity at the bazaar was decidedly apprehensive—there were too many hooves that could kick and horns that could gore. But it was important to wear the same nonchalant, slightly disdainful expression as my companions.

The first few exhibits were disappointing, even to my urban eyes. Then in the distance we noticed a shining fat flank which looked promising. One glance from the beast's eyes, however, was enough to drive us sway. It was a dirty look. In any case, she was terribly pregnant, and we couldn't see father delivering calves at this point in his rustic development.

So we moved on, between quivering flanks, kicking hooves and swinging horns, covertly watched by hopeful sellers. And then I made a fool of myself by falling in love with a calf. He could hardly stand, but kept making brave little lunges at his mother's udders. A thick fringe covered his forehead and from beneath it gazed the most lucid brown eyes I had ever seen. The mother didn't seem a bad sort either.

'This one, Mother,' I said impulsively. 'The calf's so cute.'

Some observers looked aghast, others reproachful, the rest tittered. I could imagine them saying over their bhakri and onions at night: 'Women from Bombay—wanted to buy a buffalo because the calf was cute.'

'Dear girl,' said Mother firmly, 'one does not judge a buffalo by her calf, except insofar as the calf's age indicates how long the mother will milk.'

A little later she caught sight of me staring in fascination at a superb specimen of manhood (180 centimetres tall, broad chest, challenging moustache, wicked eyes and a brilliant red turban). 'Nor,' she said, 'does one buy buffaloes because they have tall, broad and handsome owners.'

I sighed, and we moved on.

Then we came to a creature who quite took Mother's breath away. She was certainly a fine animal, though her calf was rather scraggy, and her owner didn't stand higher than a mere 160 centimetres. Having gone all around her, pinched her and patted her, and generally made her feel like an animal on sale, Mother, Krishnabai and Janabai looked at each other with the subtlest of nods. Immediately a dozen interested observers converged upon us.

'Don't offer more than two hundred and fifty,' one whispered urgently in my ear.

'She's much too "open",' confided another. 'Not filled out enough.'

As Mother stood eyeing the owner of the buffalo surreptitiously, wondering how to open negotiations, a wizened old middleman in a red-bordered shawl sidled up and volunteered. 'I'll drive a real bargain for you, lady. Just leave it to me.' The next minute he was in close but wordless confabulation with the owner. Under cover of his shawl, the middleman worked his fingers furiously. The owner shook his head. More finger twiddling. Once again, the owner shook his head.

'Look here,' Mother said, narrowing her eyes shrewdly, 'If you want to sell, sell straight to me and in words. All this twiddling of fingers just won't do.'

There was dead silence. Both men grinned sheepishly, explaining that was the only way they ever bought or sold, and then went at it with hands clutched under the shawl again. Finally, the middleman stepped back to Mother and held up five fingers.

'Five hundred!' exclaimed Mother, breaking all the age-old rules. 'Impossible.'

The middleman, a trifle abashed, went back into action, and this time came out with four and a half fingers held up.

'Don't you think you're wasting your time, old man?' said Mother very very kindly. 'I want the figure in words from the owner's mouth.'

A murmur of admiration went round. Obviously, the villagers commented, an astute woman. So through sheer exasperation, the owner blurted out, 'Four fifty.'

'Three fifty,' said Mother.

Then after he had repeated his figure: 'Three seventy-five.'

'Four twenty-five.'

'Four hundred.'

'Oh, all right, four hundred,' said the owner and the buffalo was ours.

She was led away by the nose, followed by Mother, who looked as if she might have been buying nothing more unusual than a kilo of horsegram; Janabai, looking exactly like our buffalo; Krishnabai, taciturn as ever; and myself, intent once again on dodging hooves and horns.

Once outside the enclosure, the buffalo, as custom demanded, was decorated with vermilion and milked. The pail of warm, frothing, creamy milk was passed around for all to drink from. The excitement of the bargain was over. What remained was a deep contentment—shared I guess by the animal too, for as we drank her fresh sweet milk, she raised her head and let out a deep resonant moo.

Marathi Cinema
Standing Tall

Around 1910, Dhundiraj Govind Phalke, popularly known as Dadasaheb Phalke, saw a film called *Life of Jesus* in Bombay. Bowled over by the magic of images moving on the screen, he was simultaneously imagining 'the Gods, Shri Krishna, Shri Ramachandra, their Gokul and Ayodhya' in place of Jesus Christ. He saw the film a second time and 'felt that what I had imagined was actually taking place on the screen'. He went away that day obsessed by a single question: 'Could we, the sons of India, ever be able to see Indian images on the screen?'* Two years later, he answered the question with a thundering affirmative by making *Raja Harishchandra*, his and India's first silent film.

Raja Harishchandra introduced 'the mythological' to Indian cinema, a genre that was to remain one of the staples of the industry for decades to come. The next trendsetting Marathi film was *Savkari Pash* (The Indian Shylock; 1926), directed by Baburao Painter for Maharashtra Film, Kolhapur. Based on a novel by eminent contemporary novelist Hari Narayan Apte, it introduced another genre to cinema, 'the social'. Shot on location, the film dealt with

---

This article was first published in *Frontline* on 15 October 2013.

* The entire quote is taken from Arun Khopkar's essay on Marathi cinema in 'Maharashtra—A Profile', Vishnu Sakharam Khandekar felicitation volume, ed. Achyut Keshav Bhagwat, published by the V.S. Khandekar Amrit Mahotsav Satkar Samiti, Kolhapur, 1977, with a grant from the Maharashtra State Board of Literature and Culture. Khopkar has credited the quote in his notes as follows: D.G. Phalke, 'Indian Cinema', Article No 1, from *The Navyug*, Bombay, 1917, *Phalke Commemoration Souvenir*, The Phalke Celebration Committee, 1970.

the exploitation of a peasant by a land-grabbing moneylender. Some claim that it was the first modern, realistic film in India. Others give this credit to Satyajit Ray's *Pather Panchali* (Song of the little road) made thirty years later. Be that as it may, Baburao Painter turned out not to be a dedicated film-maker and his lackadaisical ways of running the company soon caused his colleagues V. Shantaram, Damle, Dhaibar and Fattelal to break away from him and form Prabhat Film Company. Launched in Kolhapur in 1929, Prabhat Films as it came to be known, moved in 1933 to a sprawling campus in Pune. The same campus was acquired by the government in 1960 for the Film and Television Institute of India (FTII).

Some critics argue that, strictly speaking, *Raja Harishchandra* cannot be called the first Marathi film. Although made by a Marathi director with a cast of Marathi actors, it was subtitled in Hindi and English. If language is to be seen as the defining feature of cinema, then the first Marathi film was *Ayodhyecha Raja*, (The King of Ayodhya) directed by V. Shantaram for Prabhat Films in 1932. Phalke's cinematic language was perpetuated in this film, with its 'trick' shots and its frontal compositions inspired by Raja Ravi Varma's mythological oleographs. Durga Khote, who played Taramati, was the first woman from 'a good family' to act in a film. Entirely untrained at the time, she gives full credit in her autobiography to the multi-talented, highly skilled, committed owners of Prabhat Films who 'got that performance of Taramati out of me'.* Her future career in films was founded firmly on the rock of this training.

Prabhat made some of Marathi cinema's most outstanding films. Their *Tukaram* delivers a powerful cinematic experience even today. The picturization of *Adhi beej ekale* (First there was the seed), the devotional song that Vishnupant Pagnis as Tukaram sings while guarding a field against birds, stays with us as a deeply moving

* Translated into English by Shanta Gokhale as *I, Durga Khote* (Oxford University Press; 2006).

expression of bhakti. With Tukaram, a third genre was introduced to Marathi cinema, 'the devotional', depicting the lives of saints. This, too, remained an extremely popular genre for many years after.

A fourth genre, 'the historical', made its appearance in the Prabhat film, *Ramshastri* (1944). Although this film, like the historical plays of that and earlier times, was based on historical events, its purpose was not so much to record history as to make it subservient to the nationalist cause, because glorifying our historical past, inspired people with patriotic fervour. After Independence there was no place for this genre of films, but in Maharashtra, Shivaji still continued to be a popular subject for historicals.

World War II delivered a major blow to this thriving industry. Many production companies and studios folded up in the wake of the economic changes that took place after the war. Most equipment for films had to be imported, including crucially raw stock. The distribution of raw stock was severely restricted and governed by priorities that were inimical to regional films. Regional films were seen to have a limited reach when compared with Hindi films with their pan-Indian reach. Hindi films were therefore favoured in the rationing of raw stock. Although Marathi film companies had made bilingual films in the regional language and Hindi, films like *Kunku/Duniya Na Mane* (1937), *Manus/Aadmi* (1939) and *Shejari/Padosi* (1941) were all socials, propagating reformist values while the post-war Hindi film was largely escapist, financed by black money.

The audience profile for Marathi films underwent a sea of change in the post-war years. The middleclass was no longer their sole patron. It was now matched by a growing number of industrial workers who lived in the cities but whose roots were still in their villages. Catering to this new audience now became a critical balancing act for film-makers. Under the new circumstances, as many films were made on rural as on middle-class subjects. Many of them were scripted by the prolific and popular writer G.D. Madgulkar, whose name more or less guaranteed success at the box office. It is not surprising that a writer, rather than a director, held sway over the industry, since dialogue, not visual language, had become its mainstay. Words give quick and easy access to sentiment, and sentiment was what sold films. Whether it was the rural film or the urban comedy like *Pedgaonche Shahane* (The Shahanes of Pedgaon; 1952, Raja Paranjpe) and *Lakhachi Gosht* (A million-rupee tale; 1952, Raja Paranjape) of the 1950s, sentiment reigned supreme. It still does. If the extravaganza of Hindi films was one form of escape, script-enforced suffering of women and the poor leading to copious tears was another. The great achievement of the 1950s was P.K. Atre's *Shyamchi Aai* (1953), an adpatation of social activist and eminent writer Sane Guruji's tribute of the same name to mother's love. This sentimental tale won the president's medal for best feature film in the country's very first national awards.

The rural film of the 1950s introduced a fifth genre to Marathi cinema, the tamasha film. The 1959 film *Sangtye Aika* (Hear what I say), directed by Anant Mane and scripted by Vyankatesh Madgulkar, brother of G.D. Madgulkar, was the first big hit of the genre. Hansa Wadkar's outstanding performance in it literally carried the film. So significant was the film in this actor-dancer's career that she even named her explosive autobiography after it. Shyam Benegal's *Bhumika* (1977), in which Smita Patil gave a powerful performance as Wadkar, was based on this autobiography. After *Sangtye Aika*, tamasha and lavanis became de rigueur in the Marathi rural film. Soon, film lavanis invaded the repertoire of professional lavani dancers. Even *Saamna* (1975), scripted by Vijay Tendulkar, and directed by Jabbar Patel, featured a lavani, although it appeared like a gratuitous imposition on the film.

The 1970s were a time of great socio-political upheaval. Society was again questioning itself and its rulers as it had done in the pre-Independence reformist age. Shyam Benegal and later Govind Nihalani made films that created a space between the avant-garde of Kumar Shahani and Mani Kaul's films and the commercial formulae of the mainstream Hindi films. The lone representative of this new consciousness in Marathi was Jabbar Patel whose 1979 film *Sinhasan*

(Throne) was based on journalist Arun Sadhu's political novel *Aaj Dinank* (Dateline, today) and his 1981 film *Umbartha* (Threshold) was based on Shanta Nisal's autobiographical novel which made a statement about women's rights. It is to be remembered that the women's movement was part of the socio-political ferment of the 1970s.

Films like Patel's, of which there were not even a handful, were exclusively for the liberal middle-class. They were not the popular films of the time. The popular films belonged, almost exclusively, to Dada Kondke. With his background in loknatya, the urban form of the rural tamasha, he brought to the screen both its bawdiness and its double entendre dialogue. His films were about and for the industrial worker. He himself came from a mill-worker's family and knew how to tailor his films to their tastes. After the 1971 blockbuster *Songadya* (Tamasha Clown), he delivered a hit every year, entering the *Guinness Book of World Records* for the maximum number of films, nine, to run for twenty-five weeks. He was in the middle of a film when he died of a heart attack in 1998, at the age of sixty-five.

During the 1980s, producer-directors Mahesh Kothare and Sachin Pilgaonkar made films that matched the advanced technology and glamour of Hindi films. Kothare's 1985 film *Dhumdhadaka* (Fun and games) was a box office hit. He managed to straddle the tastes of the rural audience and urban youth in all his films. He produced the first cinemascope film in Marathi and later also introduced digital Dolby sound. Kothare's films did well in the eighties, but had fizzled out by the 1990s.

In 1991 *Maherchi Sadi* (Sari from the maternal home) hit the screen. Directed by Dada Kondke's nephew Vijay Kondke, it raked in money. If the uncle had entertained male workers, the nephew entertained their women. They saw the film multiple times to weep over the terrible sufferings of the heroine, played by Alka Kubal, the tragedy queen of Marathi cinema. Unlike his uncle, however, Vijay Kondke remained a one-film wonder.

The 1990s saw the emergence of the low-budget, socially committed films of Sumitra Bhave and Sunil Sukthankar. Working with unknown actors who gave strong, realistic performances, they made films on themes like water, schizophrenia, AIDS and vitiligo, winning several State and National awards. At least two of the present generation of fine film-makers, Umesh Kulkarni and Sachin Kundalkar, have worked with or been inspired by them. Both are alumni of the FTII.

In the late 1990s three factors emerged that gave Marathi films a much needed filip. With liberalization, there was more money around, and corporates, television channels and established Hindi film-production houses began to invest in them. Single screens gave way to multiplexes which allowed small budget non-star films to be exhibited. And the State began to enforce a 1969 Act that made it compulsory for cinema houses to screen Marathi films for at least four weeks in the year. Theatres violating this act were liable to have their licenses revoked or suffer a week's closure.

Shwaas (Breath) which released in 2004, thus surfaced out of a film industry that had been overcome by torpor. It won the National Award exactly half a century after *Shyamchi Aai*, and, to top that, became India's official entry to the Oscars. Based on a real-life story about a grandfather who gives his grandson a day out on the town before an operation that is to cost the child his eyesight, it pitched itself accurately in the sentimental, non-star, socially committed, powerfully enacted tradition that had always been the stamp of Marathi cinema. This was director Sandeep Sawant's first film (he hasn't made another) and was financed by three individuals, including Arun Nalawade, the actor who played the grandfather.

In 2005 came another critically acclaimed film, *Dombivali Fast*, directed by Nishikant Kamat featuring an intense performance by Sandeep Kulkarni. The story revolves around the life of a middle-class, law-abiding bank employee who single-handedly takes on the injustice and corruption rampant in our society.

Over the last eight years, the Marathi film industry has grown in a way that would have been inconceivable till the turn of the century. With more money available and some possibility of films being released/telecast, Marathi films have become a viable if still not a wildly profitable proposition. The number of films produced has increased from twenty-three in 2003 to fifty-seven in 2005, seventy-two in 2006, ninety in 2007 and a hundred in 2008. The numbers have since been fluctuating around that figure.*

The year 2008 saw the release of two unusual films, both about bulls. Umesh Kulkarni's comedy *Valu* (Wild Bull) was distributed internationally by Subhash Ghai's Mukta Arts and Mangesh Hadawale's *Tingya* was supported by Ravi Rai's production company. The film, based on the relationship between a village boy and the family bull, Tingya, won Sharad Goekar, who played the boy, the National Award for the best child actor.

In 2009, Paresh Mokashi's *Harishchandrachi Factory* took the film world and audiences by storm. Five years in the making, the film, in a sense, brought the story of Marathi cinema back to where it started. A brave and quirky film about Dadasaheb Phalke's struggle against odds to make his first film, *Raja Harishchandra*, it became the second Marathi film after *Shwaas* to be selected as India's official entry for the Oscars in the Best Foreign Language Film category.

Today Marathi cinema stands tall in the national film scenario. Directors like Umesh Kulkarni, Sachin Kundalkar (*Restaurant*), Chandrakant Kulkarni (*Tukaram*), Ravi Jadhav (*Natarang*, *Balgandharva*) and many others too numerous to be named, continue to make films driven by strong stories and excellent performances. Marathi cinema has not only arrived, but is thriving.

---

* Ninety-eight films in 2017 according to a list on Wikipedia.

On Music

'Jharokhas and occasionally majestic gates'

Three Views on Pandit Mukul Shivputra

I

Sunday evening was a very special occasion for admirers of Hindustani classical vocalist Pt Mukul Shivputra. His concert had been announced after a long gap and there was an unspoken question in everybody's mind. Would he sing or wouldn't he? Would he stay the course or leave midway? Would he react adversely to someone's face and refuse to sing? Would he even put in an appearance? Or having done so, would he go away before entering the concert hall and not return? Many such incidents had marked the erratic performing life of this amazing vocalist, and people were naturally apprehensive.

Pt Mukul Shivputra, son of Pt Kumar Gandharva, left home in his twenties to live as a recluse in a muth on the banks of the Narmada. With the muth as base, he wandered all over the country, making it extremely difficult for concert organizers to locate him. Worse, he became addicted to alcohol and drugs. Shivputra's friends, at whose homes he would turn up out of the blue, looked in vain for answers to his condition. Had his mother's death when he was still young, and his wife's death later, knocked the bottom out of his world? Had the burden of being the son of one of the most original musical geniuses of our times added to his psychological stress? Or was it some neurological disorder that was driving him to destroy himself?

These three articles on Pandit Mukul Shivputra appeared in the *Mumbai Mirror*. They have been collated for this book.

Three years ago a distressing news item appeared in the press. Shivputra had been spotted, unwashed and dishevelled, begging for money outside a temple in Bhopal. The Madhya Pradesh government offered to rehabilitate and look after him. But that hadn't worked. Recently, however, someone whose family had had a close association with Pt Kumar Gandharva, had taken him under her wing, and that seemed to have helped. On Sunday we heard the newly rehabilitated Pt Shivputra in full form, singing brilliantly before a house that was packed with his admirers.

He began his first bada khayal in Puriya Dhanashree with an extended nom tom, followed by two beautiful bandishes composed by his father. The vilambit, '*Bal Gayee Jyot*', was a deeply sombre composition. Pt Shivputra has a strong, pure, pliant voice which he modulates skilfully to add depth to his music and to emphasize the mood and meaning of the words. In this bandish, each time he hit the high note at the end of the first line, it shook you. It was like a call from the wild.

The drut bandish, '*Kahan Chala Re Piya*', came as a playful contrast to the first. The singer rendered it teasingly, his resonant voice exulting in the twists and turns of the composition which melds note and word so perfectly that you wonder which came first. Next, switching moods again, he sang '*Guruji Jahan Baithu Wahan Chhaya Re*', beginning by elaborating the second and third words before coming to the first. When he did utter 'Guruji', his voice was filled with such humility that you were moved to tears.After the interval, Pt Shivputra sang Bageshree and at once you realized there was something going on here that was hard to comprehend. Whereas the bada khayal in Puriya Dhanashree had been built up in the conventional architectural manner, block by block, his approach here was to build through a scattering of fragments. What he did before the nom tom was to sing squiggles of swara patterns in which you caught brief glimpses of Bageshree's face. This created an environment of musical suggestions which he then coalesced into the full figure of the raag. Was he searching for a new route into the raag, or deconstructing the melody to break our preconceived notions of it to enable us to see it differently? Whatever he was trying to do, the effect was both fascinating and disconcerting.

The finale of the recital was an emotionally nuanced rendering of Kabir's '*Dhun Sunke Manawa Magan Huva*' in Bhairavi.

At the end of the recital, one was so grateful that this hugely gifted singer had managed to escape his father's shadow and find his own voice. Kumarji was a genius, a pathfinder. Many of his disciples have been happy emulating the superficial elements of his style. Not Pt Shivputra. He has understood the essence of his father's music, and sought and found his own truth within it. Now that he is back amongst us, let us hope that he will sing us that truth more often than he has done in the past.

(31 October 2012)

II

Only three kinds of response were possible to Pt Mukul Shivputra's presentation of Yaman on Friday at the Nehru Centre, on the second day of the Swaranjali festival. The first could be total befuddlement laced with awe. Was this Yaman? Was this method of delineating it supposed to appeal to the listener? Must ask one of those all-knowing critics who have made Pt Shivputra a cult figure.

The second response could come from the opposite end. This was no Yaman. I know my Yaman well. And this was no way to delineate and develop a raag. I know how it is done. He simply couldn't get it right, could he? Why do so-called connoisseurs call him a great vocalist?

The third response could be something in between, befuddled but not outright dismissive, and based firmly on the established fact of Pt Shivputra's unique talent. This response is based on the evidence—if evidence were required—on his conventionally magnificent rendering of the same Yaman bandish, '*Salona Re Balam Mora*' on other occasions, at least one of which is available on YouTube.

That leaves us with three possible explanations for his strange performance. Erratic temperament, failure of some internal mechanism resulting in loss of access to knowledge and experience, and bad voice. If the former two, there's nothing further to be said. Some artists, like some human beings, are temperamental; and the loss of access to knowledge and experience is a medical, not a musical problem.

Let's look at the third possibility. Bad voice. Yes, there was much coughing and hawking. But the same bad voice didn't stand in the way of Pt Shivputra presenting a powerful Kafi tappa, '*O Miya Jaanewale*' later. One also recalls his Bageshree at Karnataka Sangh two months ago, when his voice was not a problem but his treatment was very much of a piece with Friday's treatment of Yaman. In both he was rejecting the conventional method of building up a raag through the bandish, architecturally, step by step, towards an ultimate whole.

One way or another, one couldn't escape the notion that he was making a deliberate attempt at deconstructing the melody, denying it its coherence, and the very aim of building it into a majestically towering structure. But some kind of a structure, whatever its form, surely had to be the purpose of that piece of music. Speculating, but not idly, on the impulse that lay behind his '*Salona Re Balam Mora*', one might look at what has happened in the other arts.

In literature, the idea of character, plot and event as the very foundation of fiction has been overturned by novelists to open up opportunities for creating new forms. Dancers have replaced grace and beauty with stern intensity to segue with the jagged angularities of contemporary life. Cinema has denied conventions of narrative structure, dialogue and the centrality of the chief protagonist's image. Theatre has dislodged the well-made play where the audience identifies emotionally with characters and situations, and forged new forms in which the audience is not expected to suspend disbelief, but rather to be acutely aware of the fact that the actors are actors and not the characters they are playing.

Readers, viewers and critics protested vehemently against this deliberate destruction of the old, comfortable formulae in which it had been so easy to say this is bad and this is good or this is us and this is them. Eventually, however, they were forced to admit that the new forms were not only valid, but valid in a way that was in sync with the world in which we were living. Ultimately the works of these experimenters became signposts to roads less taken, because, having broken old rules, they had created forms that held in new ways. The work of the Spanish architect Antoni Gaudi is an example of how the most outlandish (at first sight) structures, finally convinced critics that these too were legitimate ways to design and build buildings.

Pt Mukul Shivputra has not managed to rebuild yet. He has attempted to break old structures but has not been able to reassemble the bits and pieces into a self-sufficient new form. In a culture that resists change and continues to give us sublime music in the old forms, an attempt to break away, even if it fails, should make us sit up and listen. Pt Shivputra's lineage and his unique art might lead him to something genuinely new. Question is, does he have the discipline to carry it through?

(9 January 2013)

III

If you were looking for a long and leisurely evening of inspired music, Sunday was the day, Tata Theatre the venue and Pt Mukul Shivputra the singer, presented by TOUCH, an NGO for underprivileged children.

I cannot claim to have heard Pt Shivputra as often as many of his devoted admirers who packed the auditorium to bursting that evening must have done. But the few times that I have heard him, I have been filled with wonderment at the uniqueness of his genius. Three years ago, at Karnataka Sangh, he sang a brilliant two-tiered Puriya Dhanashree in the conventional way with nom-tom alap leading to the vilambit and drut bandishes; but in the next bada khayal in Bageshree, he shook the familiar ground under our seats by rejecting the conventional pyramidal architecture of the khayal to deconstruct the raag and put it back together through fragments of itself. This approach that had seemed tentative then has grown in the interim to full maturity. What we heard on Sunday was a masterly presentation of this alternative form, made effective in both the pre-interval Multani and the post-interval Jogkauns by playing down the words of the bandish in preference to nom tom and sargam.

One can see what motivated this deliberate choice. A bandish dictates the shape of a raag and its words dictate the mood. However, if a singer desires the freedom of abstraction, the only way he can gain it is by disregarding the concrete lyric. Having done so, Pt Shivputra was like an unpressured painter in his studio, using the swaras of each melody like a predetermined palette, but applying paint in his own way, at his own pace, standing back, looking at the effect, returning, adding colour, overlaying one stroke with another, till gradually the image of the raag emerged. Or, if an architectural metaphor is to be employed, one could say that, rather than a solid edifice, what he built was a light, airy structure of windows, doors, jharokhas, and occasionally, majestic gates that gradually coalesced into the contours and body of the raag.

What this method did for the listeners was to unhook them from the drama that the conventional exposition offers, where much pleasure lies in the building up and release of tension through our anticipation of each new development designed to lead to the climactic end of the item. What listeners experienced instead was an extended contemplation of Multani and Jogkauns minus dramatic flourishes. There was some internal drama going on in Jogkauns with the occasional introduction of some grace notes to which the audience responded with a collective gasp. But otherwise the music was infinite, not to be marked by dramatic closures. What added greatly to the quality of the sound was the restrained sitar accompaniment by Bhupal Panshikar.

In the absence of an overtly conventional structure, what was it then that held the listeners spellbound, so that there was none of the restless shuffling and coughing that goes on in concerts? Certainly the depth and pliancy of Pt Shivputra's voice with its endearing, non-aggressive quality, but also the magnetic force of his internal energy. Listening to him reminded me of the illuminating lec-dem I had heard only a few days before by the Bharatanatyam dancer Malavika Sarukkai, whose long, creative journey the NCPA had honoured with a week-long series of events. Speaking of the relationship between sculpture and dance, Sarukkai had demonstrated how the classic Chola bronze pose in which the Devi holds a lotus bloom in the right hand while the left arm balances it in a downward movement, is given life by the dancer focusing her energy on consciously feeling the gravitational pull earthward on the free arm. Similarly, every note and phrase that Pt Shivputra sang was given life and weight by that kind of intense, concentrated attention.

We have some amazing musicians in this country, but even the most daring only dare to innovate within the given form. Pt Mukul Shivputra is unique in inventing a form which stands as a valid alternative to the established one. The great thing is that, as his song '*Dekho Re Rut Phoolan Lagi*' and the bhajan '*Jamuna Kinare Mora Gaon*' demonstrated, he retains a deep attachment to lyricism too. The bhajan, an audience favourite, made an utterly delightful finale to what had been a sublime concert. What happier way could there be to end an exhilarating musical experience, than to go home humming '*Saware Aijaiyo*', the jaunty refrain of the bhajan?

(21 January 2016)

On Pandit Kashalkar

I do not exaggerate when I say that I would put aside just about everything of practical importance to hear Pt Ulhas Kashalkar sing—whenever and wherever. It was therefore a dugdha-sharkara (milk and sugar) occasion when he performed at Pandit Arvind Parikh's eightieth birthday celebration at NCPA's Tata Theatre on Friday, giving me two luminous reasons to be there.

Pandit Arvind Parikh is arguably the only Indian musician who has pursued two parallel lives with equal success, a life in music and a life in business. Suited, he is brisk and formidably efficient. With a sitar in his hands, he turns serene and inward-looking. His meditative music takes us far away from the frenzy of the world outside; for, unlike some other instrumentalists, he refuses to import that frenzy into his music.

All the speakers on Friday evening—Pandit Shiv Kumar Sharma, Uday Kotak, Vijaya Mehta, Dr Ashok Ranade and family friend Praful Patel, Minister for Aviation—wondered how he had managed to achieve such a perfect balance between these two lives. Perhaps part of the answer lies in the priorities he appeared to have set for himself. Someone quoted him as saying that business was his hobby and music his passion! The other part might lie in what Dr Ranade said in his characteristically witty speech. 'It is not true that Arvindbhai doesn't have vices. He has. He is a workaholic. He must have made a pact with God at birth that he would never remain idle!'

Pt Ulhas Kashalkar brings similar qualities of rigour and sincerity to his vocalism. In an interview given in 2000 to Deepak

---

This article was first published in *Mumbai Mirror* on 24 October 2007.

Raja, author of *Hindustani Music: A Tradition in Transition*, he had said, '...the process of self-discovery in a vocalist matures only around the age of forty. Until then, he does not fully understand his own training, the significant features of his own and other gharanas, his own musical temperament, or even the eccentricities of his own voice.' If we take forty years as the magical entry point into self-aware music, then Pt Kashalkar has been singing in his impeccable, evocative, unique style for at least twelve years. But I think it has been many more.

The physical aspects of Kashalkar's music are impressive. He has a sweet, supple voice with an astounding range. His notes are crystal clear even in the fastest taans, and his control over laya is effortless, a testimony to decades of rigorous practice. But there are other less tangible, more powerful virtues at work here too—a profound seriousness of purpose, a strict musical conscience, and an innate sense of proportion and aesthetic propriety. These constitute the moral and spiritual fibre of his music, irresistibly drawing critics, connoisseurs and lay listeners alike to it.

On Friday he demonstrated an aspect of his musical personality I had not known before—a delight in playing with the aesthetics of music. Familiar with his mellifluous but formal presentation of Basant Bahaar on compact disc, I was quite unprepared for what he did with the raag that evening. Beginning with a leisurely alaap which emphasized its every sensuous curve to evoke the exquisite pleasure-pain of the two seasons with which it is associated—autumn (bahaar) and spring (basant)—he moved into a different geometry altogether while filling in the voluptuous contours he had traced. He dismantled the raag note by note, moving in quick zigzags between distant notes to expose its nuts and bolts, so to say. This done, he rebuilt the raag and made it whole again. It was a stunning bit of intellectual and vocal play.

The Bhairavi that followed was steeped in deep emotion. Always a moving raag, it became doubly so because of the bandish that Kashalkar sang—'*Tum ho jagata ke daataa, rakhiyo laaj mori natha*'.

It is set in the upper octave and gives the impression of the singer calling out to God, pleading with Him for His grace. Taught to him by the late Ustad Vilayat Khan, Arvindbhai's guru, it was a touching choice to make that evening.

On Ashok Da Ranade

There are deaths that you expect and are saddened by; and there are deaths that happen so unexpectedly that you go into shock. Such a death was Dr Ashok Ranade's on Saturday afternoon, snatching him away while there was still so much life to be lived, so many books to be written, so much music to be made, so many students to be guided and so many arguments to be had with friends and fellow scholars.

Dr Ranade's approach to music, theatre and language was free. Freedom of thought is not such an easy thing to hold on to in these beleaguered times when predigested wisdom and pure cant have pushed thinking itself into a corner. Even when he spoke of aspects of that venerated thing, our 5,000-year-old culture, he would say, 'Fortunately or unfortunately, everything in India has a 5,000-year-old tradition', presenting you instantly with both sides of the ancient coin.

His was an ever questing mind and music was the prism through which he saw life and the world. Wherever music was made, with whatever instruments and in whatever language, he was there, listening, thinking, connecting. He did not believe in a hierarchy of musical forms. He studied film songs with as much application and admiration as classical music. 'Film music is the most innovative popular form we have evolved,' he would say. 'Those fellows are constantly experimenting.'

In times when narrow political interests have sought to turn Lord Rama into an election plank, Dr Ranade reappropriated him for

---

This article was first published in *Mumbai Mirror* on 4 August 2011, five days after the death of Dr Ashok Ranade.

music. The story of Rama was Rama gatha before it became Rama katha,* he said; so songs were the proper mirror to see the many images of the man who became king, avatar and finally God. He delved into folk, classical and saint poetry to come up with some two dozen forgotten songs which he composed as Ramgani (Songs of Rama), prefacing each song with a brief but illuminating glimpse into its source and form.

In his introduction to a woman's song about Rama, he pointed out that women composed songs in the ovi metre possibly because it was simple and fluid enough to allow them to sing at work. Then he raised a tangential question. 'Ovis are sung in raag Pilu,' he said. 'Why Pilu?' Here he threw in a nugget of information that his research had revealed. Pilu is the name by which an ordinary species of plant that grows by the wayside is known. Just as the plant might say, my place is not on the highway, but let me grow here, women who composed ovis were saying, we know our place in life, but let us speak of what we think and feel. By a poignant irony, the song of the simple, working woman expresses deep empathy for a King who, having family, brothers and a paragon of a wife, was still alone in life and alone in death.

The essential and most valuable quality of Dr Ranade's thinking was its firm hold on the object under examination. He didn't expect us to take what he said on faith. His approach was, 'Look. This is what I see. Do you see it? Do you draw the same conclusions from what you see as I do?' It was an inescapably persuasive and inclusive approach, very unlike scholarship that revels in opacity and exclusion.

Dr Ranade had great respect for the oral tradition and musicians whose knowledge came from tradition. 'These practitioners may not theorize the way some of us might, but that doesn't mean they are unaware of the theories that underpin their practice,' he would say.

---

* By which he meant that the songs sung for the love of Rama came before the formal presentation of the story as Ramakatha.

'Only, we must enter their language to understand their thought.' Listening to musicians was as important a method of research for him as delving into ancient books and treatises.

Within the framework of what he read, saw and heard, Dr Ranade became a free spirit of inquiry. He had no use for rules as rules. 'Rules are like a launching pad,' he would say with the smile that accompanied a thought that was about to amuse him. 'You don't take the launching pad with you when you take off.'

More the pity that the rules of life and death may not be so easily dismissed. The liveliest minds must finally bow to the vagaries of the body. His did. Unbidden and unprogrammed, death entered his watertight timetable of riyaz, research, teaching and writing and…well, that was it.

On Bhaskar Chandavarkar

Bhasakar Chandavarkar, who died ten days ago, was a very private man. People who thought they knew him knew the look, the gesture, the voice; they knew the ideas and the analytical mind; they most certainly knew the work. But few knew the person.

He was an enormously innovative music composer, but the Press rarely told us about him. No violins came out when he won the best music award at the Madrid International Film Festival for his music for the Marathi film *Bayo* (2006, Gajendra Ahire). If little newsprint was expended on him, it was at least partly because he was averse to publicity. In fact, I suspect he was averse to unnecessary human interaction itself.

I spent many days with him as a co-invitee to the Sangeet Natak Akademi's Brhaddesi festival in Guwahati some years ago. It was an exhilarating exposure to the music of the northeastern states—the Seven Sisters as they were coyly called. Bhaskar always sat apart from the others, all eminent scholars of music, dance and theatre. Many of them were trying to understand the music in terms of their own systems. This sounds like so-and-so raag, they would say, or we couldn't follow that beat—how many beats made one cycle? A wizened elder from one of the groups finally said, 'We don't understand your questions. This is just music.'

Just music is how Bhaskar heard it, not filtered through his Hindustani classical music or folk music ears. He wasn't looking for comforting comparisons between how the artists on stage were

---

This article was first published in *Mumbai Mirror* on 5 August 2009, ten days after Bhaskar Chandavarkar's death.

plucking their strings and how he strummed his sitar. He was listening with ears that were free of bias. During the week or so of the festival, I realized how open his scholarship was; how much he knew about the sources and forms of the music we heard. I was to discover later, how deeply steeped he was in every kind of music, whichever part of the world it came from.

I had invited him to lecture to the students of IIM, Bangalore, in an elective course in the arts that I had designed. He walked in quietly, set up his music system and said, 'I would like you to listen to this.' He proceeded to play us a piece of gamelan music from Indonesia, completely foreign to our ears yet completely captivating. Every point he made thereafter was illustrated by recordings of music we had never heard before. It was an ear-opening session. Practice had endowed him with a good teacher's instinct for how to engage student attention.

He had taught music at the Film and Television Institute of India in his home town, Pune, for many years. He had used the opportunity to learn the language of cinema in order to make his lectures more relevant to the students. This stint gave him a special advantage when he composed music for films. One of his proudest moments came when he heard that Satyajit Ray had seen Girish Karnad's film *Ondanondu Kaladalli* (Once upon a time; 1978) the second time just for the music. So impressed was Ray with it, that when Aparna Sen asked him to compose the music for her film *Paroma* (1985), he sent her to Bhaskar, telling her he was the better composer.

Bhaskar composed music for many significant plays too; but the one that took his music all over the country and abroad was Vijay Tendulkar's *Ghashiram Kotwal.* It would require much more than a column to analyze what he had tried to do there. Suffice it to say that he had created a parallel musical script for the play. But Tendulkar went on record saying that the music had killed the content of the play.

It was Bhaskar's great regret that most people who saw *Ghashiram Kotwal* did not hear what the music was saying. Nothing can be lonelier than to speak in a language that few understand.

On Alladiya Khan

It was on a bench on the Chowpatty sands that the renowned musicologist Pandit Bhatkhande once said to the great Alladiya Khan, 'You say you sing in the style of your forefathers. Are there any other of your family still living? And do they sing in the style in which you sing?'

Alladiya Khan, proud of the Jaipur gayaki of which he was the heir, answered, 'Yes. This is the very style in which the elders of my family sing. If you do not believe me you may go and hear them.'

He gave Pandit Bhatkhande the names of two or three elderly members of his family living in Uniyara in Rajasthan, never once thinking that Bhatkhande would actually go there. But that is precisely what the redoubtable Bhatkhande did, and having done so, came right back and challenged Alladiya Khan on Chowpatty sands. 'I have been to your native place,' he said, 'and I have heard the elders in your family sing. Their gayaki is very different from yours. It is closer to the Gwalior gayaki. Now will you admit that you have created your own style of singing?'

Deeply offended by Pandit Bhatkhande's words, Alladiya Khan cooled off towards him and remained that way till his death in 1946. Those were the days when musicians were almost arrogant in their dynastic pride, holding strongly to the knowledge they had gained at the knees of their father and uncles.

However much Alladiya Khan may have wanted to claim unswerving allegiance to the musical tradition of his forefathers, he

---

This article first appeared in *The Sunday Observer*. The date of publication is unknown.

did indeed, evolve his own style of singing. Professor B.R. Deodhar in his book *Thor Sangeetkar* (Great Singers; Popular Prakashan, 1993) tells us why.

It happened when Alladiya Khan was living under the patronage of the Prince of Amleta. This prince was a connoisseur, almost an insatiable addict of music. He would listen to Alladiya Khan sing for hours on end—during the day for the day raags, during the night for the night raags. After two years of this, Alladiya Khan realized that his voice was growing progressively hoarse till a day came when singing became impossible. He left Amleta for Jodhpur. There he waited patiently for his voice to improve. Many months went by. He prayed fervently that his voice be restored, never once losing hope. Gradually his voice returned and he could sing. But it never regained its pristine power. Then followed a period of intense 'mehnat' during the course of which he evolved a style of singing that suited his new voice. It was a difficult style, intricate in its taan patterns but short on elaborate alaaps.

The loss of voice power must have been only relative. For even today a powerful voice is the heritage of singers in this gayaki.

Dhondutai Kulkarni, tiny and incredibly youthful for her fifty-five years, the only singer whom Kesarbai Kerkar, student of Alladiya Khan, deigned to teach, asserts with pride that she does not use a mike for an audience of up to a thousand strong. It was about Dhondutai that Alladiya Khan said in 1942, 'This girl will carry on the tradition of our gharana.' Today Dhondutai says ruefully, 'Nobody has the will to put in the arduous hours of training that music demands. They want to become instant performers. I don't blame them. People can't live off their music any more. And where do they have even the space for daily practice?'

It was because Dhondutai appeared to have the will to work long, hard hours that Kesarbai accepted her as a student. And it was because Kesarbai had vowed to learn from Alladiya KhanSaheb and from him alone that he finally accepted her as a student though not before he had made her wait for nearly three years during which time she pulled all the strings she could. In those days, music was not a matter of money but 'mehnat'. You had to be the right person to stand in the direct line of descent of the old gharanas.

Dhondutai, otherwise modest, has this strong quiet assurance of being one of the chosen few. How did she come to occupy the unique position of being Kesarbai's only student?

The story goes back to the Kolhapur of the early 1930s. 'In those days,' says Dhondutai, 'it was the virtual fountainhead of music. Alladiya Khan had been appointed court singer. My father used to take me to hear him sing at the appointed hour before the aarti at the Mahalaxmi temple began. My father was passionately in love with music. He would have liked to learn it himself but circumstances willed it otherwise. So he decided to give his first born all the opportunities that he himself had so desired and never had.'

Dhondutai, the first born, began music lessons when she was five years old. But her first commitment to music came after Alladiya Khan's younger son Bhurji Khan began to teach her. That was in 1940 when Dhondutai was thirteen. Before this she had sung because her father wished her to; now she herself wanted to spend more time on music. This left her with less and less time for school studies and soon she was forced to drop out of school.

'Later, I had to make an even more important decision,' says Dhondutai in her quiet thinking voice. 'I decided not to marry. You cannot devote yourself both to music and a family. It just can't be done. My father, who had always stood by me, supported this decision. He had faced a great deal of criticism as it is because he had found me a Muslim guru and even allowed me to sing on stage. In those days when singing was considered disreputable, a woman deciding not to marry was blasphemous.'

Bhurji Khan died in 1950, leaving Dhondutai a musical orphan. She went to stay with her brother in Jabalpur. She did her matriculation. She enrolled in college. She wondered whether a university degree would not be a better idea than a life dedicated to music. Just as it seemed almost certain that the course of her life was about to change she won a Ministry of Education scholarship for music. Back she went to Kolhapur, this time to train under both Laxmibai Jadhav another illustrious teacher of the Jaipur gayaki and Azizuddin Khan, the grandson of Alladiya Khan, who had a store of the rarest compositions in his repertoire.

In 1960 Dhondutai returned to Jabalpur. A year later she received a letter from Azizuddin Khan. Enclosed was a newspaper cutting, a review of a recent concert Kesarbai Kerkar had given. At this concert, so the review said, H.R. Mahajani of *Loksatta* asked her, 'To whom are you going to bequeath this great tradition? Who will be your heir?' Piqued by the question, Kesarbai had snapped back, 'To anybody who is willing to put in the kind of mehnat I have put in to my art.' Azizuddin had decided that Tai was the only person who could accept the singer's challenge. He urged her to write to Kesarbai, asking to be taught.

'I wrote to her,' recalls Dhondutai, with a smile. 'She wrote back saying she appreciated my wanting to continue learning even after the years of training I had with renowned teachers of the gharana. She said she was old, she wasn't at all sure how she would be able to cope with teaching but agreed to give it a try.

'In a way,' adds Dhondutai, 'I think I added a few years to Kesarabai's performing life. A demanding student forces a teacher to tax himself. Kerasabai was over seventy when she took me on as a student. She had not been able to devote as much time and energy to her music as she had done earlier. My being with her rejuvenated her in a sense.'

Dhonduati narrates her first encounter with the singer who had become a legend in her lifetime. 'My father and I went to Bombay... Azizuddin took me backstage to introduce me to Kesarbai before the concert. Suddenly he asked her if she would allow me to accompany her. She paused, looked at him, then said yes. The first raag she sang was Bihagda. I knew the cheez. She let me sing quite a bit. After that she didn't sing a single raag I knew.

'The curiosity of the audience was aroused. Who was this woman singing with Surashree? There were many conjectures. Some even thought I was a blood relation.' A review of the concert in the *Maharashtra Times* took note of the stir caused by Dhondutai's presence on the stage with Kesarbai.

Why was there so much curiosity and conjecture? Because Kesarbai was reputed to be a difficult person. Temperamental, haughty, flamboyant, she was said never to have sung a complete composition for her recordings, for fear of being copied. 'But isn't that natural?' asks Dhondutai. 'After all a singer's compositions are her wealth. She does not want cheap imitations of her rare ornaments to be bartered around in the marketplace.

'As for her being a difficult person, are not all intense, passionate people difficult? I think I managed to put my finger on her pulse. She was never ungenerous with me, never temperamental. There was one concert at which I was going to sing. Mogubai Kurdikar was in the front row along with Kesarbai. Relations between them were strained. Before I began to sing, I did my obeisance to Mogubai. Later people said to me, "That's the end of you." I, too, was full of trepidation when I went to Kesarbai the next day. But her reaction to my gesture was quite unexpected. She said, "I was happy to see my daughter doing what was right and proper for the occasion".'

Lessons progressed well enough for Dhondutai but not in the tradition of teaching that Kesarbai herself had had from Alladiya Khan. Dhondutai describes a typical day in the lives of singers like Laxmibai and Kesarbai. 'The day began at five a.m. with a two-hour stint at exercising the voice in the lower octave. After breakfast came four hours of the morning raags. Then followed lunch and a compulsory two-hour rest period. At four in the afternoon began the practice session for the evening raags. The last session of the day began after dinner at about nine at night. This went on till midnight or even beyond and it was up again at five the next morning.'

Little wonder then that these singers developed a voice that was at their command at any time of the day or night to do what they willed with it.

There is a delightful story about Kesarbai in this context. It appears that after recording for a well-known company, she was told that some fault had developed in the equipment and spoilt the recording. Could she do the recording again? 'Why?' she demanded haughtily. 'It was your equipment that failed. My voice doesn't fail.'

Such were the singers who poured their pure and abundant music into the mainstream of their tradition. Writing about the gayaki of her gharana in a souvenir brought out to commemorate Kesarbai Kerkar, who died on 16 September, 1977, Dhondutai says, 'To set out to gain command over this gayaki is to commit yourself to an all-consuming passion, a vrat. It is not an easy style. There is no place here for pretty little turns and twists of the voice. The voice must flow broad and deep from the lowest to the highest notes. Every note of the melody must interweave with the beat to create a variety of patterns each of which must end gracefully, purposefully and yet unexpectedly on the sam.'

Today, in Bombay, Dhondutai observes the sixth anniversary of her guru's death with a concert. Recalling Kesarbai's prayer to God not to make her a singer in her next life because music forces all other joys out of life, Dhondutai says, 'There is one thing about which Kesarbai expressed satisfaction. She used to say that in her day "mehnat" paid off. Your dedication to your art was appreciated, your music found a platform. She said I would be unhappy because merit was no longer recognized. But I am not unhappy. Nothing can disturb the profound happiness I have within me which comes from this great and noble art which I have inherited in so pure a form, unadulterated by popular taste, unfalsified by emotionalism.'

Pandit Jal Balaporia
A Delight in Balance

With Pt Jal K. Balaporia's death, we have lost one of the few dedicated practitioners of the Gwalior gayaki in this city; and, after Pandit Feroz Dastur's death four years ago, the only remaining Parsi vocalist of Hindustani music in the country.

Pt Balaporia was only six when his father, Kaikhushroo, began teaching him raga-based songs. At fourteen, he joined the class that Sitaram Eknath Pandit of the Gwalior gharana had started in his home town, Billimoria. Even when he moved to Surat and then to Mumbai, he managed to find gurus from the gharana to guide him.

If one were to characterize in one word the effect that Pt Balaporia's music had on his listeners, that word would have to be delight. The delight lay in his chaste diction, whether he was singing in Braj, Sanskrit, Marathi or Persian, in praise of Shiva, Rama or Allah. It lay in the warm rapport he built with his audience. It lay in his own delight in all three aspects of music—poetry, swara and tala. Some of the talas that his bandishes were set to, like deepchandi, ada chautal, zhaptal, zhumra, sawari and pashtu, rarely showed up on other concert platforms. What we heard there were mostly trital and the excessively slow ektal. The latter, in Pt Balaporia's opinion, led to slackness in the construction of the khayal.

'Tala is not just a set number of beats struck at regular intervals,' he would explain. 'Had it been so, why would our great composers have created three independent talas like adachautal, zhumra and

---

This article was first published in *Mumbai Mirror* on 1 February 2013. It was written as a tribute to Pandit Jal Balporia, who died on 18 January 2013.

deepchandi, each comprising fourteen beats? The uniqueness of a tala lies in the varied lengths and tension between two beats. In the slow ektal, the lazy spaces between beats destroy the potential for a musician to create playful relationships between word, swara and tala. Only by honouring all three can you fill your music with emotion, melodiousness and balance.'

Balance constituted a fundamental precept in his training. Balance is achieved when a presentation is not stretched beyond the point where the singer has said everything there is to say for the moment. Balance is achieved when the singer makes judicious use of all eight ornaments of elaboration available to her/him, never overdoing any one of them. Balance is achieved when the singer pays due regard to the wholeness of a bandish, singing both the asthai and the antara. Eliminating the antara is like building a house without a roof. Significantly, one of the comments on Pt Balaporia's Yaman tarana on YouTube expresses wonder and excitement at hearing the antara of the tarana for the first time.

While Pt Balaporia's students admired him for the purity of his music and were ever grateful to him for his gentle guidance, what claimed their profound love were his qualities as a human being. Affectionately known as Jalsaheb, Pt Balaporia was a transparently good man who lived by the three precepts of the Zoroastrian faith—good thoughts, good words, good deeds. Strongly centred in his faith and his music, he could do what less secure souls never could: laugh at himself. His funniest stories were about his experiences as a performer on All India Radio. On one of these occasions his name was announced as Pt Bal K. Jalaporia. Passing a hand over his bald head, Jalsaheb remarked mischievously, 'I don't know where the announcer saw baal!'

Pt Balaporia's generosity towards his students was endless. On one shelf of a cupboard in the room where he taught them, was a stack of fat, well-thumbed notebooks filled with bandishes he had inherited from his mentor, Dr H.G. Moghe. 'I have so much to give, but who is there to take it from me?' he would ask. With their limited time and stressful work schedules, none of his students could commit themselves as completely to music as he had done.

He himself had all the time for them, and his beloved wife Roshan, all the warmth and hospitality. At the guru poornima last year, even when his degenerative illness had made his voice inaudible and movement difficult, Pt Balaporia sat through his students' musical offerings, listening intently, his fingers doing what nobody could stop them from doing—tapping out the talas on his knees. I have absolutely no doubt that, even in his final unconscious state, he must have been singing a tappa, a khayalnuma or an ashtapadi to himself, delighting death itself as he had delighted us.

Gayaki as Mercury

One of the most tantalizing games we played as children was when the mercury thermometer in the house broke and we got to play with the globule of heavy silvery-white liquid metal that slid out of its confinement and scattered in tiny sparkling balls all over the floor. To gather them together into one cohesive form and see them scatter again at the lightest touch was sheer magic.

The game came back to me on Saturday when we tried to contain Ustad Bade Ghulam Ali Khan's music in our understanding and it kept slipping away. The Harmony Hall in Nehru Centre was so packed that evening that one extra breath would have made it burst. There, in the course of the listening session organized by the ITC Research Sangeet Academy with the academic support of Music Forum, we saw how art can escape analytical control to do its own thing.

How to categorize Ustad Bade Ghulam Ali Khan's music was the big question we began with. How were we to understand his bountiful, energetic, no-holds-barred creativity in terms of voice, rhythm, musicality, technique, emotion, riyaz, unfolding of the raag and other criteria that pandits had evolved to pin down and assess Hindustani classical music? On the dais were Dr Ashok Ranade, Pandit Arvind Parikh, Ustad Raza Ali Khan and Satyasheel Deshpande to help us do so.

And this is how it went. Each time a category was proposed, Dr Ashok Ranade would strike it down and widen the mesh in order to help us net the truth. When it was suggested, for instance,

---

This article was first published in *Mid-Day* on 22 June 2004.

that Khansaheb's music was dominated by the shringar rasa, Dr Ranade asserted the opposite—that he sang all the rasas at all times. Musicians were impatient of the rasa theory which presumed to dictate emotion, he said. In his opinion, there were only two rasas in performance. Elation and non-elation.

That set us free. Elation is beyond rules. Elation is just simply itself and nothing else. It goes to the head. It intoxicates. That's what probably happened to the thousands of admirers who thronged to hear the Ustad perform at the numerous concerts and conferences to which he was invited. He soared and they soared with him, responding to every taan that slid out of his velvet throat in sparkling parabolas, each note perfectly formed, but gone before you could possess it.

Pundits of old had problems with Khansaheb's khayals, though they granted him consummate mastery over the thumri. Pundits always have a problem with the irrepressibly free artist. Why does he not follow the rules of the game? A classical vocalist is supposed to start with alaap, progress to boltaans and end with taans, the tempo increasing gradually as he goes along. That's how the full character of a raag is to be revealed. That's how the listener is to be led into a contemplative frame of mind, which is, after all, the goal of Hindustani classical music.

But here was a vocalist who refused to delineate a raag bit by bit in systematic progression. Its character was in his bloodstream and every musical utterance he made revealed it. Dr Ranade called him an impressionist, because he sang the overall image of a raag. He was like the painter who doesn't draw the contour of a form first and then fill it in with colour, but takes his brush directly to the canvas and reveals in the very first mark he makes, the gesture or posture of the figure he has in mind.

Not every musician could cut free from rules and take the risks that Bade Ghulam Ali Khan did; for not everybody had his voice, his confidence and, above all, his joie de vivre which together gave him the ability and desire to do so. His voice was Nature's gift. But its elasticity and control were the result of hours and hours of daily riyaz. His confidence came from a thorough knowledge of all the rules that he then chose to disregard in performance. As for his joyous spirit, that too was Nature's gift, like his voice. In many ways, he was Nature's child.

Any number of stories has come down to us about the inspiration he drew from Nature. He would observe the flight of birds with intense curiosity and attempt to emulate it in music. He sat on the parapet of Marine Drive in the monsoon and imitated, in his Miyan Malhar, the upward surge of waves as they crashed against the parapet and the crisp, froth of their return. He followed a young woman of perfect proportions all the way down a street to internalize her sensuous lines and recreate them musically later.

Actually, classical music is as far as you can get from Nature. It is the result of a gradual accumulation of layers of culture over the original foundation, which is imitation of Nature. The less 'natural' the music, the further away it is from people. Ustad Ghulam Ali Khan felt very close to folk music, which is people's music. He sang it with vigour, earthiness and elan and brought its principle of shared experience to the classical music platform. He delighted in delighting people. He delighted us too, thirty-six years after his death, with his rapid taans spun out of gossamer silk, his dizzying slides that touched each note precisely along the way, the high notes he plucked out of the very firmament, like sharp little stars of sound.

So did Khansaheb Bade Ghulam Ali Khan's music fit into the prescribed framework of khayal gayaki? The question is irrelevant. There are some phenomena so awesome that you simply accept them for what they are, grateful that such things should be.

On Manjusha Patil

Some people go to every concert there is; others only to those held by the local music circle. Many pick and choose according to the musician's star rating. Me? I'm quite happy listening to recorded music until suddenly one day I begin to yearn for a live human voice. Left unattended, the feeling can grow into a kind of emptiness, a nagging certainty that something vital is missing.

The yearning comes on most strongly in the rains. More than any other season, the monsoon is the season for music. The rain-washed air has reopened your senses to the world of sight and sound. You are filled with tenderness for all living things—man, woman, stray dog and ant—and music calls with an urgency that cannot be denied. If, at such a time, you are fortunate enough to hear a singer whose music is a celebration of life, your season is made.

Manjusha Kulkarni-Patil, presented by Sajan Milap on Sunday at the Bharatiya Vidya Bhavan, turned out to be just such a singer. That she was a seasoned performer became clear from her very first note. There's nothing more magical than the opening 'sa' when it blends so perfectly with the resonance of the tanpura that you can't tell the one from the other. Patil's 'sa' had that quality.

'I will begin with Dhanashree,' she announced. She might as well have added, 'and you will begin with a blank slate!' For, there couldn't have been more than a handful of people in that hall, old Agra gharana aficionados, who had heard Dhanashree

---

This article was first published in *Mumbai Mirror* on 20 June 2007.

before. The rest of us had only heard it as one half of raag Puriya-Dhanashree, an all-time favourite with musicians. Dhanashree by itself belongs to Ustad Vilayat Hussain Khan's repertoire, which Patil has inherited from her late guru Kanebuwa of Ichalkaranji. It is a rich, sweet raag, full of musical possibilities, which Patil explored with mischievous playfulness through a bandish in praise of the beloved. Unlike some singers, who treat the bandish as no more than a peg to hang note patterns and taans on, often singing only the first half and leaving the second unsung, Patil sang her bandish in its entirety. She imbued every word with feeling, using stress and diction with great precision to coax shades of meaning out of it. If, as the *NatyaShastra* decrees, music must include dance and drama to be complete, then Patil proved to be a complete musician. You didn't just listen to her. You watched her too, captivated by her vivacity, eloquent gestures and the convivial rapport she shared with her accompanists. Khayal gayaki offers a singer a choice of several embellishments with which to outline and paint the face and figure of a raag. Patil made judicious use of them all, always careful to maintain a fine balance between the structural and decorative elements. Her bol-alaaps, bol-taans and taans were varied in pace and pattern. Her samas were like birds alighting on water. Her full-throated voice travelled effortlessly through three octaves, never losing volume in the upper register. How could such a slim frame produce such a powerful voice, you wondered.

If Patil's Dhanashree was full of masti, her next khayal in Gowri was quiet and sombre. For now the bandish was about a woman pining for an absent lover. The nayika had changed and so had the singer's emotional range.

Patil comes from Sangli in south Maharashtra, a town that has given us many fine musicians. From the time she was twelve, she travelled every weekend to her guru's home to train. The rigour of that taalim was evident in her performance. She could command her voice to do pretty much what she wanted; yet not once did she allow her virtuosity to get the better of her music. Most importantly, while singing within the tradition, she managed to establish her own strong musical personality.

On Venkatesh Kumar

I am in complete awe of Venkatesh Kumar's music. Every time we hear him, he has something new to offer. And every time, unfailingly, he takes us to the very peak of listening pleasure.

On Sunday morning at the Dadar-Matunga Cultural Club, he began with a Lalit, not a raag one hears too often, followed by the sweet and seductive Alhaiya Bilawal and a soaring Hindol. After the interval he attempted Bhairav-Bahar. It was a failed attempt. The two raags from which it was forged, remained stubbornly apart instead of melding seamlessly. Nothing Kumar could do would stop the joints between them from creaking. However, in view of the high we reached with his Gaud Malhar and the finale, a bhajan in Bhairavi, the Bhairav-Bahar was no more than the black spot superstitious mothers put on their babies' faces to ward off the evil eye.

Venkatesh Kumar's voice has an uncommon range and power, and a flexibility to match a gymnast's body. Like a gymnast, he too performs feats that are nothing short of magical. His alaaps are quiet and thoughtful, his bandishes flawlessly enunciated, his elaborations rich with all the eight ornaments prescribed by the old masters for drawing out the beauties of a raag. His musical ideas tumble out one after the other and his taans astound by their variety and complexity. His music is all supple muscle and no flab. Somewhere, particularly in the upper octave, he reminds us fleetingly of Ustad Bade Ghulam Ali Khan.

Venkatesh Kumar has amazing lung power. He will do a full-throated ascending taan, close his mouth and hold the top note till

---

This article was first published in *Mumbai Mirror* on 13 July 2018.

you think he has stopped singing. But he hasn't. He still has breath enough to open up and bring the taan cascading down to a dramatic close. Many of Kumar's taans have a graphic quality, as though he were drawing complex lines with his voice. Sometimes he places short taans one beside the other like hatched lines. At others he executes rapid, minutely sketched zigzags before spilling out a whole sea of sound in ripples and waves. He also does intricate sargams, a musical element I'm not particularly fond of, and a variety of tihais which others consider childish mathematics, but I see as the play element in music as important as anything else for creating a richly shaded view of the raag.

Venkatesh Kumar isn't interested in mere showmanship. Every piece of music he sings is elegantly constructed. This was true even of Sunday's musically unsuccessful Bhairav-Bahar. So when he sings a tihai, the thrice-repeated phrase of the mukhada that ends on the sama, he isn't merely demonstrating his command over the rhythmic cycle. He is using the tihai to punctuate the music in order to create a transition between one passage of elaboration and another. He does other interesting things too. At one point in the Lalit, after exploring the antara, he returned to base by singing the asthai without any musical flourishes. It was like a statement that said, I've shown you a large part of the face of this raag complete with ornaments. I must now take a break to see where I started, before resuming my search for completeness. Venkatesh Kumar values the bandish immensely. It is always present like a strong skeleton, giving shape to his explorations of a raag.

This brilliant vocalist whose father was a poor folk-singer, received his training at the famous Veereshwara Punyashrama in Gadag, founded by Ganayogi Panchakshara Gawai for blind students and orphans. After the founder's demise, his student, the blind vocalist Pt Puttaraja Gawai, took over. The eminent music critic P.G. Burde tells me, Venkatesh Kumar has always maintained that had it not been for the training he received from Pt Puttaraja Gawai for eleven years, he would have been singing on trains to make a living.

Listening to Venkatesh Kumar today, you wonder whether there's another factor besides excellent training, dedication and riyaz that has contributed to his music. Perhaps something in the very soil of the Dharwad-Hubli-Belgaum-Gadag districts of north Karnataka nurtures and nourishes musical genius? It is as if the gods had said to the people of this region, open your mouths and you shall sing. Why else would this belt alone have produced vocalists of the stature of Mallikarjun Mansur, Gangubai Hangal, Kumar Gandharva, Bhimsen Joshi, Basavaraj Rajguru and Rambhau Kundagolkar, popularly known as Sawai Gandharva?

And now we have Venkatesh Kumar, unquestionably an outstanding heir to that great legacy.

Fiction

'What is our problem, really?'

Decision

The truck rumbled up to the chawl, creaked querulously and fell silent. The next moment Sakhya ran for it without thinking twice—four flights down, quick as a lick to the back of the chawl, in and out of slush, through the stink of piss, around the rubbish heap, across the maidan, through the crowds and then wherever his steps would take him.

Where? Sakhya had to ask himself soon enough. Wherever you stand in Mumbai, you see streets going off in every direction. When Sakhya stopped running to catch his breath, he could not figure out which way to go. Here or there? Down this road or that? Sakhya was thoroughly confused. Why did I run off like that, he wondered. I'll go back. Home.

Sakhya stood at the corner of a square like a block of wood, numbed by the thought of going home. He did not want to go home, never, particularly not that day. Of all the forty families in the chawl, Gaja had to go pick him to play Parvati. So many girls were dying to play her but Gaja said: 'Nope. It has to be a delicate boy. If someone teases the girl, we'll have a riot for nothing.' Just then somebody had called out in a disguised falsetto, 'Ay Sakhya.' And Sakhya had turned into a frozen statue where he sat.

Just the memory of that call was enough to get his feet moving again. They moved automatically, without giving Sakhya a moment to think which way he should go. They followed only one rule: avoid

This story first appeared as 'Sakhyacha Nirnay' in Marathi in the 1999 Diwali special issue of *Anustubh*.

every road leading back to the sea. They wanted to be far away from dhols and bands, away from the Ganpatis.

As the distance between him and his home grew, his fear waned. Gradually it freed itself from the frozen muscles around his heart and slid down and out through his feet. It was far behind him now. So were his father's bloodshot eyes, Parshya's stony face and the ripple of Gaja's amulet-bound muscles.

~

Gajanan stood deliberately flexing his arm in Parshya's face, saying, 'Sakhya can go to hell. Just tell me, are you keeping your pansy brother's word or you want to have it out with me?' Parshya's eyebrows meet over a fine nose that comes down, straight as an arrow, from under their thick, jet black bow. Parshya said nothing. He simply looked Gaja in the eye. A buzz of voices was growing around them: 'Come on, Parshya', 'Let it go, Gaja. Leave it.'

'No, I won't let it go,' Gaja roared. 'When I say something, it happens. It's my word.' Now they grabbed Parshya—by his sleeves, his trouser belt, whatever came to hand. 'Move it, Parshya. Stop wasting time.'

Parshya was being dragged backwards. But his eyes did not move from Gaja's face bloated with drink. It was only when Gaja swung around and started giving orders that Parshya, too, turned to climb the four flights of stairs to their room. Someone called in a high falsetto, 'Hey Parshya, don't forget what goes under the sari.'

Parshya did not look back. He went straight into the room. No one was at home. His father must be drowning himself somewhere in drink. But the room was stuffed tight with his stink. Parshya took the mirror from its corner; picked up the razor; stripped; scraped off his moustache; put powder on his dark brown face; painted a large kumkum sun on his forehead; and unfolded the fake zari-covered flashy red sari bought from the contributions. He had seen his mother wear her sari every day in the servants' quarters at Baisaheb's. He wore it now as she had. He stuffed the front of the blouse with balled up scraps of old cloth, clipped on a nose-ring, slid golden and green glass bangles on his wrists and was ready.

Downstairs, there was a lot of shouting happening on the truck. The statue of Bal Ganpati was being hoisted. A small forest was being created around him. A peacock, its fanned-out plumage studded with multi-coloured lights, was going to dance in it. Gaja was barking orders. The last five years he had been hobnobbing a lot at the lower levels of the political ladder. Gulabwadi was his beat. He collected the most contributions and all the local riots happened under his leadership. The numbers of people who bowed before him was increasing by the day. People had begun to address him as Gajananrao.

Parshya was clammy with sweat sitting in the stuffy room. He dabbed lightly at the drops on his forehead, wiping off the frown between his eyebrows along with them. His face and mind grew calm. He picked up the mirror and held it up to his face. He started. An involuntary cry escaped him: 'Aai!'

~

The day Father killed Mother, Sakhya had not gone to school. He had pretended to go but came back. It was Baisaheb's day at the hospital. She would go, ask what the patients wanted, distribute magazines and write letters for them. It would be dark by the time she came home. If Sakhya had played hooky on one of those days, she was none the wiser. On other days she would get upset. She used to pay for Parshya and Sakhya's books and satchels. Yet, on days when she had house guests or a party, she herself would keep Parshya back from school to help with the extra work. Sakhya was younger and weaker. He was never given a day off from school. So he would give himself a holiday once in a while on Baisaheb's hospital days. He would drop his bag with the security guard and go off on a loaf. In the evening Parshya would scold him. Mother would also yell. But after a day of fun, Sakhya didn't care. On that day Sakhya had flung his bag at Security and gone skipping off towards the public garden. He wanted to go to the garden where Mother took Baisaheb's grandson when he came to stay. In the evenings there would be horses there with feathers on their heads, and a merry-go-round. At this time of the day the merry-go-round was covered in tarpaulin and secured tightly with coir ropes.

But the swings were empty. There was not a soul in the garden, except for a couple of men snoozing under the trees. The swings were his alone. He hopped from one to the other in turn. He swung high into the sky. His head felt light. He did not want to stop. But then he saw his father emerge on unsteady legs from the lengthening shadows of the trees. Sakhya was in the air when he noticed him. He used his thin feet to stop the swing. The swing wriggled and writhed like a wounded animal and whined to a stop.

Sakhya's eyes were fixed on his father who had skirted the garden and was walking away, muttering to himself. Sakhya skipped off the swing and followed him at a distance, his legs trembling. His father too knew that this was Baisaheb's day at the hospital. So it was also his day to ask Mother for money and to thrash her black and blue if she did not part with it. Sakhya thought of his mother. She must have finished lunch and was probably relaxing for a few easy minutes to make paan and eat it before returning to her work. Sakhya was furious with the security guard. Why did he let Father in though Baisaheb had warned him not to? He had said just one thing to Sakhya: 'He is your mother's husband.'

Sakhya's father was climbing the stairs to the servants' quarters. He could hear his footsteps. He dared not follow him further. He crept under the staircase and crouched there trembling, fingers in his ears. But they were bony and his father's voice went right through them. A string of his father's vile expletives burst around him like fireworks. His mother only said: 'Okay. So I'm a whore. But why are you a pimp? Go earn your own money for liquor.'

'Pimp? Pimp, am I?' His father's voice had gone berserk.

His mother screamed.

Then nothing.

Then silence.

When his father came pounding down the steps and had gone far enough, Sakhya rose. He climbed the stairs on trembling legs. He sat down beside his mother, now still. He moaned. Parshya came home from school. Sakhya was still moaning. Parshya shook him hard. 'Talk, can't you? How could you just sit? Didn't even yell?' Parshya's voice cracked. Sakhya only moaned.

In the evening Baisaheb spoke soothingly to Parshya and Sakhya. 'If you make a police complaint, your father goes in. Who will you be left with then? You have a father. He has a room. Hold on to them. That poor soul is gone. Nothing's going to bring her back.'

Parshya said, 'We'll stay here. I'll do Mother's work. I can do all her chores. Let Father go in.' Parshya's voice was tearful.

Baisaheb stroked his head. 'No, Parshuram. I live alone here. I need a woman to help me. You're still too young. Go to school. When you're old enough, I'll find you a job.'

Baisaheb wangled a death certificate from a doctor she knew. Mother's body went into the electric incinerator the same night. Together Parshya and Sakhya cleaned up the servants' quarter till it shone. Then they picked up their satchels and the tin trunk which held theirs and their mother's clothes and began walking towards their father's room. Those who saw them go, whispered. Thapa, the security guard, lowered his head. They went out of the gate. They crossed the road. A double-decker bus thundered by between them and the housing society. Its sweeping hauteur wiped away all that lay on the other side.

~

Parshya tried to open the trunk that stood in the corner gently at first. But when it would not give, he yanked it hard. The bolt flew open. Inside lay two saris, two blouses and a small tin box. Parshya opened the box. In it was a glittering chain, yellower than gold, but not gold. Had it been gold, Father would have drunk it up long before. Parshya lifted the chain out of the box and put it round his neck. He carried the mirror to the window. Standing amongst the motes that swirled round and round in the beam of sunlight that came through, he brought the mirror up to his eyes. The light caught the chain. It glinted. Mother too had stood before Baisaheb's mirror once, delighting in it. Parshya was home to help tidy up after the big party on the previous evening. He had gone to Baisaheb's room to ask where he could put the glass bowl he had in his hand. Seeing his mother, he had involuntarily exclaimed, 'Looks nice.'

Mother was embarrassed. She removed the chain quickly and tucked it into her waist.

'Did Baisaheb give it to you?' Parshya had asked.

'Rubbish. Does Baisaheb give me everything?'

'Who then?' Parshya had persisted. Mother had looked at him, smiled and said, 'I bought it myself. With the five rupees the guests gave me.'

~

'Parshya! Ay Parshya!' someone called from below. 'Where the fuck are you?'

'You want the ten-day Ganpati to go on the twelfth day?' That was Gaja. Parshya hung the mirror up in its corner, bolted and locked the door and went down, stumbling over the sari. The women and girls snickered to see him. Somebody wolf whistled. None of these things affected him. He shook off the hands that were trying to help him up. He climbed on to the truck by himself and sat solemnly beside the Bal Ganpati as he had been instructed to—left leg over right knee, right arm around the shoulders of the statue and eyes fixed ahead. As soon as he had taken his place, a cry of '*Ganpati Bappa Morya*' went up. The trumpet sounded its first cracked notes, croaked a couple of times and started playing '*Chhaiya chhaiya*'. The truck lurched forward and began to move. The band went ahead; boys, girls, men and women followed behind, dancing; the truck with Bal Ganpati sitting in his forest brought up the rear. Beside Ganpati sat Parvati, looking straight ahead without blinking as much as an eyelash.

The truck was moving. The band was playing. The dancers were dancing. Those in charge of fireworks were bursting them. Meanwhile Parshya was beginning to feel as if he was going to faint. The bedlam dimmed before his eyes. His ears echoed. His right hand grew stiff. His left leg tingled with pins and needles. The sweat poured from under his prickly wig, making rivulets through the powder on his face and dropping off his chin into his lap.

He withdrew his right arm gently from around Ganpati's shoulders. He cracked his knuckles quickly one after the other. He lifted his left leg off his right knee and stamped it a few times to get rid of the pins and needles. Then he shifted his position, turning a little towards the statue, resting both feet on the ground. Now he put his right arm around Ganpati again and fixed his eyes on him. All he had eyes for now was the graceful curve of his trunk, his modak-filled belly, his snugly crossed legs, his high forehead, his hair turned back from it in waves and, again and yet again, his serene, tender gaze. That is all he saw. That is all he wanted to see. He wanted to hold Ganpati close to his heart. Listen to his stories. Tell him his own. Soon Parshya was talking to Ganpati. He did not notice he was doing it; nor did anybody else.

~

As the sun went down, Sakhya felt a sudden pang of loneliness. He sat on the Marine Drive parapet. The waves of the monsoon sea crashed against the rocks below his feet and broke. Their spray struck his face and turned into streams that dripped down it into his collar. He pulled his knees up against his chest and hugged them with both arms. Alone, he stared at the sun that hung now like an upturned pot over the horizon.

~

'No women are going in,' Gaja shouted, looking slyly at Parshya. The statue was set on a servant's head. Two of Gaja's friends set off with him towards the sea. Parshya followed. Gaja had not planned to go;

but when he saw Parshya, he too went, cursing him. The last rays of the sun danced on the waves. When they were far in where the water was calm, no longer burbling and spuming towards the shore, Gaja's friends lowered the statue from the servant's head. Parshya, standing nearby, had eyes only for the baby god. And then, even as he watched, one of the men slipped, knocking the other's arm. Bal Ganpati, supported by six hands, now toppled over and entered the water head down, legs up. Parshya's breath caught. Without a second thought, he dived in. His eyes could not make out a thing; but he flailed his arms in wide circles, searching. Finally they touched the statue. He hugged it close with both arms, brought it up, then slipped it gently back into the sea.

When Parshya came up he did not see a single known face in the crowds through the gathering dark. He waded to the shore, his sari, drenched and heavy, wrapping itself round his legs. The salt water entered the innumerable mosquito bites on his legs, making them sting. But he kept his balance even as he stumbled.

The truck was parked at a distance. He walked with great difficulty. Gaja saw him from afar. He lost his temper. 'Get rid of that sari. Come on. No time to wait.' Another voice said, 'You're asking a woman to strip?' The women in the truck sniggered secretly behind their pallus. The girls in skirts and salwar kameezes laughed outright. Gaja felt powerful. 'Woman, is it? Then we know what to do with her.' He pounced on Parshya and stripped half the sari off him in a single move. A smell of liquor surged out of his mouth, entered Parshya's nose and mouth and spread through his body. Parshya's temples burned. The veins in them danced. The women in the truck watched with shocked eyes. Gaja's hand lunged out again. Holding the half-stripped sari against his chest, Parshya roared, 'NO!' The word was enough to excite Gaja and his friends even more. Somebody lifted Parshya's wig off his head. Someone else grabbed his nose-ring. Somebody plunged a hand in his blouse. 'Fuck! It's not coconut shells. It's cloth. Softy-soft.' The balls of cloth slipped out of the blouse. The necklace broke. Parshya kicked for all he was worth.

He hit out and bit to keep his honour intact. Then somebody tugged at his chain. That is when Parshya threw off the sari he was holding close and ran like the wind. As he ran, he spat again and again to get rid of the bitterness in his mouth. He wiped the hot tears from his eyes and moaned in memory of the honour he had lost.

~

It was only because the security guard knew Parshya and Sakhya that he had allowed Sakhya in and let him spend the night under the stairs of the old servants' quarters. He assumed that Sakhya had run away because his father had thrashed him. 'But remember,' he said, 'I'm going to tell your father if he comes by.' Then he warned, 'And listen. Just this one night. Tomorrow morning you'll scram. Yes?'

'Swear on my mother, I will.'

Sakhya felt at home under the stairs. Music drifted out of the house across the way. A moist breeze blew in puffs from afar, giving him goose bumps. There was silence all around. Sakhya moved back to lean against the wall. The cool wall calmed his mind. Sitting there, he closed his eyes and fell asleep.

~

Parshya was panting like a pair of bellows when he reached Security. His face was covered in maps of powder. His forehead was smeared with blood-red streaks of kumkum. Tatters of his blouse flapped from his arms. Below it all were his blue shorts. The security guard stared at the sight of him as he muttered, 'Yes. Sakhya came a couple of hours ago.' Parshya turned to go in and Thapa could not resist asking, 'Do you act in plays?' Parshya's non-sequitur, 'No, I've come to take him home,' baffled him further.

Parshya did not see Sakhya in the dark under the stairs. But he sensed him. He bent low to enter. A figure came awake with a start. 'I guess you haven't eaten.' Parshya sat down beside the now visible Sakhya and held out a paper-cone of dry bhel. Parshya and Sakhya ate together.

'Let's go home,' Parshya said, screwing up the empty cone. Sakhya would not budge.

'Come on, let's go,' Parshya said, getting up.

'Gaja will beat me.' Sakhya's voice came out small.

'Why?'

'I didn't do Parvati.'

'But I did.'

'You?'

Parshya caught hold of Sakhya's hand and moved it over his face. 'Feel the moustache?'

'No. But why did you do Parvati?'

'To keep your word.' Parshya stripped off what remained of the blouse, balled it up and wiped his face clean with it.

'But they mustn't have teased you.'

'Why not? Sure they did. But I didn't pay attention. I was Parvati.'

'So where's the dress?'

'They pulled it off, the bastards. Come on.'

Sakhya got up. They began walking. Home was an hour or so away. The fourteenth-day moon floated above them. Distant drums and pipes played '*Dhak dhak dhak, choli ke peeche kya hai*' (What's behind the blouse?), and '*Bholi surat dil ke khote*' (Fair faces with dark hearts) along with the latest hits.

As they walked, Sakhya asked in a small voice, 'Ay Parshya, you think we should join Gaja's gang?'

'Why?'

'Then we don't have to be afraid of anybody. Gaja will even straighten out our father.'

'I don't want to. You go if you want.'

'How can I go without you?'

'Why? Are our legs tied together?'

'No, yaar. How can we be enemies?'

'So don't go.'

A sob escaped Sakhya. 'I'm scared.'

'You think Gaja isn't?'

'Gaja? Get out. He's got power.'

'There are people with more power. Gaja needs ten men to do anything.'

Sakhya became thoughtful. 'But he is the most powerful in our chawl.'

'Still I don't want to be with him. You go if you want.'

'He'll beat us up.'

'He beats up his gang members too.'

'So what shall we do?'

'You decide for yourself. I know I'll never go with him. I don't care if I die.'

Parshya looked at his younger brother's face and relented a bit.

'You want to decide, right? Then look here.' He drew their mother's chain from the pocket of his shorts. He held it before Sakhya on an open palm. 'If you choose the empty fist, you go with Gaja. If you choose the fist with the chain, you stay with me.'

Parshya put both hands behind him. The brothers stood on the pavement. Before them rose their chawls dark as death, faces ripped, stomachs leaking, feet cracked, ready to collapse and bury two hundred families under brick and mud. Parshya stood shifting the chain from this fist to the other behind his back. Then he held both fists before Sakhya. Sakhya broke into a sweat as he glanced at them turn by turn. 'Ay Parshya, I don't want this. I want to be with you.'

Parshya's face relaxed. He said in a soft voice, 'But let's see what your fate had in store for you. Choose.'

Sakhya tapped each fist in turn, muttering their old playground rhyme, 'Addam, taddam, tadtadbaja.' He slapped the fist where the rhyme ended. The fist was empty. Sakhya broke into a fresh sweat. Laughing, Parshya threw an arm around Sakhya's shoulders and the two crossed the road and entered the chawl.

The Dog and I

Lost in thought, the dog sits on the second step of the Irani restaurant and I am in my chair, both guarding our places, he in his way, I in mine. This is my fourth dog. He'd just given up his mother's teats, wandered around looking for his place in the world, found this step and settled down. That was twelve years ago.

The previous dogs had come the same way, grown up on this step and died one day, run over by a car or killed by a disease. I have followed this cycle from my unemployed days to now, when I have retired.

I wonder why all these dogs have preferred this particular step of the restaurant to settle down on. Perhaps I know. When a pup comes here first, it kind of lingers outside, its eyes on the owner. When the owner spots the pup, he gives it a steady stare. There's no sympathy or anything like that in his eyes. Just conditions: you want to sit there, sit, but do it at your own risk. You will not step into the restaurant. You will not expect anything from me. This said, the owner gets back to work. But most importantly, he doesn't name the pup. No Tommy, Raja, Rover and all that. We call him dog. Just that. Dog. A pup that accepts these conditions, indeed one that has been looking for just such a place, settles here for good. For the rest of his life, he shelters here in the blazing afternoons and returns at night to sleep. In between he roams the streets for food. The funny thing is, not a single bitch has made her life on this step. It's always male dogs.

This story first appeared as 'Kutra ani Mi' in the 2004 Diwali special issue of *Saptahik Sakal*. It has been translated from the Marathi by Shanta Gokhale.

This dog is old now. His grey coat, once glossy, has faded. He sits here all day. This one's not going to die in an accident or anything like that. Old age, more likely.

My eyes are fixed on him, not only because he's directly in my line of vision, but also, and more importantly because, staring at the dog on the step has been a lifelong pastime with me. Moreover, he is doing nothing and I am doing nothing. Not only is he doing nothing, but he is sitting completely still, head resting on his front paws and both ears down. This dog was never particularly frisky. When he sits, he sits like a still life. If you look hard and long at a still life, you begin to see many things. Some prove useful in life, and others fill you with the joy of discovery. Let me define what I mean by still life. Take this chair, for instance. It is still. And out there the dog, too, is still. But there's a difference between the two kinds of stillness. The chair is involuntarily still. Which means it can't move even if it wants to. No, that's not it. It can't even want to because it cannot want. Ergo, it can't move unless someone moves it.

The dog on the other hand can move, get up and run if he so wishes. Despite this, if he sits like a still life, the stillness is significant. Sitting still then is not lack of action but a form of action. It follows from a choice. A chair has no choice. It just is. How long can you stare at a chair, however skilfully made or attractively carved? How long?

But I can stare at a dog for any amount of time. The reason is that, although he has chosen to sit still at this moment, he might suddenly change his mind the very next moment. The still life has moved. I'm interested in catching that precise moment of decision and trying to guess what prompted it.

What I'm going to narrate now happened many years ago when I was unemployed. In those days I had a friend who was also unemployed. It wasn't like we'd both planned to be unemployed together. We were independently unemployed like everybody else, but at the same time. My friend was called Eknath. Some time before my unemployment ended, he disappeared. I haven't met him since. But in those days we used to come to this restaurant every day to share a cup of tea and the free newspaper. We often said to one another, 'Isn't it funny we're in the same boat but neither has an oar?' The thought wasn't originally ours, nor was the metaphor. Both came from the English phrase 'sailing in the same boat'. One day one of us, don't remember who, realized that it made an excellent description of our state. We began to use it quite freely then. It made us feel like brothers. Human beings love getting entangled in relationships. Social creatures, all of us.

So after we'd finished reading the newspaper, and after we had shrugged our shoulders at each other, we ordered a cup of tea and shared it. Some days he drank from the cup and I from the saucer. Other days, I drank from the cup and he from the saucer. Tea done, we roamed the city on foot, seeing, hearing, doing whatever came free. We returned home at night, he to his, I to mine. I had my mother at home. She cooked for people to look after me. He had... I never asked.

Gradually we discovered places where films were screened for free. We gathered that Jehangir held free exhibitions of paintings. We also realized that European and American cultural centres had something or the other going on all the time. We got to know places where you could hear music concerts for free too. By an odd coincidence, at one of these venues, a dog would come regularly with an elderly woman. The others had got used to his presence. Once it became known that the duo created no hassles, they were allowed to enter the hall freely. The old lady would nod off as soon as she found a seat. The dog would sit erect, listening to the music. If he didn't care for it, he left quietly, dug himself a shallow ditch under a tree outside, curled up and slept. I rather envied him. It often happened that I didn't like the music either. But I had to stay put. To kill time. I didn't have the option of going out and snoozing under a tree. One day we were at the French cultural centre to watch a film. We didn't understand a word of it. The dialogue was in French and the subtitles were in English. The first language was foreign to us and the second had always eluded us. A double whammy. But our purpose in being there was not to understand the film. The auditorium was air conditioned, a shelter from the blazing furnace outside.

So we entered the French bastion and slunk into two corner seats. The film had already begun. The auditorium was dark so Eknath fell asleep. I began to watch the screen with wide-open eyes. It's my misfortune that I can't sleep any old where. Not that I regret it. I never envied Eknath his ability. Moreover, I've always been ready to watch things over long periods of time with my eyes wide open. In fact, I love doing that.

So I was watching the film with concentration. The images seemed to be moving at a certain pace. I caught their rhythm. I was captivated. Then suddenly, the camera came to rest on a woman's still face. It was the lead actress. A woman who had been moving and talking all this while was now a still life. But my body still thrummed to the earlier rhythm. It wanted that rhythm back. The image on the screen remained frozen, denying me that satisfaction. But gradually, the thrumming came to a halt. I grew calm. I gazed at the face on the screen. I took in its inclines and plateaus, its lines, its moles, its eyelashes. It was as though a landscape was unfurling before me. Then suddenly there was a movement. Almost imperceptible. The merest twitch at the corner of the lips. Then the face began to fade. Other images faded in. We were back to the earlier rhythm and the story moved on. It was a long film. But even now, thirty years later, I carry that face somewhere inside me. It floats up sometimes to confront me, and it happens again. The twitch at the corner of the lips.

The moral of the story is: the longer you observe a still image or the more time you have to do so, the sharper your vision gets. Sometimes I suspect I even see things that aren't there. I've gained a lot in life by watching dogs turned to still life on this step. I have a feeling I'm going to learn a few things from the present dog too. He's grown decrepit now and his saliva flows rather copiously. But he still has a firm hold on the essence of who he is—a dog. While he lies on this step, I can tell by the particular droop of his ears, what thoughts are racing through his mind. He's trying to figure out where those sounds are coming from, of raised voices and music that we've been hearing for a while now. Once he decides what they mean, he will know what action to take. I am curious about the action, because the dog is old now.

Many years ago, I had waited as I am waiting now, to see what the dog of those times would do. I didn't know whether Eknath had found a job, or simply upped and left, or killed himself. But from being with me he was suddenly not there. After he stopped being there, I had more time to gaze at the dog. Around that time Aai had said, 'If the newspaper ads aren't helping, go meet the saheb whose contact our saheb has given you. Even a peon's job is still a job. The contact had assured our saheb that the prospects would be good for the lad if he was smart and reliable.'

Aai had a few favourite English words. Contacts and prospects were two of them. She had heard them frequently as she served dinner to the saheb and his wife. Over the years she had even grasped their meaning. She knew that they carried the power to banish permanently all worries about food, water and shelter. What stumped her was why I, despite having a contact in hand, was blowing it off. She had spoken of her bewilderment to me, mildly at first, and then with growing irritation.

To be honest, I didn't have the decisiveness it takes to blow things off and all that. Even more importantly my mind was free of silly ideas like why would I do a peon's job when I had a B.Com degree. The only problem was, I couldn't decide when to present myself at the contact's door and in what manner.

You don't need to ask such questions with newspaper ads. They make everything absolutely clear. Your application must reach them by such-and-such date. They will let you know their decision by so-and-so date. In the event that you are called for an interview... I never was, but had I been... The call letter will inform you where to go, what time to go and what documents to take along. Product ads tell you what clothes to wear for interviews and what shaving cream to use. Booklets of model answers to interview questions are available. An old suit that had once belonged to the elder son of Aai's employer lay in my trunk. I had saved a newspaper clipping that illustrated how to knot a tie. In this case, I didn't know where to get hold of the information that would tell me how and where to meet the contact, the best time to meet him, what to wear, in which words to address my request to him, what style of speech to use. Aai said, 'Get hold of an astrologer and let him tell you the most auspicious time to meet him. When the stars are right, everything falls in place.' I had no patience with Aai's thinking. Eknath was always running to astrologers. Auspicious times came and went. He remained jobless and may even be dead now. Why, Aai's elder brother himself had been told he had a windfall coming. Had it ever come?

I didn't say all this to Aai. I don't like getting into arguments. Instead I continued to go through the newspaper as usual. Then one day I decided I would meet the contact. I set the newspaper aside and was about to get up when the still dog on the step moved. That one was pitch-black except for a vertical line of white on the forehead like the mark of a Vishnu devotee. The dog had stirred from his sleep, got up on all fours, shaken himself, turned his head and looked me in the eye, then flopped back. Why was he still there, I remember wondering. This was the time when he set off with thoughtful mien and dignified steps for the overflowing garbage bin in the next lane. I had often seen him there. I had even envied him as he stood on his hind legs, sniffing at the trash and extricating precisely what he wanted. I had often muttered to myself, lucky blighter. Are you hungry? Dinner is served. Are you sleepy? The bed is ready. This was real freedom. But that day he was immobile. Perhaps the nip in the air had tempted him to curl up again and snooze. How was that going to put food in his stomach?

Just then, a man in shorts entered the restaurant. There are two categories of shorts. One kind gets washed every night and is worn the next day. The other is selected from a pile in the wardrobe. The wearers of both kinds eat pao, but the dog seemed clued in to the sociology of shorts. Before this one, two other men in shorts had come and gone, but the dog hadn't stirred. Yet when this man bought his pao and was paying, the dog sprang up and made a thin whining sound in his throat. The man turned to look at him. The dog fixed his gaze unswervingly on him. The sentiment in that gaze was clear. It said, you are my saviour, you the Almighty without whom nothing moves. Seeing those eyes and the devotional song that the rhythmically wagging tail was singing, the man's heart melted. 'Give him a pao too,' he said, and threw an extra coin on the counter. The owner threw a pao at the dog. The dog's mission was accomplished.

I rose. I made sure Aai's employer's note for the contact, which I'd been carrying around in my pocket, was intact, straightened my shirt and set off. It was evening by the time I reached the contact's home on foot. I stood outside the building waiting for his car to arrive. The idea was to draw his attention to myself as he got out of the car with a sibilant 'Saheb'. The tone had to approximate the dog's whine. Once the saheb turned to me, I was to raise my eyes, but not open my mouth till he said, 'What is it?' Or perhaps not open my mouth at all. Just rely on the look in my eyes. Words can cause unnecessary confusion. So when he said, 'What is it?' I was to simply hold out the note of introduction to him. He was likely to be tired at the end of the day and might feel irritated about having to read the note. That was the time to tell him with my eyes that he was my saviour, etc. I wasn't to feel bad about not having a tail, just compensate for the lack by bringing my hands together.

The look in my eyes and the way I shortened my height by bending slightly at the knees must have pleased the saheb. He instantly gave me his card and asked me to report to his office the next day.

Done. I had a job. Aai distributed pedhas. Using the same technique with my eyes, knees and voice, I rose from being a peon to becoming the saheb's personal assistant. When someone gave me a baksheesh, I accepted it with a smile. But I never stuck out my hand expecting one as my right. That is why every dealer who came to meet saheb heaped praise on me as a 'very honest man'. When I retired, the saheb gave me a gold watch and said, 'It's going to be difficult to get another ideal secretary like you.' He was right. I had learnt much on the job, all by myself. Nobody had taught me about the right time to keep my eyes open, and the right time to keep them closed; when to listen attentively and when to listen but pretend you hadn't heard. Besides learning all these things on my own, I also learned to see trouble coming because of colleagues' envy, and sidestep it. That's all very well; but I had to stay alive to do all this. That I did stay alive was owing to the smartness of the black dog.

Dogs usually don't challenge the challenger. They know their limits. Rarely do they bite off more than they can chew. They practise the general principle of not being where they don't need to be. This was the lesson I learned from that dog and have lived to tell the tale. I must admit though, I did hesitate for an instant; but wisdom dawned on me right away and I took to my heels. That day, we had heard similar sounds to these. They hadn't come from one direction but from all around. Groups of people kept gathering at every corner, whispering and scattering. Offices were closed. I was in my usual chair. I was observing how the dog's black coat, coloured by hoodlums last Holi, glinted in the rays of the declining sun. He was lying quietly, his head resting on his front paws; but his ears were alert. They turned in all directions to catch the sounds. His tail was very still. Not relaxed-still. Tense-still. Exactly like this dog's tail is right now. I was looking at him steadily, without blinking, without even swatting the fly that had settled on my hand.

The distant voices had come quite close now. If not for the dog, I'd have assumed they were headed somewhere else. Our neighbourhood was known to be peaceful. There were no riots in these parts even during the Independence struggle. News of stabbings and descriptions of spurting jets of blood came from other places. I was four then. I clung to Aai when I slept. My dreams were full of stabbings and spurting jets of blood. For some reason I connected my uncle, who loved scaring me, with the mayhem. I grew very afraid of him.

But even a peaceful neighbourhood like ours can occasionally explode and rivers of blood run. That's why I kept my eyes fixed on the dog. When the voices came close enough for us to make out the words, the sitting dog sprang up and ran out, zigzaging like lightning. I stood by my chair for a moment, looking at the hotel owner. The next moment, I pushed my chair aside and followed the dog. The dog sprinted left into a lane. I followed. He crossed the main road. I crossed it too. Without once looking back, the dog made for the beach. The second his feet hit the sand, he stopped, panting. Then he circled a spot twice, decided it looked good, dug a shallow ditch and went peacefully to sleep.

I admired his decisiveness. I sat there, letting the sand slip between my fingers. The feel of the sand trickling through my fingers had a soporific effect on me. When my trance broke, I realized the dog had vanished. Suddenly I felt very alone. I got up and set off for home. The restaurant was devastated. The chairs and tables had been pulled out and lay in a burning heap on the road. The restaurant owner lay next to it, his glazed eyes staring up at the sky. That's how smart that dog was.

It is for this reason that I've been watching the old dog so intently. I don't know what I can expect from him. The voices are coming closer. His ears are alert, his tail tense, but his gaze is uncertain. Confused. It is the confusion of old age. You can see there's no future for him. No prospects. When you have prospects, your gaze is focused.

Actually animals don't have prospects in the real sense of the word. That's what the play I saw the other day suggested. A dog and a tiger cub get acquainted. The dog knows the human species inside out. The tiger cub is very curious about human beings. The dog tells him a few things about them. One of the things is that human beings have prospects. The cub is as keen to see a human being as it is to figure out what its prospects are. When the dog brings the cub to a human settlement, the excited cub raises itself on its hind legs—like Man—to see whether it can spot its prospects anywhere. At the very moment that it stands up, it sees Man and its prospects both at the same time. A gunshot rings out. The expectant joy on the cub's face freezes into an expression of surprise. It slumps gently to the ground.

I am thinking of that story as I sit here watching this dog. The restaurant owner sees the doubt in my eyes. 'He can't see very well these days. Will probably die soon,' he observes.

'What are these voices?' I ask.

'Only Allah knows,' he says shrugging. 'Must be a riot somewhere.'

'The voices seem to be coming this way.'

'Could be.'

'Won't you put up the shutters?'

The restaurant owner is silent for a while. Then he says, 'This time they must be coming for the principal next door. It is college admissions time.'

The voices have now reached the end of the lane. The dog stumbles to its feet. You can see a mob approaching. Over fifty toughs, each armed with a sickle or axe. The dog stands there trembling. The moment the mob enters his field of vision, he is off. He runs helter-skelter. The mob is blind. The dog, too, is blind. He weaves in and out between their legs like a runner in a game of kho-kho. One of the men kicks him hard in the side. The dog hits the ground, yelping in agony. The crowd begins kicking him around like a ball. They kick him all the way to the principal's house. The principal has locked his door and vanished. That incenses the mob further. They slash at the dead dog with their blades and go away.

This is the difference between man and dog. The dog doesn't know what old age means. He has no idea of cause and effect. He doesn't have the capacity to figure out what consequences will follow which action. Actually, there isn't much difference between this dog's age and mine. If he is thirteen or fourteen, I am sixty. At this age you can't run like the wind. So you employ other strategies. You become absolutely still, like a lizard on the wall, pretending you're not there at all. The mob went past the hotel. Had we made the slightest move, they'd have pelted stones at us. But I sat still as a stone. Seeing me, the restaurant owner also turned to stone. There was no way anybody could have told we were there.

Anyway, in all this commotion, a skin has formed on my tea and it's gone stone cold. In the old days I'd have drunk it anyway. But now, with my retirement benefits in the bank, I can afford to order three or even four cups of tea one after the other if I choose. Just as I raise my hand to call for another cup, a tan-coloured, spindly legged but keen-eyed pup peeks into the restaurant. The present owner does what his dead father would have done. He stares at the pup. The pup hovers by the door. It sizes up the owner with one eye. With the other it, examines the steps. Then, folding its legs under itself, it settles down calmly on the second step.

The Felicitation

That was the first time Shekhar and I had gone to see Vatsalabai. Since then we've visited her so often, together or separately, that we've become familiar with every single tread-worn step of the staircase leading to her house. We were Liberal Arts students at College; Vatsalabai was a professor of Biology. So the possibility of any contact between us was remote. We had heard that she was a very good teacher. But she would either go straight to the library after her lectures, or go home. Her contact with students was confined to the lecture hall.

We had also heard that when she first returned from overseas with her doctorate, she had been far more informal, sipping tea in the canteen with the students, laughing, debating animatedly, making jokes. That was in the late 1960s and early 1970s. The legends of that period were still circulating in college. But it did not seem even remotely possible that the Vatsalabai we knew could ever have been or done anything like that.

People say that it was after the Emergency that she underwent a sudden, complete and absolute change. One of her closest friends was arrested during the Emergency. He was brutally tortured. His fingers were broken, his body hair ripped out. Every form of fiendish savagery that men who taste power can devise to torment their fellow men was tried out on him.

When he emerged from prison, he was no longer the same. His fingers were twisted, the hair on his head had gone white, his chest

---

This story first appeared in Marathi as 'Satkar'. It has been translated from the Marathi by Ranjit Hoskote.

was a hollow case. Vatsalabai took him into her home. She lavished her love on him. But he had already been marked by death. He was, in effect, dead. All that remained was for his breath to actually stop. One day, that too came to pass and Vatsalabai snapped her ties with the world.

No one can say for certain who had relayed this story by word of mouth for twenty years, until it reached our generation. No sooner are such stories set in motion, than they begin to circulate freely on campus. They float in the air, they sway with the grass. You stumble across them at every step. Their connection with reality has long ago been severed. They have become realities in their own right.

Vatsalabai's story doesn't end there. After her friend's death, she dressed only in white saris for a while. The stiff, starched whiteness of those saris matched her emotion-drained face. Some people say that she looked, in those days, like an archetypal Mother Goddess who had drunk all the poison in the world and survived.

Then she took to sitting and writing in the library. Like one possessed, she would cover page after page with writing every day. Gradually, her face regained its former appearance. Its severity disappeared and it grew serene. Her favourite colours began to show up in her clothes again. She threw herself into her teaching with a new enthusiasm. Her love for her subject shone once again on her face; her eyes, however, seemed to be conducting a silent dialogue with someone beyond the students. People wondered whether she could see her students at all, so completely did her line of sight bypass them.

When Shekhar and I joined the college, Vatsalabai had only a year to go before retirement. To us, Vatsalabai was a dark-complexioned, somewhat wrinkled, neat, beautiful little idol dressed in a sari. She always wore a smile, not false but not wholly convincing either. She was a mystery to us.

In the last year of her tenure, a collection of her short stories was published under the title *Grains of Sand*. Because we were so curious about her as a personality, we swooped down on the book, read the stories—and were struck dumb with amazement. Just as some important insight into life was being offered to us in these stories, it seemed to slip out of our grasp; or so we felt, and this plunged us into a state of unease. We sensed that, like her smile, Vatsalabai's stories too were poised at a frontier of some kind.

Last year, *Grains of Sand* won a State award. An occasion had presented itself at last, we felt, when we could deluge her with all the questions we wanted to ask about her literary universe, about those stories which were so fantastic and yet seemed more real than the reality. We went to Principal Rao and placed before him our proposal that the college host an official felicitation for Vatsalabai.

Principal Rao said, 'Okay, let's give her an official felicitation.'

Vice-Principal Sane asked, 'But who on earth has read her stories?'

'We have,' we replied.

Then Mrs Kripalani said, 'Why would non-Marathi students attend the felicitation? Hold it as a Marathi Association event. That should take care of it.'

'Her work is of considerable stature,' we said. 'The scale of the felicitation should be in keeping with that. We can always request Vatsalabai to deliver her address in English.'

In due course, a felicitation committee was set up. At its first meeting, Professor Hazare, head of the Marathi department, said, 'There's a distinct non-Marathi quality to Vatsalabai's stories. They don't seem rooted in our soil. Besides which, they're quite incomprehensible. Too difficult for the average person to understand.'

Shekhar spoke up, 'I don't know if a college student qualifies as an average person. But we certainly understood her stories. They're not the slightest bit difficult. They're just strikingly original, that's all.'

Professor Jahagirdar of the Economics department, who otherwise never spoke, said, 'We must organize a felicitation for Vatsalabai. That is our duty towards culture.'

'It's only natural that you should feel that way,' retorted Professor Patil of the Statistics department. 'She's from Nagpur, isn't she?

You've travelled the world, seminaring here, there and everywhere, but your sentiments are still bound up with Nagpur.'

Principal Rao rebutted this remark: 'It isn't right to be parochial in all matters.' Professor Patil came right back: 'But there should be no objection to being pragmatic in all matters, surely.' Sliding forward in his chair, he continued, 'Why exactly do we wish to felicitate this lady? To express the respect, the admiration we feel for her. On such an occasion, shouldn't there be a respectable number of people who would want to turn up to hear her speak?'

Once he had raised this point, the general secretary of the students' union, Upendra Sharma, chimed in: 'Professor Patil is right. Students won't be interested in attending such a function.'

'Then let's organize a public felicitation for her,' I said. 'That way at least her admirers beyond the walls of this college will get a chance to hear her speak.'

'Where are these admirers of hers?' asked Professor Hazare, making a face. 'The lady's such a recluse, such an island unto herself that people in our literary circles begin by asking who she is in the first place!'

'Well, what's your decision then?' asked Principal Rao. 'Should we abandon the idea of felicitating her?'

At this, three or four voices spoke together. While it wasn't possible to ascertain who precisely was saying what, the substance of what they were saying added up to: 'Certainly not. What an idea! Of course we must host the felicitation. No question about that. How can we not?'

For a long while after that, no one said anything at all.

Finally, Principal Rao broke the silence. 'Right, so we go ahead. But we have to decide what form it will take. We have to ensure that students attend it in large numbers. Otherwise, it will seem as if we've used the pretext of honouring Vatsalabai to slap her in the face.'

'Frankly, we don't think there's any need for a jam-packed hall,' observed Shekhar slowly. 'All the students of the Marathi department will be there. Then there will be a few students like us. There are five or six Science students who are interested in Literature—they'll come. That should be more than enough.'

Professor Hazare pulled a long face. 'We get the dregs, you know, the dregs. What possible interest can they have in the kind of stories Vatsalabai writes? I'm certainly not prepared to offer a guarantee that all the students of our department will turn up. The girls will be there, but you'll have to persuade the others.'

Silence spread again over the gradually darkening room. The onset of darkness infused every individual's silence with a momentary sense of release from his or her public responsibility. Many believe that their first public responsibility, while discussing literature, is to put on a solemn face; the darkness gave all the tensed muscles in the room a chance to relax at last. In that wilting atmosphere, Sharma's voice rang out loud and clear: 'What is our problem, really?' His tone bespoke the confidence of one who has taken the proceedings firmly in hand. 'A group of people A wishes to host a felicitation for a lady B at a venue C. For this programme to go off successfully, we need a sizeable number of students in the audience. Now the trouble with the lady B is that her public image is zero. For which reason, she doesn't have the capacity to draw a crowd. But if the chief guest, the person invited to honour her, is a crowd-puller, our problem would be solved at once. My suggestion is that we invite Rajeev Vijapure to be the chief guest.'

Principal Rao's peon turned on the light at that moment, and by its illumination, the faces of all the professors in the room seemed to be glowing. Professor Patil raised his hand three times in manifest enthusiasm: 'That's a good idea.' Encouraged by the approving nods around the table, he went on, 'After all, Rajeev Vijapure is also a credit to our college.' At this, Professor Hazare asked timidly, 'But didn't the college ask him to leave during his second year?'

'Rumour. Mere rumour,' scoffed Professor Sane. 'The truth is something else altogether. By his second year, he began to receive so many offers that it became impossible for him to attend college regularly.'

'Well, that's all right then,' said Professor Hazare, heaving a sigh of relief.

'And even if there was some controversy, all that was ten years ago,' said Professor Patil. 'The lad has done Maharashtra proud since.'

'Is that right?' asked Professor Jahagirdar, surprise writ large on his face. 'What does this boy do? What sort of offers are you talking about?'

Principal Rao scratched his chin and threw a piercing look in his direction: 'Jahagirdar, do you ever lift your head from your books and look at the world around you? The next time you do so, you'll see the face of this "boy" on five out of every ten Hindi movie posters.'

I cleared my throat. 'This is not acceptable to us.'

Shekhar backed me. 'Are the sort of people who will land up to see Rajeev likely to be interested in Vatsalabai's speech?'

Principal Rao kept his eyes steadfastly on his fingernails. 'We'll have to put this to vote,' he said. 'Raise your hands, all those opposed to the idea of inviting Rajeev Vijapure to be chief guest at Vatsalabai's felicitation.'

Three hands went up: Shekhar's, Professor Jahagirdar's and mine. The other professors simply bent their heads and looked down. Sharma, on the contrary, threw back his head and imitated a rooster crowing at daybreak. This crowing was the rage just then, having been popularized by Rajeev Vijapure in his latest film. The gist of the song that opened with it, plainly put, was: *Hey babe, if the sun himself wakes up to my crowing, who says you won't?*

I spoke up. 'Why don't we simply cancel the felicitation instead?'

'No, no, no,' everyone shouted. 'The felicitation must go ahead.'

Baleful glances were directed at us.

'Why are you so bitterly opposed to Rajeev?' roared Professor Sane. 'Rajeev Vijapure may not have excelled at studies. But do you think it's an ordinary feat to succeed in the world outside, as he has done?'

'And in the world of Hindi movies, at that! He's raised the banner of Maharashtra aloft in Hindi movies, no less—not in our third-rate

Marathi films,' said Professor Patil. 'This Ganesh Chaturthi, all of Maharashtra danced to his beat.'

At this, for no particular reason, everybody burst out laughing, which produced the illusion that all the questions surrounding the felicitation had been resolved; and the conversation turned to matters of organization and protocol: who would take the invitation to Rajeev Vijapure, who would escort him to the venue, who would invite Vatsalabai, fetch her? How to inaugurate the function? How many bouquets to get? Whose responsibility was the traditional gift of honour, the shawl and coconut, and last and most important, what snacks were to be served? This last point provoked a lively debate. Professor Jahagirdar suggested a simple menu of idli-chutney and coffee.

Professor Sane said, 'Why is it that sabudana khichri and piyush are never suggested? Why do we always look to the south for inspiration when it comes to snacks?'

'Well, look north then. Let's have samosas,' returned Professor Patil, who was famous in college for his witty observations. When he spoke, people burst spontaneously into laughter. They did so on this occasion too. After the laughter had subsided, some suggested patties, others suggested batata-wadas. Finally, the batata-wadas won out.

'And green-chilly chutney to go with them!' said Professor Patil, licking his lips in anticipation.

Since the plan seemed solidly in place, everybody got up to leave. Then Principal Rao asked, 'Sharma will go to fetch Rajeev, but what about Vatsalabai?'

'We'll fetch her,' said Shekhar and I together. Shekhar muttered, 'But we find the whole idea of Rajeev Vijapure felicitating Vatsalabai unacceptable.'

Principal Rao only raised his eyebrows and looked at us through his thick glasses. But Professor Sane exploded: 'You find it unacceptable? Just who do you think you are?'

Professor Hazare, who was speaking after having maintained a long silence, intervened soothingly, 'They're young, Mr Sane. They're idealists. As they should be, at their age.'

Cooling down somewhat, Professor Sane said, 'But to reject the views of the majority is simply...'

Unable to find a word strong enough to convey his feelings, he settled instead for blowing his nose loudly into his handkerchief.

~

That was how the first opportunity to go to Vatsalabai's house came our way. Our faces soured, our heads bent, we walked up the worn stairs of that chawl-like building to invite her to the felicitation. Climbing alongside us, on the left-hand-side wall, were thick, black heavy-duty electric cables. In the long common balcony of every floor, there were children playing bat-ball or killing one another with toy guns. Girls were playing hopscotch and last-letter-new-word. Every door on the way to the last single-room apartment on the third floor stood wide open. And in every room, a TV set shone in its place of honour. And from every TV, a variety of noises, including snatches of English and Hindi dialogue, canned laughter and shrieking, assailed the ear.

The door to Vatsalabai's house was shut, though. I knocked at it. From within, a voice said, 'Do come in, the door's open.' On hearing this voice, we cracked up in a fit of laughter. Given our image of Vatsalabai, we had expected her voice to be deep but melodious. The voice we had just heard was like something a clown might affect to amuse his audience. I barely managed to get my laughter under control and was about to knock again, when we heard the sound of a bolt being drawn back, the door opened, and in a deep, melodious voice, Vatsalabai asked us, 'Who are you looking for?'

From behind her, the earlier voice spoke again. 'Do come in, the door's open.' And a parrot flew out to welcome us, and perched on Vatsalabai's shoulder.

'Don't you put him in a cage?' I asked.

'No,' said Vatsalabai.

'Won't he fly away?'

'He's free to, if he wishes.'

'Hasn't he ever flown away?'

'Not yet, he hasn't.'

'Do come in, the door's open.' The parrot extended his invitation again, and we stepped laughing into the house.

Vatsalabai's room was furnished in an austere but tasteful manner. There was a harmony among the objects. The walls were a light ash-grey. The curtains, tablecloth and other furnishings were red. Everywhere, there were hints of earth colours, red and moss-green. One wall was covered from floor to ceiling with wide, open bookshelves. On them stood neat rows of books, systematically arranged, each book bound in an identical-looking cover. The books stood in a pattern, classified according to the colours of their covers. Those colours, too, were ash-grey, red, moss-green, black.

'I can't see very well without my glasses,' explained Vatsalabai, divining the question implicit in the manner in which we were looking at the books. 'I can't read the letters, but I can make out colours easily. That's why I've bound all the books on a particular subject in covers of the same colour. And on the spine of each book, I've written the author's initials in large, bold letters. That's how I am able to stand here and read the letters on the spine of every book, even if it's on the topmost shelf.' Placing tumblers of cold water before us, she continued, 'And when they're your own books, you can identify them just by their shape. All you have to do is climb on the stool and take them down, your hands go unfailingly to the ones you want. What are your names?'

'This is Shekhar. I'm Neelima.'

'Did you want to see me about something in particular?'

'Yes,' said Shekhar. 'We heard that you don't have a phone. That's why we've descended on you like this, without notice. Otherwise we would have requested you formally for an appointment.'

'A phone,' she muttered. 'It'll arrive someday, I imagine. I applied for one, years ago. Sometimes I ask myself, do I really need a phone?'

While Vatsalabai was speaking, I had been concentrating on the kitchen—which lay beyond where she sat—trying to listen for the sounds of another presence in the house. Once again, she divined the motive behind my actions. She said, 'I live alone.'

None of us felt like stirring to break the silence that followed. Each of us hoped that someone else would break it, sooner or later. But no one seemed about to speak—not Shekhar, not Vatsalabai, not the parrot or anyone. Overwhelmed by our emotions, we were reluctant to raise the matter of the felicitation, but it had to be done. And then the parrot said, 'Do come in, the door's open.'

We laughed. 'Is that the only line he knows?' asked Shekhar.

'Oh no!' replied Vatsalabai. 'Sometimes he embarrasses me. If he doesn't like a visitor, he starts saying "Ta-ta" every five minutes. But he is shrewd in his judgement of people, I must admit. Well, what was it you wanted?'

'We want to host a felicitation for you at the College. To celebrate the award that your collection of short stories has won,' I said.

'So you're students of the College, are you? Oh no, let's not have a felicitation or anything like that.' In one sense, I felt relieved at her reaction.

'Was this the reaction you expected?' she laughed.

I fumbled for a reply. 'Yes, no, the fact of the matter is…' I began to mutter, when she cut through with a direct question. 'Well, tell me why.'

I took a deep breath and launched into the story of how the idea of the felicitation had come to us and what the felicitation committee had done with it.

Vatsalabai said nothing at all. She leaned back in her chair and sat looking out of the window. So distant did she seem from our conversation that we began to wonder if she had become occupied with some other thoughts altogether. Then, suddenly, she said, 'I think I ought to accept your invitation. I've virtually lost all contact with the world since I retired. That simply won't do. Right, tell me when and where it is, and what it's going to be like.'

~

The day of the felicitation dawned, and the butterflies fluttering in our stomachs began to receive support from every other part of our bodies. I lost my appetite and Shekhar's insides were in such a churn that every now and again, he would break into a sweat. We had decided to go and fetch Vatsalabai at four in the afternoon, and Sharma would go at roughly the same time to fetch Rajeev from the studios. Since Rajeev was in a hurry to get back, it had been decided that the felicitation part of the programme would take place first, and Vatsalabai's speech would come afterwards.

When we reached Vatsalabai's home, we found her ready and waiting for us. She was dressed in a dove-grey sari with a crimson temple-border. As was her custom, she wore no ornaments on her hands or in her ears. Just the spectacles on her nose, the watch on her wrist.

'I'm nervous,' she said calmly. 'It's true that one shouldn't break away from the world. But solitude seems so congenial these days. It's terrifying to see the emotions on people's faces.' Then, smiling mischievously, she said, 'That's why I've got these spectacles on. I'm going to read out my speech, so my text is all I need to be able to see. I haven't taken my glasses for distance.'

In the taxi, Vatsalabai said, 'What I said about the glasses is literally true, mind you. The road ahead looks like an abstract painting to me. It'll be your task to lead me to the stage and seat me in my chair.'

We had tea in Principal Rao's office. Professor Patil said to Vatsalabai, 'You've grown even thinner than you used to be.'

Professor Sane said, 'But you look fresh nonetheless. Retirement suits you, doesn't it?'

Mrs Wagh of the Marathi department said, 'What a stunning sari! But your saris are always like that, of course.'

Professor Jahagirdar said, 'I've been trying to get inside your stories.'

'You've been reading them?' Vatsalabai asked.

Professor Jahagirdar replied, 'Some of them. I enjoyed the story about the trade in human organs, it was wonderful. Once I've read them all, I'll give you my critical appraisal.'

Professors Sane, Patil, Hazare and all the other professors assembled there were tucking into their batata-wadas. Their sniffling noses indicated the pleasure with which they were tackling the spicy green-chilly chutney. The programme was due to start at five, but even at six o'clock, there was no sign of Rajeev Vijapure. Finally, it was decided that we would all move slowly in the direction of the hall. When Professor Patil, who was in the lead, stepped onto the stage from the side-door, the hordes gathered in the hall crowed in one voice and burst into song: 'The rooster said the sun has come up, the hen will come out too, *kukucch-ku*!'

Professor Patil raised his hand for order and signalled, through his expression, that he was about to say something witty. 'Possess your souls in patience,' he said. 'The rooster has yet to arrive. We are only the chickens.' The hall resounded with laughter, thunderous clapping and whistling. In the midst of this uproar, Shekhar escorted Vatsalabai on to the stage and helped her into her chair. I sat on one side of her and Shekhar sat on the other.

Vatsalabai said, 'One can pretend to be blind by wearing the wrong pair of spectacles. But what's to be done with the ears? How many students have gathered here?'

'The hall's packed,' I said.

'And how many of them, do you think, have read my stories?'

Crestfallen, I said not a word. But Shekhar said, 'Your admirers are sitting in the front row.'

'How many are they? Describe them to me,' said Vatsalabai.

'Kedar Ranadive: curly hair, blue shirt, glasses, slightly protruding teeth. Prajna Nalavade: green salwar-kameez, bobbed hair, long earrings. Pheroze Keravala: very fair, long hair tied in a ponytail, a gold earring in his right ear, black T-shirt, jeans.'

'Keravala? A Parsi?'

'That's right. But he's from Solapur. Speaks excellent Marathi. And with a perfect Solapur accent too.'

'That's splendid, then. Three readers in front of me and you two on either side. It's the five of you I'll address.'

While we were talking, the professors on the stage had begun to get restless. Rajeev had still not turned up, and the uproar in the hall was rising in a crescendo.

Principal Rao said, 'We ought to get started.'

Professor Sane said, 'Let's get Vatsalabai's speech over and done with. Rajeev will surely arrive by then.'

Principal Rao said, 'No. That will not be proper.'

An idea occurred to Professor Patil. 'Sir,' he said to the Principal, 'do you recall the boy who staged a mimicry performance for the College Day celebrations? Shall I ask him to come up and entertain the kids? While he keeps them busy, I'll go and telephone Rajeev. I have his mobile number.' Patil's face glowed with the pride of intimate acquaintance with so trendy an instrument as the mobile phone. Rao nodded and Professor Patil rose to his feet. The bedlam in the hall subsided somewhat. Professor Patil raised his hand. 'Silence please,' he shouted. The bedlam subsided further. Then Professor Patil began to speak: 'I fully understand how eager you are to see Rajeev Vijapure. But what we are experiencing today is the tremendous effort that goes into his achievement of such popularity. An hour ago, Rajeev called us from the studios on his mobile, saying that he might be slightly delayed getting here, and he's apologized to you in advance.'

Clapping, whistling, hooting, catcalls.

'Rajeev should be here any moment. But as an appetizer to prepare us for our encounter with the real Rajeev, why don't we have an imitation Rajeev? Samir Sharangpani, alias Rajeev Junior!' Professor Patil raised his voice and shouted in his best emcee manner.

Thunderous applause. A chorus of whistles. Patting his mane

into place, Samir took the stage in a single leap. Without pausing for breath, he snapped his fingers and began to dance to the tune of '*Kukucch-ku*!' The hall responded by clapping in time with the beat. Some people clambered up on the tables and began to dance on them.

The number had entered its last stanza when, as though cued by some director's call of 'Action!', Rajeev Vijapure suddenly appeared on the stage and began to dance along with Samir. The audience went crazy. Hardly had the dance ended than the request went up: 'Dialogue! Dialogue!' Without batting an eyelid, Rajeev took off: 'Son of a bitch, I will drink every drop of blood in your body. Until then I will neither eat nor sleep. Scoundrels like you have plunged my beloved motherland into filth. If young men like me don't rescue her, we should call ourselves insects, not men.'

In the midst of the thunderous applause that met these lines, Rajeev's formal presentation of the traditional shawl and coconut to Vatsalabai took place. Since Vatsalabai couldn't see a thing, Shekhar and I supported her from both sides and helped her to her feet. Rajeev gave her the shawl and coconut and touched her feet with great reverence. Then, having touched the feet of all the professors on the stage, he stood before the mike. In a voice choked with emotion, he began to speak, using the Hindi of moviedom. 'The day I was thrown out of this college—that's right, I was thrown out of this college—that very day I swore an oath that one day I would return, having achieved something in life. And when I was invited to be present on this auspicious occasion, I thought perhaps that moment has come, that I've reached the pinnacle I wanted to reach. Having said this, I will take my leave of you. Jai Hind! Jai Maharashtra!'

Rajeev included everyone in a comprehensive namaskar and then, tossing his locks, he quit the dais and was gone. Seeing their hero vanish from before their eyes so soon and so unexpectedly, the students raised a pandemonium all over again. Those who had been waiting to ask for Rajeev's autograph at the end of the programme now began to pour out of the hall through both its exits. When both doors had been substantially jammed by the stampede, a tide of students surged on to the stage and poured out through the wings. Some of the people on the dais were swept away by that tide; some swam and made it ashore, while others drowned. Shekhar and Vatsalabai were among those who drowned. First, Vatsalabai was thrown down from her chair. When Shekhar stepped forward to help her, he too was thrown to the ground. I saw all this from where I was, clinging tightly to the bars of a window on one side of the stage.

Gradually, the tide ebbed. The hall grew peaceful. I left the window and ran to Vatsalabai. My eyes were streaming with tears. Shekhar was trembling all over. That's when Professor Jahagirdar's voice came from somewhere, 'Vatsalabai's all right, isn't she? Was she hurt?' He came limping through the side-door on to the stage. He asked again, 'Where's Vatsalabai?' To his quavering question, there came a ringing reply, 'I'm right here. And I'm doing fine, thank you. I'm just slightly bruised.'

Jahagirdar was followed by Ranadive, Keravala and Prajna. Prajna's kameez was completely torn down one side. Ranadive brought some water for Vatsalabai and Professor Jahagirdar. Prajna set right the overturned flower-vase on the table and Keravala stood the toppled chairs on their feet again.

Professor Jahagirdar began to apologize for the contretemps that had taken place. Vatsalabai said, 'Don't feel badly about it. I'm perfectly fine. Only, I've lost my glasses; could someone look for them?' Keravala found the glasses in a corner of the dais, broken. 'That's all right,' muttered Vatsalabai, putting them away in her handbag. She took out another pair of glasses and put them on. Surveying the expanse of the empty hall, she said, 'Now there's no harm in looking out across the distance. How nice it feels! Peaceful. Now then, shall we sit down and have a proper chat?'

Game!

At the stroke of five thirty, Dighe presents himself at the Tarnaka Sports Club in shorts and a loose sports shirt, both Tinopal-white. His body is that of a young man although he is within spitting distance of forty-five. Because he knows this, he puffs out his chest as he walks. It is with a particular pride that he strokes his flat stomach in circular motions with his left hand. It is with a particular style that he whirls his badminton racket through the air with the other hand. Mrs Dighe, clumping along beside him, diminishes him somewhat. And so he does not say a word to her as he walks, and in order to prevent her from saying a word to him, he keeps up a tuneless whistling.

Dighe steps onto the court and takes a deep breath. The air is warm and close but it fills him with energy. Meanwhile, Mrs Dighe sighs her relief as she deposits her ample posterior into the nearest armchair and then uses the end of her sari to wipe the sweat first from her face and then from the folds of her belly.

'No one here yet. Good. Now if only Kumar manages to get here on time, I'll get a singles match. Bloody doubles means you get no exercise. Just some meaningless running about.'

'Aaho, no singles and all, aahn? You might hurt your knee. Not to mention body pain.'

Dighe falls to whistling. What is she on about? Why must she always say something like that? Thirty years I've played baddie; that must count for something. And as for my knee, does the word footwork mean nothing to her?

This story first appeared in Marathi in *Abhiruchi*. The date of publication is unknown.

'Hey Kumar, forty winks or what?'

'Who has time for naps, Kaka? Afternoon show, so I got late.'

'Bunking college, rascal?'

'What, Kaka? Don't you read the papers? Colleges are still on strike.'

'What to read in the papers? It's like asking for a daily headache. Come, gird up your loins and face your fate.'

'Them's fighting words, Kaka. Is that a challenge?'

'Hey Kumar, no challenge-schmallenge, aahn? He thinks he's a young buck, this one. There he has a daughter of marriageable age and instead of finding a suitable boy, he's here chasing shuttlecocks.'

Dighe begins his tuneless whistling. Why must I endure this, day after day? When she comes, I lose all my games. Why can't she just go and sit with her Leelatai until I'm done? But no, she has to stick her oar in every time.

'Aaho, Kaku, he may not be young but he's still a player to beat.'

A roseate happiness spreads through Dighe at these words. It inspires him to lob the shuttlecock at Kumar, albeit in friendly fashion. For a while, they just trade shots, warming up. Dighe doesn't push himself, doesn't run around much. While he would never admit this to Mrs Dighe, his bloody stamina isn't what it used to be. He has to save himself for the match.

'Come on, come on. Let's start. Ready, Kumar?'

'Oh yes, any time.'

And then she arrives: the New Member. She's just started showing up. A slender body but she plays a mean game of badminton. And she's nice to look at. No, not just nice. *Rather* nice. She doesn't say much. At least not with her mouth. But her eyes? Her eyes are different. Her eyes are eloquent. Dighe's left hand strokes his stomach, still reassuringly flat, and then goes to his head to check that his hair is in the shape it should be.

'Come on Kumar, stop drooling.'

Kumar flushes and in his confusion hits the net and loses the first point.

Dighe has some tried-and-tested shots. He has worked on them for nearly thirty years. He can direct the shuttlecock as surely as a coachman directs his horses through a touch on the reins. Today he is in full form. Sometimes the shuttlecock whistles past Kumar's ear; sometimes it kisses the net and sways there, like a wounded bird, before toppling gracefully into Kumar's side of the court. Kumar scuttles and flutters after it. Dighe is in the zone; he wins point after point and after each one, he sneaks a glance at her out of the extreme corner of his eye, and then he smiles—a Very Special Old Pale smile. His smile says: 'He's a young man. Give him time. How long can a mouse last against a lion?'

But then he discovers that she in turn is watching Kumar out of the extreme corner of one eye. This makes Dighe hustle to return Kumar's shots. He begins to run and swerve. He dives. And as he leaps, his hair, his carefully arranged hair, ruffles up and begins to look like a book fallen open, its soft white pages turned by the breeze. But Dighe has no mindspace for his hair. As his points accumulate, he loses restraint, loses himself in the game. Often The New Member says in her sweet voice, 'Good shot' or 'Bad luck'. Dighe is flooded with happiness to note that she can tell a good game when she sees it. When I hit that sweet drop shot, she exclaimed, 'Too good' with exactly the right amount of excitement. And she was right. These young men think a good game is about beating the shit out of a shuttlecock, as a dhobi beats the dirt out of the clothes. Their only weapons are their youth and strength. But can you hang your brains on a nearby tree, like the monkey in the fable, and hope to win?

Dighe tots up thirteen points. Two more to win. Kumar the Buffoon is at eight. He keeps looking at her and trying to strike macho poses. First, get your game right, laddie. Then see how the ladies line up.

But now Dighe is tiring. To cover this up, he whistles as he throws the shuttlecock into the air and then hits it before he's even drawn breath. But who knows why, he misses his shots now. Returning one of Kumar's better-placed shots, his feet get entangled with each other. He feels a muscle cramp in his chest and his knee reminds him of its existence. He sits down, pretending to spot a lace that has come undone. He undoes a lace and ties it up again and he puffs like a bellow as he tries to catch his breath. When he gets up again, he intercepts a secret smile passing between Kumar and The New Member. When they see he is back on his feet, both wipe the smiles off their faces but Dighe has seen those smiles, he has decoded them and he is now in a fine rage. These kids think I'm done? Go, go. I'll beat fifty-six Kumars before I tire.

Kumar is now playing a gentlemanly game. He returns Dighe's shots with care and he keeps an eye on him as he plays. And The New Member says, 'Well returned.'

Nevertheless, the game slips out of Dighe's hands. He runs now, runs without thinking. My racket must connect with that… How can it not? And yet it does not. Kumar wins point after point; now it's thirteen-all and soon he's taken the lead and is steaming ahead. Fourteen, fifteen, sixteen, seventeen…all to Kumar.

'Fight, come on, fight,' she says and that sweet voice gives Dighe the courage to try and wrest the game back. He tries his sweet shot and for a moment, the shuttlecock balances on the net, a ballet dancer en pointe. Kumar won't be able to return that one…and then it slumps into Dighe's court.

Game! Dighe leaves the court. As always, he holds himself erect because he is afraid that he is going to collapse. He gathers the vestiges of his energy to paste a sporting smile on his face, now pasty and pale. 'Well played,' he says to Kumar and with the same false confidence, he pats his ruffled hair back into place. And he drops into the chair next to Mrs Dighe.

Dighe tries to keep his lips together but his breath huffs and puffs as it forces its way out. A huge bell seems to be tolling in his chest: gann, gann. Each note hits his ears and slices a path through his neck and into his brain.

And into this tolling another sound, the thunder of a train entering a tunnel.

'He brought his death on himself…' and 'Well, a Venus-fly trap will always get you' and 'False pride, what can you do?'…thud, thud, thud. Ask not for whom the bell tolls, the belle took her toll on thee. The train thunders on, bogey after bogey, and the darkness in the tunnel swallows them again and again, again, again, gann, gann.

Dighe walks beside Mrs Dighe in silence. His shoulders are slumped, his head is down. His racket hangs from his fingers, a branch snapped off a tree by a careless storm. That deep belling note has ceased but Mrs Dighe's train is still on track. Any moment now…

And so Dighe tries his tuneless whistle again, but somehow, like a shuttlecock caught in a net, the notes get stuck somewhere between his teeth.

Shakespeare Take Two

'Rhythms of the Bard'

I Am Not What I Am

[*The green room after a show of* Othello]

Othello/Harry: In this vast and empty space, unmarked by ought that breathes; on this dull plain where sun nor moon shed light; nor yet do night's dark shades reside. In this barren, unrewarding domain, where no tree grows, no bud raises its head, I freeze and grow unutterably small. But you Iago, you swagger still as you did when our feet did rest on the comforting warmth of wood, curtained by velvet on either side.

Desdemona/Celia: [*Laughing*] Come down to earth, my love. Here there is none to sigh and applaud. Here there are only mirrored surfaces, throwing back at us our truest visages. Here are globes of unnatural light that guide our eager hands each night, as we paint our transformations… From Harry to Othello, Celia to Desdemona, Dick to Iago.

Othello/Harry: Would that I were still the Moor, that most excellent and noble warrior, so piteously betrayed by one who, seeming white, didst have a blackguard's heart bent on destroying two innocent lives.

Iago/Dick: He speaks still in the rhythms of the Bard, with hollow words that ring as false as a bell from chain to rim wide cracked. If you must hold fast to your robes, oh not so noble, not so valiant, Othello; return you to the stage where I, divested of my coat of mail, shall play Iago as he was meant to be.

[*He sheds his costume and stands in his vest and long underpants. As the play proceeds, he and the others change into their street clothes.*]

DESDEMONA: Oh for shame thou unseemly man, thou dost forget my presence here.

OTHELLO: Besides which in that empty hall, no audience sits to cheer us on...

IAGO: ...or yawn and boo as happens oft. Me? I need no audience as you do, for your sonorous speeches, your grand and empty gestures. I am and will be, audience enough for me. The man with the quill erred grievously, failed both by nerve and philosophy, when he cast me in human mould. A happy harpy I should I have been, one of Macbeth's three in habit and kind; neither man nor woman nor creature winged or pawed, but a force from beyond the pale; returning, when done, to its inchoate space. [*Long pause*] And now, having shed my garments here, I would shed these archaic rhythms too, so we can be, just she, me and you. [*Pause. Deep sigh of relief.*] Phew! That feels good. The time has come old fellow, when I must say, straight from the shoulder: the Bard got it all wrong.

DESDEMONA: Now that's rich. All wrong? How?

IAGO: In making me human. A human being is supposedly fashioned by that grand idea called God. The Bard would not have permitted himself to grant even distantly, that this divine entity, this paragon, could have created anything so totally unworthy of the word human as I am. Even a villain has a saving grace or two. But me? Not one. Did I love my wife? Most certainly not. Did I have a friend I was loyal to, for more than one-sixtieth of a moment? Nope. Was I brave? Not even in bed as Emily would have happily granted. Indeed, I held bravery a most foolish thing. So what was the Bard to do with me? It must have struck him as he scratched his glossy pate that even a villain who has not a single saving grace, still has a few reasons to hate. So he gave me a couple of psychological props. It seems to have mattered little to him whether they stood or fell at the merest blow of a passing breath. He had done the best he could. In any case, all said and done, Iago was not the hero of the tale. And so I announced myself jealous of Othello; pretended rage at Cassio's preferment and showed how deeply I did hate the darkness of Othello's skin.

OTHELLO: [*Sneering*] Your archaic rhythms are creeping back my friend. You are unfair is all I can say. I do not think you ever spoke word or phrase that declared such a despicable hate.

IAGO: Think you not? Then think again. What make you of these words then that Iago throws in Brabantio's face? 'Even now, now, very now, an old black ram is tupping your white ewe.' Black? White? Be they needless colours that mean nothing but the sound they make?

OTHELLO: True. Too true. You hated my skin, hated that in my blackness I should win a white woman, lead an army of all-white men, where you were but a bearer of the flag.

IAGO: Pah! Psychological props that only got in the way.

DESDEMONA: In the way of what, Iago? They explained much of what you did.

IAGO: Why then have critics spilt all that ink holding them futile, flawed and flimsy? The truth of the matter is, fair lady, it is you that I wished to destroy, for no other reason than that you were you and I was I. Othello was only my means. What was he anyway, without his sword and armour, and his never-ending bombast?

OTHELLO: Do not say bombast, Iago. Poetry.

IAGO: Have it your way. Bombastic poetry. 'Like to the Pontic sea / Whose icy current and compulsive course / Ne'er feels retiring ebb, but keeps due on / To the Propontic and the Hellespont…'

Knew his geography well, did the Bard. But, like you, he failed at the sticking point; failed to nail the truth that stared him in the face. You were Macbeth, I a harpy, turning you whichever way I liked. But she? Desdemona? She needed neither sword nor armour nor words nor God to be good. Just plain and simple good. There was no joy in destroying you. You were only incidental to my grand plan. The purity of her goodness, her truth, her love were the affront to the Evil that was me. She had to be destroyed. And it was good it was done. Or else, as I did predict to Brabantio, you would have littered the world with a race of middlings, neither white and good like her nor black and stupid like you, but merely grey and mediocre and downright dull.

OTHELLO: You are a racist, I see it now. You say black with such vicious force.

DESDEMONA: You said that to my father? You said so in those very words?

IAGO: A little differently. You were not present there when I made the merry prediction. You were...how do I put it delicately...busy seeking the pleasures of the body. No, I did not use those words. What I did say when Brabantio, woken from his sleep, came down in his gown frothing at the mouth, disbelieving the news we bore, was, 'Zounds Sir...'

DESDEMONA: You swore?

IAGO: I confess I did, it being a habit of the tongue.

DESDEMONA: It could not have put you in Father's good graces.

IAGO: I was not there to seek those graces. I had a graver purpose in hand. I said, 'Zounds Sir, you are one of those that will not believe in God if the devil bid you. Because we come to do you service and you think we are ruffians, you'll have your daughter covered with a Barbary horse; you'll have your nephews neigh to you; you'll have coursers for cousins and jennets for germans.'

OTHELLO: I would have sliced your tongue for that, had I but been present there.

IAGO: I would have kept my tongue tied up had you been there. Think me a fool that would prattle on with no concern for who was there and what he might feel impelled to do?

OTHELLO: So your wickedness began even before we sailed for Cyprus?

IAGO: Wickedness? Is that not the word mothers use for their naughty milksops? Ooh that's wicked my little pet, I see you have not eaten your egg; how then can you grow strong like Dad? [*Laughs at his imitation*] Respect the man who has taken your lives. Give him his proper name. Devil.

DESDEMONA: I would if you had horns, and a forked tail to boot.

IAGO: Woe is me. This is what I mean. You have it all, dear lady—the fair skin, the golden hair, the blue eyes, the sweet voice and, if I may make so bold as to assume, the sweet breath too. But Good lacks one good thing. Humour, which people call the spice of life. Would you really have the devil announce himself with horns and hooves and fangs, slimy green saliva, perhaps? I must confess I lack these outward shows. For devils would lose their custom if they declared themselves in so crude a fashion. Had you but read the bald and bearded one with greater care, you would have known, 'The devil hath power t' assume a pleasing shape.'

OTHELLO: Bald and bearded one? Who might you mean?

IAGO: Our maker perhaps? Look not so horrified. I mean not God; for that is for me an empty word. I mean the man with the quill, the greatest, the pride of this damp and insular land. For while this isle once rode the waves, conquered every scrap of soil in sight, then lost it all in time, returning to being nothing but itself, an isle; our maker even now rides the waves, expanding his empire from shore to shore, never stopping, not even now four hundred years after he was laid to rest. Hail Emperor William Shakespeare, all hail! Fain would I honour him with a middle name more thunderous than the common William, but none was entered in his certificate of birth. If we believe the diligent thousands who have plucked the smallest bolts and nuts from his works to examine and declare their marvellous mettle, length and breadth, then he was just old Will, no more, no less.

DESDEMONA: You are merry at the cost of a poet who had more talent in his little toe than you have in your entire frame...

OTHELLO: …Filled as it is with vile contempt for all that is good and great.

IAGO: Woe is me again. Oh dreaded piety that will not let men laugh. You Othello and you Desdemona, did make the most perfect match; save colour. Had you been left to your crumpled sheets and the witless pleasures you found beneath, you would have begotten idiot babes who would have been the very bane of this already cheerless world. But that was not to be, for the devil took charge, and sent you to the bourne where you most properly belonged.

OTHELLO: Whereunto you, too, were dispatched.

IAGO: Oh yes, but with a subtle difference. I would have you recall, I said not a thing in my defence. Neither wept nor whined, but went in silent dignity. But you? You were still full of hot air even after my wife, a mere woman, had called you gull, dolt, ignorant as dirt. Speak me that speech, I pray, so I may laugh again.

OTHELLO: What speech? No speech of mine made anyone laugh.

IAGO: It did me. The one with frills and furbelows made to catch the world's sympathy.

OTHELLO: I shall make no speech. Here there is no world to hear.

IAGO: True. So true. You always craved more ears than you could count. But now you must make do with mine. Speak me the speech, I pray.

OTHELLO: It was no speech. I spoke from deep within my heart.

IAGO: Then your heart was no deeper than your tongue. You said to those who came to arraign, 'When you shall these unlucky deeds relate…' Unlucky? Was that all they were, your wife lying dead in all her chastity, murdered by your hands?

DESDEMONA: When I hear that speech, dead as I am, I too wonder why I loved him so! [*Laughs weakly*]

OTHELLO: Say not so, dear Desdemona. Listen with care and you shall hear in those words the depth of the love I bore you. [*Striking a pose, appealing to her*] 'When you shall these unlucky deeds relate,

/ Speak of me as I am. Nothing extenuate / Nor set down aught in malice. Then must you speak / Of one that loved not wisely, but too well; / Of one not easily jealous, but being wrought, / Perplexed in the extreme; of one whose hand, / Like the base Judean, threw a pearl away / Richer than all his tribe; of one whose subdued eyes / Albeit unused to the melting mood, / Drop tears as fast as the Arabian trees / Their medicinal gum...

IAGO: [*Laughing loud and long*] Enough enough… I can take no more. Oh my horned tribe, have you ever heard such froth, such foam, such fizz, such fog? Dear Othello, do you hear yourself or do the sonorous strains of your voice so block your ears that you cannot hear what the whole world does? For had you heard yourself, even you, had surely bowed your head in shame. Such verbiage. Such hypocrisy. Such hollowness! No wonder you compared your tears to gum dropping off Arabian trees whatever or wherever they may be. So stuck were your eyes with that gum Othello, I doubt you noticed that you wept alone. [*Laughs out loud*]

DESDEMONA: You are cruel. Too cruel for words.

IAGO: To that, dear lady, I do plead guilty. 'Tis a professional virtue I practice assiduously. When I hear those lines each night dear Moor, I cannot help but believe the man with the quill was having you on when he danced them on your tongue.

OTHELLO: How say you that? Having me on? What means it, having me on?

IAGO: If you would only deign to step out of the seventeenth century into now, you would have your answer straightaway. 'Having you on' is ragging you, ribbing you, pulling your leg? [*Weary*] Making a bloody sport of you? As flies to wanton boys are we to th' gods, / They kill us for their sport. Sport? Fun?

OTHELLO: You need not go on. I understand.

DESDEMONA: It is not the man with the quill but this devil in human form that is having you on.

IAGO: My lady, that was sharp. Keep company with me a few more hours or years and you will return blow for blow. But may I say the speech is not of my making, but comes from the Bard's mischief-filled quill? I only gave it meaning. There lies the lady pale as her smock and your concern is not her, but you? That you should be well thought of? Is that how God-believing humans love? Does remorse come tied up in satin bows?

DESDEMONA: How would you have it then? That noble Othello should go to the gallows with the world still unknowing of how he came to be a…a…I stumble, I cannot bring myself to say it.

OTHELLO: Say it my dear. I will love you still.

IAGO: Let me say it for her. A murderer. Wasn't that the word your virtuous tongue tripped over? But he was something worse. He did not merely kill you. He killed Good. That is what I wish you understood.

DESDEMONA: He was not alone to blame. You have yourself claimed, the killing was your own first and last intent.

IAGO: With that you put your finger on the throbbing nerve of my pain. It should have been me and me alone that committed that philosophical deed. It would have been so, had the Bard had courage to paint me the devil that I was. Ours would have been an equal battle. You would have fought for your life, for you would not then have been weak with love as you were when Othello came, black hands outstretched to squeeze the life out of your milk-white neck. In the battle between you and me, the Bard would have created an astonishing scene. But he balked. He paled. He feared the wrath of God. A God that could not countenance Evil overcoming Good.

DESDEMONA: You assume you would have won? You do not believe I would have fought till fatigue got you, your blows slowed to a sluggish sloth, then ceased altogether and you retired, forked tail tucked tight between your legs?

IAGO: Bravely spoken, fair lady. A believer in God, you cannot believe that we are equals of exact measure. You cannot believe that in this world of God's alleged creation, Evil exactly balances Good. You believe instead, that Good will always and forever be victor. How? Without killing? You say you would have fought, not killed. Good does not kill. That is its weakness. Evil kills. That is its business and its strength.

DESDEMONA: [*Tired*] It is too late to do much about it. The Bard has written and moved on. But tell me, do you truly hold yourself higher in understanding than him? That you know better the beat of human hearts and how human destinies work? How language, poetry and drama are crafted to make meanings beyond words? If so, how would you have us play the final scene of menace and death?

IAGO: By changing the play from start to end to make me the inevitable hand of death. Your ruthless, remorseless nemesis, I. Then would it be just us, face to face. Where this go-between would have no place.

OTHELLO: How dare you call the valorous general of a great army a go-between?

IAGO: How? By being more truthful to my beliefs, more subtle in my thinking than you were or could ever be. Desdemona and I are the two poles. Equal in strength, she Good, I Evil. We are natural opponents. But you? What are you? Let me tell the world. You are like a great big wave that rolls towards the sandy shore, making a loud and resounding roar that people hear with fear and awe. And then? Then at the shore, it breaks. Turns into airy fairy surf, mincing and purring along the sand. Our Bard has a pretty phrase for it: full of sound and fury signifying nothing.

OTHELLO: And all the battles I have won and the scars I have suffered? Do they count for nought?

IAGO: I do not speak of you as a soldier, but a man amongst men. And women [*Bows to Desdemona*]. I will go further. I speak of you as unaccommodated man. Another bull's eye from the Bard. He certainly had a feel for the phrase, *le mot juste*. A poor, bare, forked animal, unaccommodated man!

DESDEMONA: You sad, sad man. You cannot speak two lines without the Bard's support; and yet you put yourself above him in understanding of human destiny. He, in his spectacular wisdom, tells you more about the human condition in one word than you could in a thousand.

IAGO: And yet, fancy words or not, I know this Othello inside out. Which is to say I know the out. As for the in…he has none. What is he then, this unaccommodated man? Did he woo you? He did not. He told you tales of courage and pain and you did love him for them. Did he love you? He did not, for he loved himself overwhelmingly more. Did he trust you? He did not. He allowed a woman's handkerchief, the merest wisp of embroidered cloth, to churn him into such a storm as made him blind to all that was good, turned into a mere blood-lusting beast. And when he had done his gory deed, and learned that he had sorely sinned, how then did he image himself? When Lodovico asked, 'What shall be said of thee?' he said without a moment's pause, 'An honourable murderer if you will; / For naught I did in hate, but all in honour.' Honour? Whose honour, I ask. His own. The tawdry honour of a tawdry man.

DESDEMONA: You too killed your wife in coldest blood. Was that to you an honourable deed?

IAGO: The Bard was kind enough to me not to have sullied my tongue with that sin-aggrandizing word, honour. Honour's the quilt beneath which cowards hide their most dishonourable deeds.

DESDEMONA: You were a coward too. You killed Emilia because you knew her words were the rope that had fashioned your noose. You killed her because you were too much a coward to die in true remorse for your craven diabolic deed.

IAGO: And what pray was my deed? That I urged Emilia to steal that scrap of cloth from you? That she who supposedly loved you, declared you the purest creation of God, did not once ask me why I wished to have it so urgently? It was not I that stole it. It was she. It was her stealing that caused your husband to believe in your infidelity. He insisted on proof. Emilia supplied it. Had she not, you would not have died. So the final judgement between Othello and me must be, that I was true to myself and he was not. Warriors do not kill women, the least armed of human beings. That makes me more a man than he. What is he? An ironclad silo stuffed with straw. A hollow thing that dares call itself man.

OTHELLO: Iago, you have laughed enough. This must be your very last laugh. I know the source of this verbal filth. Its rotten root is envy, buried deep. Your vile bile rots in your gut all day and oozes each night all over the stage. I watch you snigger, I see you smirk…

DESDEMONA: Why watch? Why not just play your part?

IAGO: As Iago does, unhappily though it be, knowing that the truth, granted him in a sharp and knowing line, is something other and bigger. 'I am not what I am,' he says. Think, Othello, what that means. I am not what I am. I am not the true me.

OTHELLO: I do not care who you think you are, knowing that you desire to be the Moor. To strut your hour upon the stage, make the very speeches you say you deprecate. You cannot bear to be the rat you are, scampering from hole to hole, nibbling this and nibbling that. It is not your great and vaunted evil, but your mean and gutter jealousy, that coils around my neck each night, smothering my lines, giving them the lie. I'll have no more of it. Iago shall die.

CELIA: Harry, surely you mean not that. He argues not on personal count. He argues a deviant philosophy.

HARRY: Philosophy be damned. I have no use for it. He harms me every night. It is him or me. [*He whips out his sword and rushes at Iago.*]

CELIA: Harry, stop. You are not yourself. [*Grabs his hand*]

HARRY: Let go. I'm too far gone. This villain has had his final laugh.

DICK: Not yet, my friend. There is one left. You mix real life with life on stage. That sword you wield has a blunted tip. Utterly harmless to human flesh. This is the time for the Bard's best line. Keep up your bright sword for the dew will rust it. Celia, take him home. He needs to rest.

[*Harry collapses in a chair, fatigued beyond words and closes his eyes. Celia collects her bag. Hands Harry's to him.*]

CELIA: Come, my dear. It is time we quit this venomous, foul and filthy air.

HARRY: [*With a wan smile and a shrug*] How silly of me. How truly insane to be so wrapped up in a play that I knew not the real from the fake. Forgive me, dearest Dick. I was overwrought. Tomorrow we shall be together again. Iago. Desdemona. Othello on stage. I hope you forgive me for today.

DICK: Of course I do. Let us go. This was but a run-through of a play in my head. The clash of Good and Evil. I am obsessed.

HARRY: Thank you, Dick. But I was forgetting. [*Rummages around in his bag*] I have here something for you. A gift. Ah here it is, the very thing. [*He pulls out a pistol and aims it at Dick.*]

CELIA: What are you doing, you foolish man? [*Rushes to stand between the two men just as Harry pulls the trigger. She collapses.*]

HARRY: [*Down beside her, howls in grief*] Celia! My darling! My life, my love! You devil. Beast. Accursed scum. See, just see what you have done.

DICK: I? No. Oh my God! What…

[*Harry rises swiftly, swings around, aims at him and shoots. Then turns the pistol on himself and pulls the trigger. He falls. The manager rushes in. Takes in the scene.*]

MANAGER: Bloody hell. Here is a pretty scene to make your hair stand on end. What ho! Who's there?

[*The doorman rushes in followed by four men. They stand in silence looking at the carnage.*]

MANAGER: The Bard always knew, didn't he? That life was but a walking shadow, a poor player, that strutted and fretted his hour upon the stage and then was heard no more. So too did these three strut and fret their hour upon the stage and shall be heard no more. Take up the bodies, my men. Such a sight as this becomes the stage out there, but here shows much amiss.

[*The men lift the bodies. Slow march out.*]

END

Rosemary for Remembrance

Writer's note: I see this as intimate theatre, to be played without the burden of technology.

[*Ophelia sits on a bench stringing a garland of flowers.*]

OPHELIA: One way or another,
It has always been death for us.

GERTRUDE: [*From within*] What did you say, my dear?

OPHELIA: One way or another,
It has always been death for us.
Remember how the breath was squeezed
Out of my cousin Desdemona?
What had she done?
She had known only one thing—to love.
To love a man whose stories of distant
Lands and battles she had listened to
With wonder in her eyes.
In those clear blue eyes,
He was a paragon of male virtue.

GERTRUDE: [*From within*] Poor child.

OPHELIA: 'Think on thy sins,' he said,
fury turning his eyes red.
'They are loves I bear you,' she said,
truth deepening the blue of her eyes.

[*Gertrude comes out with a plate of biscuits. Ophelia lays aside the garland and nibbles daintily on a biscuit.*]

OPHELIA: These are delicious. Did you bake such for Hamlet?

GERTRUDE: What? In the royal kitchen amongst the knaves?

OPHELIA: [*Giggles*] I suppose not.

GERTRUDE: 'Queen Gertrude dons apron for only son', the gossip pages would have said today. 'Royal recipe in box'.

[*Both laugh*]

OPHELIA: The queen of hearts
She made some tarts

GERTRUDE: [*Sighs*] That is one thing I never was.

OPHELIA: What?

GERTRUDE: The queen of hearts.

OPHELIA: But you were, my lady. The queen of two hearts:
Your first husband's and then your second.
Two men loved you and you loved two men.

GERTRUDE: You use the word love with such innocence,
Ophelia, my dear. What does it mean—love?

OPHELIA: Desdemona was love.
Had he but looked deep enough
Into the crystal blue of her eyes,
He would have seen nothing
But love shining there.

GERTRUDE: You are still with Desdemona.
That man had no sight to see
Anything but his own self.
His eyes were like abscesses, turned inwards,
Pouring their pus into his heart.

OPHELIA: That's not true.
He was, in his way, noble, my lady.
The pus was Iago.
Oh, why did the noble Moor trust him?
He who had seen so much of the world,
Could he not see the viper
in that monster heart? [*Pause*]

GERTRUDE: Men trust men. Eat your biscuit my dear. It'll soon go soft. Look at the sky.

OPHELIA: [*Looks up*] Just one sliver of blue in all that grey.
That's how she was too: clear and blameless.
'Kill me tomorrow. Let me live tonight,'
she cried piteously. [*Pause*]
'Let me live but half an hour...
but while I say one prayer.' [*Pause*]
He called her strumpet.
Did he even think what that meant?

GERTRUDE: Men use those names for the women
They abandon, rape and kill.
They need to believe the women
They do those things to, deserve
To have those things done to them.

OPHELIA: Even now, how it hurts that your son called me unchaste; although I tell myself it was not me he was speaking of, but himself. It was his own honesty that he doubted. He said so himself.

GERTRUDE: Did I not say it? Men!
Eyes always turned inwards upon themselves.
They—the centre of the earth.

OPHELIA: He spoke the truth did he not, when he said, 'Be thou as chaste as ice, as pure as snow, thou shalt not escape calumny'? [*Pause. Laughs loud and clear, choking on her biscuit*] He did not mean me of course; for he knew I was not chaste as ice or pure as snow where he was concerned.

GERTRUDE: How so, my child? Your face always so transparent, the veins that showed through, filled with purest blood. [*Pause*] Even now as I sit here, I see your face, still so warm...floating on the icy water... suffused with innocence like the flowers that lay strewn across your breast—those that you took with you when you fell from the riverbank, and those that fell after, like a shower, to guard you against the flood. Even in death, you were purity itself.

OPHELIA: [*A smile still playing on her lips*] Not so my lady. I was not so innocent nor so chaste and pure as the world imagined. Not when he said, 'To a nunnery go.' Before that for sure. But not then.

[*She picks up another biscuit and nibbles at it.*]

GERTRUDE: How so, how so?

OPHELIA: I cannot answer that. For I do not know
Even after all these centuries
what is pure and what is chaste.
Certainly I did not know it then.
I was not of an age to reflect,
to separate how the world thought
from how I thought or should think.
I did not know myself in the world of men
—of father, brother, lover.
On their tongues 'chaste' sounded
like God's rule and I went by it.
Father ordered. I obeyed. Was that wrong?
To walk in that passageway, book in hand
as he had instructed me to do, waiting
To waylay Hamlet? To pretend
to be alone, knowing they were
hiding in the shadows, my father and my king.
That was a terrible falsehood. [*Pause*]
But no, it was not a falsehood at all.
I was indeed alone in that dark corridor,
the weight of the book in my hand,
the weight of my heart in my breast.
I feel it still. [*She takes Gertrude's hand and places it on her chest.*]
I was more alone then than I had ever been before.

GERTRUDE: Do not blame yourself, my child.
The times were not right for us to choose
Otherwise than that which we were ordered to do.

OPHELIA: Are the times right now, these many centuries later?

[*Gertrude looks at her and they both laugh.*]

GERTRUDE: Would you look your father in the eye
Even now and say, 'No sire,
I will not do what you desire of me,
For it goes against my conscience
and my heart?'

OPHELIA: My heart! What was it?
Just an organ that beat and beat
Till the day it stopped.
What did I know of its desires?
My father and Claudius the king,
hiding in the dark, their cunning eyes on me,
what did they care for my desires?
They knew theirs, and knew their power to make
me the means to take their desires to fruition.

GERTRUDE: You had to do what you were instructed to do.

OPHELIA: When all that was within me told me otherwise?
I should have wept like the rains that pour
From the skies in Cherapunji to hear Hamlet say,
'To a nunnery go.' I should have pleaded my cause with him,
'When fathers and kings order, what can a simple maid do?'

GERTRUDE: [*Laughs out loud*] Pleaded your cause with him while they watched? That would have given Willie's story such a turn, as would have sent it flying out of the orbit set for it, never to be found again. With fathers and brothers and lovers, there are writers too in the world of men. It was the man with the quill who settled our destinies....

OPHELIA: ...who crafted a willow branch so weak,
it would not take the weight of a frail waif like me.
I had not meant to die.
I wished so much to live.
Life had been so sweet.

GERTRUDE: But he had meant you to die.
You had to be the reason for your brother
to kill my son and my son to kill your brother.
Men with quills have always made
the brave and noble kill each other for us.
So we may be held responsible
for the wars we never wanted.

OPHELIA: One way or another, it is always death for us, is it not?

GERTRUDE: It is. [*Sighs*]
But between your death and mine,
there lies a gulf. You did not
choose your death. I did.

OPHELIA: How so, my lady? When you raised
that goblet of wine to your lips,
offered you by your own loving husband,
you could not have known that in its amber depths
lay a black pearl that would poison your
body and take your life.

GERTRUDE: [*Pause. Very quietly*] I did. I did know.
We keep our lips tight shut, for men cannot endure
women who speak. But there is no power,
no will in the world that can make us
keep our eyes and ears and minds shut.
For in Nature, if not in the world of men,
we are human. We see and we hear and we gather
in our minds our own sense of the world.

OPHELIA: What sense of the world made you drink
from a goblet you knew to be poisoned?

Did you not wish to live? You, a queen? [*Pause*]
Was it your guilt that made you
volunteer your life to death?

GERTRUDE: My guilt? What guilt? Why 'guilt'?

OPHELIA: My lady, did you not hear it whispered in the court
That Claudius your husband had murdered
His brother the king? Did you not hear it whispered
That you had held your tongue and turned your eyes away
To help him in his evil plot? Did you not hear it whispered
That the ghost of your first husband had urged Hamlet
his son and yours, to avenge his murder?
Were your ears not open to those whispers?

GERTRUDE: Indeed they were. And indeed they heard. [*Pause*]
Yes they heard; but they did not turn what
they heard into arrows to pierce my heart.

OPHELIA: How so, my lady? How could your heart
not be pierced a thousand times, a thousand
million times, till it turned from a throbbing
muscle of life into a monstrous mass of guilt?
The king who was killed by the usurper of his throne,
was the man you loved. The man you loved had
killed the man you once loved: the man who fathered your son.

GERTRUDE: You accuse me of too much, my dear.
You accuse me of love for the king, my first husband.
You accuse me of bearing his son. But I will let that pass.
I drank from the accursed goblet because
I knew who it was meant for. [*Pause*]

OPHELIA: What means, my lady?

GERTRUDE: It was a black pearl. The same

That I had once seen given
to a chambermaid who was with child.
She carried a nobleman's guilty secret in her womb
For which she had to die. God knows,
My father's court was full enough of bastard sons.
One more could have done no harm.
But the nobleman's wife would not have it.
She it was who forced the pearl
down the chambermaid's throat.

OPHELIA: Why do you speak of chambermaids
when my throat grows dry
waiting for what you have to say?
You do not tell me so let me ask
For whom was that pearl meant?

GERTRUDE: It was meant for the man you loved, my dear.
It was meant for my beloved son.

OPHELIA: Dear God. Why would the king want
dear, gentle Hamlet dead?
His mind was distempered,
but surely that did not earn him death?
So cruel a death?

GERTRUDE: [*Long pause*] Murder ends nothing. It multiplies itself
Till murdered and murderer lie side by side.
That is the law of life. My cousin Macbeth
Thought he would murder and be king.
He was king, but only long enough to see his
Dear lady lose her mind and die a piteous death;
To watch as Nature itself marched upon him
To fell him while in his fullest sap.
His kingship died as it was born. [*Pause*]
The man with the quill knew the laws of Nature
And he knew the laws of Men only too well. [*Pause*]
But let me answer your question directly.

I had foolishly thought that the black pearl
alone carried death. I had foolishly thought,
By drinking my death, I would ensure life for my son.
I was naive. My husband the king was not.
He had devised a second carrier of death.
If the first failed, the second was sure to find its mark.

OPHELIA: And what was that second? [*Pause*]
Dear God, I think I know.
I fear to hear what I know.

GERTRUDE: The tip of the rapier that drew his blood was poisoned too.

OPHELIA: The rapier that my brother, brave Laertes held.

GERTRUDE: The very same.

OPHELIA: Dear Laertes, so brave of heart, so true to all that was true.

GERTRUDE: Not always so, more is the pity. The king, having murdered one, had to murder all. It was a vortex into which Laertes, too, allowed himself to be sucked.

OPHELIA: My brother Laertes? Not always true? Ready to kill with cunning?

GERTRUDE: Not always true. He who was so matchless with
the rapier that he could have touched Hamlet
in the first instant and won the match, carried
poison in his hand and murder in his heart.
'A touch, a touch' the courtiers would shout
and see their Prince fall.

OPHELIA: He murdered against all courtly rules?
My brave brother Laertes?

GERTRUDE: He most tragically did.

OPHELIA: He who taught me to see the evil in the world,
did not hear the evil that was spoken in his ear?

GERTRUDE: When the tongue that speaks is the king's,

the ear that hears is enslaved.

OPHELIA: Oh the pity of it, that kings' tongues grow so distant from the seat of their consciences! But you loved the man that spoke the evil, even more, they say, than you loved the man whose life he took, from where began this brutal cycle of killings. Did you not see the blackness of his heart? How could you love him then?

GERTRUDE: That word 'love' again. [*Sighs*] Tell me, what is 'love'?

OPHELIA: My lady, what does your question mean?

GERTRUDE: It is a question that women ask when past the age of flushed cheeks and beating hearts but before all is dead within.

OPHELIA: I must think myself fortunate to have gone before I knew such a day of emptiness.

[*Gertrude picks up the garland the girl has finished stringing and puts it around her own neck.*]

GERTRUDE: How does that look on me?

OPHELIA: [*Eyes and mouth wide open*] Truth to tell...

GERTUDE: Tell it. When all the lies are told, the only thing that remains in shining brightness is truth.

OPHELIA: Truth to tell, my lady, begging your pardon, it does not become you.

GERTRUDE: No? Think you it is better thus?

[*She winds the garland around her head.*]

OPHELIA: [*Laughing*] Nor that either.

GERTRUDE: Laugh my dear, laugh. Do not stop your laughter. Let it peal like morning church bells.

OPHELIA: I did not mean to laugh, my lady.

GERTRUDE: Why? Let us laugh together

[*She laughs out loud. Ophelia is reluctant to join in, but is soon infected and laughs till the tears roll down her cheeks.*]

OPHELIA: [*Wiping her eyes*] Is it not strange that the very glands
that run with sorrow run with laughter too?

[*Gertrude puts the garland around Ophelia's head.*]

GERTRUDE: There. That is its proper place: with youth and faith in love.

[*Long pause as she admires the effect*]

No, I did not love the king my first husband,
Nor the king my second. It was not love but logic
That took me to the altar the second time.

OPHELIA: My lady? I do not understand.

GERTRUDE: Think upon this. What is a queen?
The wife of a king, the mother of a king.
What life is left to a queen when a king dies?
Who is she? What must she do?
Whose shadow is she to be? Who is she to serve?
Nothing and nobody. The castle becomes
A dungeon and she a ghost, left to flit
Within its dank, dark walls, seeking some
Deep crevice in which to hide
Till her son grows old enough to wear the crown.
I must count myself fortunate that Claudius's eye
Fell upon me with the greed of possession.
Greed drove him. He had a greed to possess
All that his hated brother had possessed.
Logic taught me to see this and to dissemble love.

OPHELIA: You had no choice?

GERTRUDE: I had no choice.

OPHELIA: And with the first?

GERTRUDE: No choice then either. That was a match
Made on the battlefield, a healing patch
Between war and treaty. [*Pause*]
The king who won that battle,

soon to be my husband,
was a valiant warrior...but he was not a man.

OPHELIA: Not a man, my lady?

GERTRUDE: Not a man. You will not understand my meaning.
You did not live long enough for such understanding.
I too did not understand it then, for I too was of an age
Not to know that beds were not battlefields.
I took the King's struggles in the royal bed to be
What men did when they took wives to their chambers.
[*Pause*] Then came that spring. Many years later.
The King away on one of his eternal wars.
The air heavy with the honeyed scent of the golden cowslip.
It was then, in those too few magical weeks,
that knowledge came to me of what it was
to be a woman and what it was to be a man.
[*Pause*] Why do you smile that secret smile?

OPHELIA: You say I did not live long enough
for such understanding. But I did.

GERTRUDE: You did?

OPHELIA: I did live long enough, my lady, just long enough.
[*Pause. Looks around*] I have spoken of this to nobody,
Not even to myself.

GERTRUDE: You wish to speak of it now?

OPHELIA: I would not have wished so before.
But perhaps I may, now that the times are changed.
And yet I do not know if I can, or even if I should.

GERTRUDE: You need not if you do not wish it.
But I believe I know what you are about to say.
I believe I knew even then.
We always know, do we not?

There are signs that tell us.
But we choose to ignore them,
seeking comfort in blindness.
I have long since given up that comfort.
Of blindness.
Deafness.
Silence.

OPHELIA: [*Looks around again. In a whisper*]
It was the night of the play.
You must remember that terrible night.
You called Hamlet to your side,
And he said 'Here's mettle more attractive.'
And laid his head in my lap.
It was only to tease my father, who could
do nothing about it for the king sat beside him.
That amused Hamlet.
But for me, it was an exquisite torture
such as I had never known before.
His head in my lap set something a-tingle
there that would not stop but grew,
till I thought it would choke me.

GERTRUDE: [*Distracted. Gets up, walks about*]
I hardly saw Hamlet or you. I only remember
the sweat that pricked my armpits as the play
got closer to a reality I had not witnessed,
but had for long suspected.
The king flew into such a temper
as was terrible to behold.
I ran into my chamber, trembling,
afraid for Hamlet.
I asked kind Polonius, your father,
to hasten to where Hamlet might be
and summon him to my chamber instantly.

OPHELIA: I was there.

GERTRUDE: Where?

OPHELIA: In the place where Hamlet came.
When the king and you and your retinue
hurried away, I hung behind.
Nobody paid heed to me.
I was there, hiding behind a tree
biding my time till those others,
Horatio, Rosencrantz and Guildenstern left.
They talked and talked and talked.
And I asked myself: is this the time to talk?
Long sentences my lady, long sentences
Like dull snakes uncoiling under the moon.
Then the worst happened. My father came running
To summon Hamlet to you. And I despaired.
Now he too would talk and talk
the way you know he always did. And I feared
Hamlet would go with him and the others,
leaving me to burn alone in my pent-up body.

[*Pause. Deep breath. Smile*]

But Hamlet did not go. He sent the others away.

GERTRUDE: The man with the quill did that
to give Hamlet another soliloquy.

OPHELIA: That was no soliloquy. Just bragging.
Nothing so moving or so fearful as the first.
'To be or not to be'. The despair of that
tore into my heart. Please be, please be,
I called out mutely, knowing I would not be heard.
[*Long pause*] But I would not have broken into
That soliloquy even if I had had the chance,
For it was not about him alone.
It was about all of us,
and about life itself
that is forever shadowed by death.

This one, under the moon,
was just some angry, overblown bluster.
'...now could I drink hot blood,
And do such bitter business as the day
Would quake to look on...'
I let him spend his bravado,
then ran to him and stopped him
with my lips, senseless as I was
to all else save the throbbing in my thighs.
I pressed myself upon him.
The heat of me lit a spark in him and there,
under the moon, with the fragrance of
Night flowers around us, we coupled.
I knew then what man was, what woman was,
What Nature was. [*Pause*]
He was the first to wake from that scented dream.
He rose and cast upon my sated body a
look of so fierce a fury that I sprang up to hold him.
He tore himself away and walked,
Nay, almost ran from me.
'Let me be cruel,' he shouted, still in his soliloquy.
'I will speak daggers to her,' he spat out,
Hurrying out of my hearing and into your presence.

GERTRUDE: Perhaps you and the moon and the flowers
had shown him life, however transiently;
for he did not speak daggers to me.
He had done so before.
Those daggers were still planted deep in my heart.
When sons are cruel, they turn mothers into open
wounds that never stop bleeding.

OPHELIA: I stood under the moon afraid of his words.
And yet, my body sang. You did not hear that song.
Nobody did but me. It was the song of the body,
The song of my body.

Not my dear cousin Desdemona's song of willow.
Although, had I known it then,
the willow was not too far away from this body.

GERTRUDE: The song I heard was piteous.
It was your dirge for your father.

OPHELIA: [*Sings*]
And will he not come again?
And will he not come again?
No, no, he is dead.
Go to thy deathbed.
He never will come again.

GERTRUDE: You scattered flowers.
There's rosemary, that's for remembrance
you said. I held the sprig of rosemary
you gave me and remembered.
Memory was like a sudden stone
weighing unbearably on the heart.
Moments, months, years, wasted
With the acts of kings and courtiers.
I heard your song, but not a tear
Flowed from my eyes.
Stones do not weep.

OPHELIA: No tears from my eyes either. My father was dead.
My lover, whom I only now knew, was alive.
I was split. I had two bodies, two hearts.
One body moved to the river. The other pulled me back.
In the river was death. In the flowers was life.
Under the water was death. Under the moon was life.
My heart was a cold emptiness. My heart was a tingling spring.
I wanted to drink from that spring for ever and ever.

I hung my flowers upon the branch of the treacherous willow.
I wanted to give them a swing.
A very gentle swing that would scatter
Their scent in all of heaven's air.

GERTRUDE: And the bough gave way.

OPHELIA: And the bough gave way.

[*Long pause. Ophelia takes the garland from her head and places it in her lap.*]

GERTRUDE: That moonlit night took you and he and me
And everybody else into that final darkness.
For a few precious moments before then, you
had seen life burst into colour. Me?
I had seen its colours but once,
In that long ago spring, too long ago for the colours to keep.

OPHELIA: Will you speak of it now or am I still
not of an age to understand?

[*Gertrude smiles and carries the plate of biscuits in.*]

GERTRUDE: [*Voice from within*] It was a page...

OPHELIA: A what?

[*Gertrude comes out.*]

GERTRUDE: A comely page. A boy of some eighteen summers
who played the harp and sang.
His voice was so exquisite sweet,
that its echo erased all other sounds
from this gross world. The page would play
and sing for me and I would listen
in my loneliness. I did not know his name,
nor did I need to know. It was enough
that I knew his voice, understood what he sang
and why he sang. I needed to feel that voice upon me.

In me. [*Pause*]
When I felt it grow in me day by day,
I sent him away.

OPHELIA: And your husband the king...

GERTRUDE: ...accepted the child as his.
Kings are captive to their subjects' expectations,
As we are to theirs. His subjects expected him
To bear a son and a son was born.
That was enough.
Nobody asked why there was only one,
And none thereafter. [*Pause*]
In the eyes of the world, his duty was done.
In his own eyes, he was full of shame.
He never entered my chamber again.

OPHELIA: Hamlet's sire, a page who played the harp!
I often wondered. Hamlet's soft and slender fingers!
Not a warrior's, I would think. Their touch was
still upon me when I sang,
'Here's rosemary for remembrance'.
I smelt the rosemary and remembered
The crushed grass under our bodies
That had smelt of it too, so warm and moist.

GERTRUDE: I wish I too remembered the fingers that
Played upon the secret strings of my body.
I smelt the rosemary you so wanly gave me
But could not remember a thing
About that long ago spring.
It is sad, but good too, that
Memories of the body do not last.

OPHELIA: Oh my lady, I am so truly sorry for that.
How much more tragic that makes your going:
So barren, so wasteful, so utterly without meaning.
Hamlet died and there was music to announce his death.

Fortinbras said, 'Bear Hamlet to the stage like a soldier.'
But you were just a body.
'Take up the bodies,' said Fortinbras,
of you and of the others,
Bodies without names.

GERTRUDE: No, it was not tragic.
In the last moment it was not tragic.
It did not matter then what Fortinbras said.
It was not for what he or the future would say
That I had died. I had died for my son...and...

[*She picks up the garland of flowers from Ophelia's lap, lifts it to her face and takes a deep breath of their fragrance. When she lifts her face, it is glistening with tears.*]

...and I was rewarded in death.
In that last moment between life and death,
when my breath was ebbing out of me, gasp by gasp,
I heard my beloved Hamlet's voice. [*Pause*]
Fatally wounded himself, he asked,
'How does the queen? How does the queen?'
No longer angry, no longer venomous,
he was the loving son he once had been,
his anxious, caring voice, asking 'How does the queen?'

[*Pause*]

In that last moment before death, I lived.

END